D1346945

THE **BIG** BOOK OF
**GREAT BRITISH**
**RECIPES**

ROZ DENNY

# THE **BIG** BOOK OF GREAT BRITISH RECIPES

## 365 Delicious and Treasured Recipes

DUNCAN BAIRD PUBLISHERS

LONDON

In memory of Catherine, Effie and Alice – all fine home cooks.

The Big Book of Great British Recipes
Roz Denny

First published in the United Kingdom
and Ireland in 2007 by
Duncan Baird Publishers Ltd
Sixth Floor
Castle House
75–76 Wells Street
London W1T 3QH

Conceived, created and designed by Duncan Baird Publishers

Copyright © Duncan Baird Publishers 2007
Text copyright © Roz Denny 2007
Photography copyright © Duncan Baird Publishers 2007

All rights reserved. No part of this book may be reproduced in any form or by any electronic or
mechanical means, including information storage and retrieval systems, without permission in
writing from the publisher, except by a reviewer who may quote brief passages in a review.

The right of Roz Denny to be identified as the Author of this text has been
asserted in accordance with the Copyright, Designs and Patents Act of 1988.

*Managing Editor*: Grace Cheetham
*Editors*: Stephanie Evans and Mary Allen
*Managing Designer*: Manisha Patel
*Design*: Carole Ash at Project 360
*Studio photography*: William Lingwood
*Food stylist*: Bridget Sargeson
*Prop stylist*: Helen Trent

British Library Cataloguing-in-Publication Data:
A CIP record for this book is available from the British Library

ISBN: 978-1-84483-449-5

10 9 8 7 6 5 4 3 2

Typeset in Trade Gothic
Colour reproduction by Scanhouse, Malaysia
Printed in China by Imago

*Publisher's note:* While every care has been taken in compiling the recipes for this book, Duncan
Baird Publishers, or any other persons who have been involved in working on this publication,
cannot accept responsibility for any errors or omissions, inadvertent or not, that may be found
in the recipes or text, nor for any problems that may arise as a result of preparing one of these
recipes. If you are pregnant or breastfeeding or have any special dietary requirements or medical
conditions, it is advisable to consult a medical professional before following any of the recipes
contained in this book. Ill or elderly people, babies, young children and women who are pregnant
or breastfeeding should avoid any recipes containing raw meat or uncooked eggs.

UNLESS OTHERWISE STATED:
• All recipes serve 4
• Use medium eggs, fruit and vegetables
• Use organic, free-range produce whenever possible
• Use fresh herbs
• Do not mix metric and imperial measurements
• 1 tsp = 5ml
  1 tbsp = 15ml
  1 cup = 250ml

# CONTENTS

# INTRODUCTION

British food is often described as 'good plain cooking',
implying that it is perhaps a bit dull. Given our rich agricultural
and pasture land, centuries-old heritage of cultural diversity
and regional culinary distinctions, there is certainly nothing
plain about making the best of fresh natural foods. We are,
after all, a nation of farmers and fanatical gardeners. So
instead of 'plain', I would like to celebrate British cuisine
as the very best of 'good home cooking'.

The demographic history of the British Isles is one of
waves of migrants over thousands of years. We are certainly
no pedigree nation! And the food that is served at our tables
has reflected this constant change. It is true to say that for
the last 40 or 50 years, at least two generations of young
Britons have grown up enjoying a very mixed diet, which
reflects foreign travel, immigration and now instant global
communications. Pizza, lasagne and curry are now more
familiar to almost half the population of these islands than our
so-called traditional dishes. But now it seems younger Brits
are discovering their culinary roots for the first time, either
from TV chefs and countless food programmes or from older
members of their own families who can still serve up a tasty
meat pie or homemade trifle.

# WHAT IS BRITISH FOOD?

During the 17th and 18th centuries Britain emerged as a great sea power. It was also a time when our food was regarded as some of Europe's best. Merchants introduced new produce from the New World and the Far East, and some ingredients that had been the sole preserve of the nobility became more available and more affordable. Increased tourist travel in continental Europe added a growing French and Italian influence on British cuisine. French was the main language spoken in Europe and both its cooking and culinary phrases were taken up by the English. After the French Revolution in 1789, Britain offered refuge not only to fleeing aristocrats but also to many of their cooks and chefs who took up positions in great country house kitchens. This explains how mayonnaise, omelette, soufflé, ragout, béchamel, meringue, ramekin and casserole became standard terms in our kitchen manuals and recipe books.

During the zenith of the British Empire in the 19th century the foods of the Indian Raj, the West Indies, Africa and other colonial outposts were brought to the motherland by returning merchants and civil servants. Kedgeree, chutney, mulligatawny soup, curry and punch became firm favourites at home while imported foodstuffs from the colonies, transported in faster ships, meant that many previously luxury foods were more readily available.

By far the biggest influence, though, took place in the latter half of the 20th century with growing multi-culturalism and package holidays 'abroad'. Now, it seems, more people in the UK have tasted olive oil than British suet or beef dripping. And we can get almost any food at any time of year air-freighted to our shops – despite the environmental concerns. Many recipes in this collection reflect and celebrate this cosmopolitan culinary heritage. There is Korma alongside Cottage Pie, 'Spag Bol' next to Steak and Kidney Pudding, Welsh Bara Brith and Battenberg Cake. In short, a microcosm of our constantly changing world.

## A COOK'S TOUR OF BRITAIN

Britain may appear a tiny dot on the global map, but it is blessed by its latitude, is surrounded by seas rich in marine life and has a high percentage of fertile land. It benefits from the ameliorating effects of the warm Gulf Stream current sweeping up past Ireland and around north-west Scotland. This ensures a relatively temperate climate and extremes of weather are generally rare. Mild temperatures, a generous rain supply (maybe too much on occasions) and highly efficient agriculture (dating from the great 18th-century agrarian reformers such as 'Turnip' Townsend and the Duke of Bedford) mean we can produce bountiful harvests. Britain's geological formations are also very varied for such a small landmass, resulting in many differing soils and microclimates. Despite these natural advantages, with a growing population of over 60 million we cannot hope to produce all our own food, and must rely increasingly on imports. None the less, small entrepreneurial farmers and market-garden producers are flourishing by concentrating on speciality crops or reviving old varieties of plants and rare farm breeds, catering for the increasingly discerning customer. Good food lovers in Britain have exciting times ahead.

## NORTH, SOUTH, EAST, WEST ...

Generalizations aside, the traditional heartlands of Britain still produce their specialities. The flat, drained lands of East Anglia and the east coast of central England, from the Fens up to south Yorkshire, supply many traditional foods – asparagus, sprouting from crowns buried in sandy mounds, baby new potatoes, game birds from the many private and increasingly commercial estates, as well as geese, turkey and ducks. Catches of fish and seafood are landed, especially around the bulge of the Norfolk, Suffolk and Essex coasts where the Romans created their oyster beds in Colchester and West Mersea (they are still thriving 2,000 years later) and fishing communities dress Cromer crabs. The picturesque Blackwater Estuary, just 50 miles from London, is home to one of the world's most famous producers of sea salt, Maldon salt. These delicate crystal flakes are culinary stars from Tokyo to Spain and California.

Kent, the fabled Garden of England since Tudor times when Henry VIII required the fruit growers to improve their apple and cherry orchards (perhaps encouraged by his Kentish-born second wife, Anne Boleyn), still maintains its reputation for top-quality fruit, despite competition from imports. Here, too, hop growers supplied the real-ale breweries with the vital flavouring for British beers and ales.

The counties of the south coast (Kent, Sussex, Hampshire, Dorset, Devon and Cornwall) delight food lovers with creamy cheeses, marshland sheep from Romney Marsh and Pevensey, soles from Dover, scallops and dabs from Rye, cakes and pies, bacons and hams from countless small farms, early new season potatoes from Cornwall and the near sub-tropical Scilly Isles, farmhouse ciders and scrumpy. The shores of southwest England have long produced a healthy supply of crabs and seafood from Brixham, as well as plump, oil-rich mackerel from Cornwall, monkfish and species of shallow water fish such as hake, John Dory and sea bass (much of which has been bought even before it is landed and spirited away to European and Japanese markets). The southwest is also the land of rich pastures producing creams for butter, cheese, golden Cornish icecream and the unique par-cooked clotted cream to dollop on scones or spoon on hot sweet fruit pies and crumbles.

From Cornwall the coast sweeps up to Wales, where foods of the Celtic ancient Britons still feature. One is laverbread, a type of seaweed, which you can buy online. It is the same as nori, as used by the Japanese to make sushi, but in Wales it is an accompaniment to roast Welsh lamb, which is prized the world over for its sweet and slightly salty flavour. Welsh cooks, on the margins of good farming land, are masterly at making stews and soups using barley and leeks, or serving up tasty cockles gathered from the beautiful bays and beaches, eels from the Severn Estuary, meaty liver faggots in onion gravy, cheesy toasted rarebits and the lightest of scones, warm from the oven and oozing with melted butter.

## ... BRITAIN'S BEST

The heart of England, the Midlands, the very hub of the Industrial Revolution, is also rich in cultural history – it is after all the birthplace of Shakespeare. This, too, is where landowners of great estates took pride in building up fine herds of cattle, sheep and pigs, some of which we know today as the rare breeds still cherished and promoted as fine-quality beef, lamb and pork. Rolling arable fields yield high-quality grains, orchards in Hereford and Worcester give bumper crops of cider apples while the Vales of Evesham and Belvoir produce soft fruits, stone fruits and asparagus spears. The hedgerows here yield rich commercial pickings too, both fruit and flowers, among which are the elderflower blossoms, gathered on a sunny day in May or June and steeped to make fragrant cordials.

The great northern counties of Lancashire, the Peak District and the Lake District have their regional specialities – black pudding, toffees, hillside lamb, sweet yeasty breads and cakes, Morecombe Bay shrimps and of course, two of our great British cheeses: creamy blue Stilton and tangy Lancashire.

On the northeast coast (Northumberland, Durham and Cleveland together with England's largest county, Yorkshire) local food producers excel with cheeses (crumbly Wensleydale), hams from York, fish from Hull and some of the UK's most popular ales and beers; this is the land of the 'amber nectar'. It also is an area that prides itself on home baking from Singin' Hinnies and Stottie cakes to apple pies (served with a chunk of cheese), teacakes, pikelets and Harrogate toffee.

And over the border we go into Scotland where, like Wales, the canny farmers and cooks have made a virtue of turning less than ideal conditions of colder, brisk weather and less good soils into producing top-quality foods from the tranquil lowlands in the south to the wild and romantic Highlands and Islands. Scottish foods read like *Who's Who* in the world's gourmet club – raspberries, heather honey, shortbread, oatcakes, Shetland lamb, wild and farmed salmon, Finnan haddock, Arbroath Smokies, Stornoway black pudding, hand-dived scallops and lobsters from clear deep-water lochs – not forgetting whisky and the inimitable haggis with Neeps 'n' tatties. With a long heritage of home baking, Scottish émigré cooks took their cherished recipes for cakes, biscuits and breads to colonies in the New World, Australia and New Zealand.

Across the water, Ireland's less harsh climate and landscape of roll-ing green hills nourish dairy cattle producing rich milk, and (together with a buoyant economy) have encouraged the new European citizens to set up speciality cheese dairies, bakeries and other small food businesses. Quality Irish beef and fish appear on menus the world over, from salmon fished in clean rivers to rope-grown mussels in Bantry Bay. The Irish, always keen on gatherings, celebrate their food culture with festivals to draw in not only visitors but also the enthusiastic local producers.

All of the British Isles, whatever the region and season, have a long history of using free foods – fruits, blossom, leaves, mushrooms, nuts, seafood, samphire and seaweeds, and small game such as rabbits and hares. Hedgerow hips, berries and crab apples are stewed into jams and jellies; sloes steeped in gin; elderflowers made into a sparkling drink; wild herbs and leaves such as garlic leaves, fat hen, sorrel, watercress, nettles and dandelions go into salads and soups, along with mushrooms, includ-ing chanterelles, girolles and ceps found in beech forests and woodlands.

## GREAT BRITISH CHEESES

The impact of two world wars on British food and cooking when everyone had to 'dig for victory' and endure strict rationing was marked, even after rationing ended. Our once diverse cheese industry was badly affected and only now, over 60 years on, are we enjoying a renaissance of quality artisan cheeses. Cheddar may be the most imitated cheese in the world but many traditional cheese-making skills were lost during World War II and subsequent attention has been concentrated on rebuilding the nine regional hard cheeses known as the 'Territorials': Cheddar, Caerphilly, Cheshire, Stilton, Double Gloucester, Red Leicester, Derby, Lancashire and Wensleydale. There are very many more fine British cheeses.

Good cheese is like fine wine – the raw product reflects the soil, aspect, climate, welfare of the animals and even when they are milked, morning or evening. The skill and imagination of the cheese maker give individuality and character. With some of the best farmland in the world it is no wonder the growth in British cheeses has gathered speed among both traditional cheese-makers and new enthusiasts bringing fresh ideas. We have mould-ripened Brie styles, goat's and sheep's milk cheeses (hard and soft), Raclette and Parmesan types, logs and pyramids and creamy blue cheeses to rival the great European cheeses. Central to this rebirth of the home cheese industry are the British Cheese Awards.

Several British cheeses, such as West Country Cheddars, Stiltons and Lancashires, now hold EU classifications protecting their names and quality – Protected Designation of Origin (PDO) and Protected Geographical Indication (PGI). Several lesser-known regional cheeses have also been awarded PDO status. Read the labels before you buy. Cheese labelled 'Farmhouse' indicates that it is made in smaller dairies, not big factories.

Some personal favourites, starting with traditional Territorials, would be:

**CHEDDARS** – first recorded by name around AD1500. The best Cheddars can take up to 18 months to reach full maturity. Look for Montgomery, Quickes, Keens and Westcombe. The international Slow Food movement also works to protect classic Farmhouse Somerset Cheddar.

**STILTON** – the ultimate creamy blue British cheese. These cheeses can come only from Derbyshire, Leicestershire and Nottinghamshire (and not, ironically, from Stilton, the Cambridgeshire village where this cheese was apparently first served to travellers who feasted at the Bell Inn). Best known are Colston Basset, Cropwell Bishop and Quenby Stiltons. Dovedale is a creamier softer Stilton-style cheese that spreads like a Brie.

**LANCASHIRE** – crumbly and buttery. This is a blend of morning and evening milkings, wonderful for toasting or serving with hot apple pie. White lighter cheeses are made from single milkings. Most Lancashire cheese is eaten in the region. The best known is perhaps Kirkham's.

**WENSLEYDALE** – a tangy, crumbly white cheese from Yorkshire, popularized in the animated films *Wallace and Gromit*, frequently served with apple pie or fruit cake. A variation is Cotherstone made in the Yorkshire village of the same name.

**CAERPHILLY** – (the Welsh miner's cheese) a mild and slightly acidic cheese, perfect for salads.

**CHESHIRE** – reputably Britain's oldest cheese, mentioned in the Domesday Book. Best known is Appleby's Cheshire (which is actually made in Shropshire). There are white, golden yellow and blue varieties.

**DOUBLE GLOUCESTER AND RED LEICESTER** – deeper in colour with a rich flavour, making them good for cooking. They are made from single and double milkings.

**SAGE DERBY** – lightly pressed with mottled layers of green sage.

The list of fine farmhouse artisan cheeses, using cow's, ewe's, goat's and even buffalo's milk, is growing. Some are variations of traditional Territorials; others are completely new styles: semi-soft, mould-ripened, charcoal-coated, etc. Many are prize winners at both national and international levels and are well worth seeking out.

From England there is Ilchester, Lincolnshire Poacher, Stinking Bishop, Cornish Yarg, Swaledale, Bonchester, Buxton Blue, Dorset Blue, Blue Vinny, Beenleigh Blue; from Wales, Y Fenni (flavoured with ale and mustard) and Pantysgawn; from Scotland, oat-coated Caboc, Crowdie, Isle of Mull, Lanark Blue; and from Ireland, Durrus, Cashel Blue, Gubeen, Coolea, Cooleeney and St Killian.

**COOKING WITH BRITISH CHEESES**  Many of the recipes in this collection require a firm cheese for cooking. These I refer to as 'Cheddar type' – but you can vary the flavour by choosing any of the traditional Territorial cheeses above. Gruyère and Parmesan are sometimes called for, reflecting the European influence in older British recipes, or those we have adopted, such as good old Spaghetti Bolognese (page 75).

## A HERITAGE OF EATING

With this readily available supply of fine produce and a relatively prosperous population, it is not surprising that food and feasting play an important part in the cultural life of Britons. Until recently, there were still regional variations on when meals were taken. Main meal times varied markedly from south to north. In the south, including the Home Counties around London, a two- or three-course meal would often be taken around midday when office workers could return home to lunch. The leisured or middle classes would stop for a little snack around 4 pm – afternoon tea (see page 169), followed by supper (a light hot meal) at about 7 pm or – for formal occasions – an elegant dinner at 8, starting with clear soup, a hot main course, dessert (pudding) and cheese or a savoury, a small tasty mouthful to clear the palette. A colder climate and the paucity of heating in the homes meant that our forebears needed a greater calorie intake than modern families and consequently had appetites that seem positively gargantuan by today's standards.

In the industrial heartlands of northern England, Wales and Scotland, workers had a shorter midday break and so returned from the factories hopeful of a hot main meal around 5 pm, which they called High Tea. This would consist of a homely dish such as simple stew or fish with potatoes, eggs and cheese with bread and butter, followed not by a rich dessert but a slab of homely cake and all washed down with mugs of tea or ale. The menfolk would then retire to their local pub and down several pints of locally brewed beer before returning home around 9 pm for another snack – or supper – again, some cake or a chunk of cheese. Thus, amusingly, the words 'tea' and 'supper' mean different meals to Britons depending on whether they come from the north or south.

Leisure time involved a tradition of eating. Village halls, sports pavilions, fêtes and festivals have all played host to parties, with people often bringing their own home baking or plates of cold cuts (sliced meats), chutneys, potato salads, crusty cottage leaves, sausage rolls, cakes and biscuits. A large hot water urn ensuring a good supply of tea and, for more merry occasions, a local publican might bring a barrel (or more) of ale. During summer months, features of rural Britain still are local cricket matches between village teams, with the essential tea table for weary players (and their long-suffering partners) groaning with plates of sandwiches, cakes, egg flans and scones washed down, of course, with plenty of hot tea and fruit squash. Another popular annual event is the agricultural show, where locals proudly display prize vegetables (leeks, marrows, carrots or onions) from their allotment or back garden, nourished with secret nutrients from compost heaps. Perfect cakes – Victoria sponges, gingerbreads, fruit cakes and scones – along with pots of perfectly set jams and squares of creamy fudge will be poked, sampled and judged – the winners content with a small cash prize and a large rosette to secure their reputation until the next year.

## FEASTING AND FESTIVALS

The British Isles has a wealth of festive foods, many based on religious
Christian origins. The year starts with Twelfth Night (6th January) followed
by Shrove Tuesday in February, when pancakes are made to use up rich
foods from the larder in preparation for 40 days of fasting during Lent.
Easter signals the end of plain fare and a return to meat eating, often with
a lamb roast (to commemorate the paschal lamb) and a rich fruity Simnel
Cake (page 182) and Easter Biscuits (page 192). Summer is light on
religious festivals but social eating takes over, ideally outdoors. From
those cricket matches to tennis parties, barbecues, family celebrations,
weddings and, of course, picnicking, the British love to take their chances
with the weather and plan outdoor eating, perhaps with a marquee set up
just in case the rain clouds gather. September sees a return to festivals
based on the Church calendar (albeit it with less regard to the religious
element these days) – there's Harvest Festival, when the fruits of the
harvest are displayed in churches and services are held to give thanks
for this natural bounty, Michaelmas (29th September, traditionally the
start of the goose season) and Hallowe'en, which is now a big commercial
operation. In between many regional favourites are still held, such as
the Feast of St Oswald in Grasmere, Cumbria, where Gingerbread (page
193) is baked. Other towns and villages uphold traditions that date back
hundreds of years, including cheese rolling (chasing truckles of cheese
downhill), pancake tossing and apple bobbing. One British festival has a
blatant political meaning: the 5th November, Guy Fawkes' Night, when
Britons unite around a bonfire, watch firework displays, eat fat sausages
(bangers) and sip mulled ale or spiced wine to celebrate the deliverance
of Parliament in 1605 from the Gunpowder Plot.

## THE GREAT BRITISH CHRISTMAS

No festival is more popular or celebrated than our traditional Christmas,
and throughout this book you will find many recipes suitable for festive
feasting. Start on Christmas Eve with Baked Salmon with Hot Beetroot
(page 55). On the big day itself, toast the forthcoming feast with a special
Christmas Punch (page 213), followed by Roast Turkey with Stuffing,
Giblet Gravy (page 111) and Cranberry and Port Relish (page 206). For
dessert, there's Christmas Pudding (page 147) and Rum or Brandy Butter
(page 206), Mince Pies (page 143) or Strawberry Trifle (page 158). You
might offer chutney (pages 206–209) or sweets (pages 192–197) as
presents and, of course, the ultimate cut-and-come-again Christmas Cake
(page 182).

   Boxing Day (26th December) is a day for a splendid buffet, which
might include Spiced Silverside of Beef (page 98), Mustard Glazed Ham
(page 91) and Turkey Pie (page 112), all enjoyed with winter salads and
baked potatoes.

# BASICS

You don't need a lot of equipment or fancy skills to cook good food, just a decent set of heavy-based saucepans and two or three non-stick frying pans is a fair start. Invest in a solid roasting pan and a couple of baking trays and bun tins: they will last for years. A cast-iron casserole is more than useful, because you can put it in the oven or on the hob. Many cooks wouldn't be without a food-processor these days, but a hand-held electric mixer will suffice for most baking tasks.

You'll find some basic recipes on the following pages, showing you how to make stocks, sauces, pastry and other integral parts of the recipes in the book. Many of the recipes are very easy – even if you're new to cooking – but it may be helpful to know a little more about jam-making.

## JAM-MAKING

Making jam is not an exact science, so recipes are only a guide. Fruits should be ripe but not overripe and most need to be gently cooked first in plenty of water until tender before sugar is added and boiled to a set.

Jams and fruit jellies react with sugar, fruit acids and a substance called pectin to give a set. Lower sugar jams give a softer set than higher levels. For a firm set, allow 1kg sugar per litre (or 1lb sugar to 16fl oz of cooked fruit pulp). Modern jams have a lighter set, with 750–800g (1lb 10oz–1lb 12oz) sugar per litre (1¾ pints, 4 cups) of pulp.

### EQUIPMENT
You will need a preserving pan with a heavy base for slow simmering. Alternatively, small quantities of jam can be made in a large saucepan. Always stir with a long-handled wooden spoon so you don't get splattered with boiling jam. A sugar thermometer helps, as does a wide-neck metal funnel for pouring into warm jam jars. For clear jellies, you will need a fine flannel jelly bag and a hook to hang it from, or use an upturned stool.

### TO CHECK FOR A SET
First place two or three small plates in the freezer to chill. Boil the pulp and sugar until it drips from a wooden spoon rather than runs straight down (called flaking). Spoon a small ladle of jam onto a chilled plate and wait for 5 minutes or so, then push the jam or jelly away from you and hold the plate up to the light. A slight skin should form and wrinkle. If no wrinkle appears, continue to boil the hot sugar pulp for a few minutes longer, then repeat the exercise.

### PREPARING CLEAN JAM JARS
Any screw-top jar with a metal lid will do, or use preserving jars (for syrups and vinegars use glass bottles). Heat in a low oven until hot so the jam won't crack the glass when it is poured in (use a metal jam funnel). Most modern jam jars hold around 400ml (14fl oz, 1⅔ cups).

# BASIC RECIPES

## Chicken stock

**MAKES** about 1 litre (1¾pints, 4 cups)   **PREPARATION TIME** 10 minutes   **COOKING TIME** 45 minutes

2 tbsp vegetable oil
8 chicken wings
1 onion, chopped
1 carrot, chopped
1 stick celery, chopped

1 bay leaf
2 sprigs of thyme or tarragon
sea salt and freshly ground black
   or white pepper

1   Heat the oil in a large pan and brown the chicken wings until golden, then add the vegetables to the pan and cook for 5 minutes. Pour in 2 litres (3½ pints, 8 cups) water and the herbs. Bring to the boil.

2   Season lightly and simmer, uncovered, until reduced by half (about 30 minutes), then pour off the stock. Cool and chill. Can be frozen.

### VARIATION

### Beef, veal, lamb or game stock
Use 1.5kg (3lb 5oz) fresh bones instead of chicken wings. For game bird stock use the backs and small legs of birds after breasts are removed.

## Fish stock

**MAKES** about 600ml (1 pint, 2½ cups)   **PREPARATION TIME** 5 minutes   **COOKING TIME** 25 minutes

about 500g (1lb 2oz) fresh white fish bones
1 small onion, roughly chopped
1 carrot, roughly chopped
1 stick celery, chopped
1 bay leaf

2 large parsley stalks
1 blade mace, optional
½ tsp black peppercorns
1 small wineglass (175ml, 6fl oz, ¾ cup)
   white wine (optional)

1   Put the bones, vegetables, herbs, peppercorns and wine (if using) into a large pan with 1 litre (1¾ pints, 4 cups) water. Bring to the boil, then simmer for 20 minutes and strain before use. Can be frozen.

## Court bouillon

**MAKES** about 1 litre (1¾ pints, 4 cups)   **PREPARATION TIME** 5 minutes   **COOKING TIME** 15 minutes

1 shallot, sliced
1 small carrot, sliced
1 stick celery, or ¼ small fennel bulb, sliced
2 sprigs of fresh thyme

1 bay leaf
150ml (5fl oz, ⅔ cup) white wine vinegar
   or dry white wine
sea salt and freshly ground black pepper

1   Put the shallot, carrot, celery, herbs, vinegar, 1 tsp salt and some pepper into a large pan with 1.5 litres (2¾ pints, 6 cups) water. Bring to the boil, cover and simmer for 15 minutes and strain before use.

# Béchamel sauce

**MAKES** about 600ml (1 pint, 2½ cups)　**PREPARATION TIME** 10 minutes plus infusing　**COOKING TIME** 5 minutes

750ml (1¼ pints, 3 cups) milk
1 small onion, sliced
1 small carrot, chopped
1 stick celery, chopped
1 large bay leaf

2 sprigs of thyme
a little grated nutmeg or 2 blades mace
25g (1oz) butter
2 tbsp flour
sea salt and freshly ground black pepper

1　Heat the milk with the vegetables, herbs and spices and simmer for 3 minutes. Remove, infuse for 1 hour, strain the milk, return to the pan and reheat until very hot.
2　Melt the butter in a non-stick pan, add the flour and cook for 1 minute on a low heat. Gradually beat in the hot milk, stirring well until smooth and creamy. Season to taste.

# Quick white sauce

**MAKES** about 500ml (18fl oz, 2 cups)　**PREPARATION TIME** 2 minutes　**COOKING TIME** 5 minutes

2 tbsp butter or soft margarine
3 tbsp flour
500ml (18fl oz, 2 cups) milk

¼ tsp dried thyme
a little grated nutmeg (optional)
sea salt and freshly ground black pepper

1　Put everything into a non-stick pan and bring slowly to the boil, stirring until thick. Simmer for 1–2 minutes.

# Bread sauce

**MAKES** about 500ml (18fl oz, 2 cups)　**PREPARATION TIME** 5 minutes plus infusing　**COOKING TIME** 5 minutes

1 shallot, stuck with 3 cloves
1 bay leaf
250ml (9fl oz, 1 cup) creamy milk
100g (3½oz, 1 cup) fresh breadcrumbs

120ml (4fl oz, ½ cup) single cream
knob of butter
a little freshly grated nutmeg
sea salt and freshly ground white pepper

1　Place the shallot in a non-stick pan with the bay leaf and milk. Heat to boiling point, remove and let stand. Strain the milk, reheat until almost boiling, then beat in the breadcrumbs. Season, stir in the cream and butter and add the nutmeg.

# Basic batter

**MAKES** 6 x 20cm (8in) or 4 x 23cm (9in) pancakes　**PREPARATION TIME** 5 minutes　**COOKING TIME** 10 minutes

250ml (9fl oz, 1 cup) milk
100g (3½oz, ⅔ cup) plain flour

½ tsp sea salt
1 large egg

1　Whiz together all the ingredients in a food processor, or sift the flour into a large bowl, make a well in the centre, drop in the egg and half the milk then gradually combine with a whisk, adding the remaining milk little by little at the end.

**TO MAKE PANCAKES**

Heat a large, heavy-based, non-stick frying pan until hot, rub with oiled kitchen paper. Use a generous ladleful of batter for each pancake. Cook until holes appear, then flip over for a few seconds to cook the other side. Slide onto a plate, cover with foil and keep warm while you make the rest, oiling the pan as necessary. For sweet pancakes, add 2 tbsp icing sugar to the basic batter recipe.

# Shortcrust pastry

**MAKES** 3 x 275g (9½oz) blocks  **PREPARATION TIME** 10–12 minutes  **COOKING TIME** as recipe

500g (1lb 2oz, 3⅓ cups) plain flour
1 tsp sea salt
250g (9oz) butter, chilled and cut into
   small cubes

1 large egg, beaten
about 2 tbsp ice-cold water

1  Whiz the flour, salt and butter in a food processor to form fine crumbs. Mix in the egg and pulse until the mixture forms clumps.
2  Tip into a bowl and draw together with your hands, sprinkling with cold water until it forms a smooth but not sticky dough. Knead lightly and then divide into 3 blocks. Wrap in cling film for use as required. Will freeze for up to 3 months. Allow to thaw completely and knead lightly again before use.

# Sweet dessert pastry

**MAKES** about 1kg (2lb 4oz), or 3 x 330–340g (12oz) blocks  **PREPARATION TIME** 10 minutes  **COOKING TIME** as recipe

250g (9oz) butter, softened
180g (6oz, ⅞ cup) caster sugar
3–4 vanilla pods or 1½–2 tsp vanilla extract

2 large eggs, beaten
500g (1lb 2oz, 3⅓ cups) plain flour

1  Beat the butter and sugar until smooth and creamy in an electric mixer. Slit open the vanilla pods and scrape the seeds into the mixture with the tip of a sharp knife, or add the extract.
2  With the motor running at slow speed, gradually add the eggs then the flour in stages. As soon as the mixture comes together as a crumbly mixture, stop the motor. Remove the mixture and knead it with your hands to a smooth dough.
3  Divide into 3 blocks, wrap in cling film for use as required. Will freeze for up to 3 months. Allow to thaw completely and knead lightly again before use.

# Rough puff pastry (feuilletage)

**MAKES** 425g (15oz)  **PREPARATION TIME** 10–15 minutes  **COOKING TIME** as recipe

250g (9oz, 1⅔ cups) strong plain flour
1 tsp fine sea salt

250g (9oz) butter, at room temperature but
   not soft, cut into small cubes
about 125ml (4fl oz, ½ cup) cold water

1  Sift the flour and salt into a large bowl. Mix the butter into the flour with a table knife. Don't rub in. Mix in enough cold water to make a firm rough dough. Cover with cling film and chill for 20 minutes.
2  Knead lightly and quickly then shape into a smooth rectangle on a lightly floured board. Roll it in one direction only until it is 3 times the length, approximately 15 x 50cm (6 x 20in), ensuring the edges remain straight and even.
3  Fold the top third down to the centre, then the bottom third over that. Give the dough block a quarter turn (to the left or right) and roll out again to 3 times the length. Fold as before, cover with cling film and chill for at least 30 minutes before rolling to use.

# Suet pastry

**MAKES** about 425g (15oz)   **PREPARATION TIME** 2 minutes   **COOKING TIME** as recipe

250g (9oz, 1²/₃ cups) self-raising flour
125g (4oz, 1 cup) shredded suet
1 tsp sea salt

freshly ground black pepper
ice-cold water, to mix

1   Mix together the flour, suet, salt and pepper, then stir in enough cold water to make a firm but not dry dough.
2   Knead lightly then divide into 8 balls for dumplings or roll out for steamed puddings.

# Vinaigrette

**MAKES** 250ml (9fl oz, 1 cup)   **PREPARATION TIME** 2 minutes   **COOKING TIME** nil

160ml (5¹/₂fl oz, ²/₃ cup) olive or sunflower
   oil, or half and half
4 tbsp white or red wine vinegar

1 tsp French mustard
sea salt and freshly ground black or
   white pepper

1   Put all the ingredients in a jam jar, add seasoning to taste and screw on the lid tightly. Shake well to blend. Store in the fridge and shake before each use.

# Apricot glaze

**PREPARATION TIME** 1 minute   **COOKING TIME** 3 minutes

1 jar apricot jam
2 tbsp fresh lemon juice

1   Spoon the apricot jam into a small saucepan. Add 2–3 tbsp water and the lemon juice. Heat gently until runny then rub through a heatproof sieve into a jug and decant back into the jam jar.

# Real custard

**MAKES** 300ml (10fl oz, 1¹/₄ cups)   **PREPARATION TIME** 5–10 minutes   **COOKING TIME** 5 minutes

250ml (9fl oz, 1 cup) whole milk or
   single cream
1–2 tbsp caster sugar
1 vanilla pod, split, or ¹/₂ tsp vanilla extract

1 large egg
2 egg yolks
1 tbsp cornflour (optional, for a thick custard)

1   Heat the milk with the sugar. While it is heating, scrape the sticky seeds from the vanilla pod, if using, into the pan with the tip of a sharp knife, or add the extract.
2   Beat the egg, yolks and cornflour, if using, in a heatproof bowl. When the milk starts to rise in the pan (i.e. scald), tip it gradually onto the yolks, simultaneously beating with a whisk until smooth. Pour back into the pan and stir over a very low heat until the liquid thickens then immediately pour back into the bowl and, for extra flavour, add the vanilla pod. Cover with cling film and cool. Remove the vanilla pod before serving.

**Note** For making ice creams, use either double or whipping cream, twice the amount of sugar, and omit the cornflour.

# CHAPTER 1

# SOUPS, STARTERS & LIGHT DISHES

Browse through an old British cookery book and you could well be surprised by the number of imaginative soup recipes it contains. Mrs Beeton's first book from 1859, for example, devotes almost 60 pages to soups, many of which would not look out of place in today's modern food magazines. Soups can be a light first course to a dinner or a hearty main meal, perfect for lunch or a tasty supper. Delightful regional names like Partan Bree and Cock-a-leekie reflect country traditions, while soups like Mulligatawny are more exotic with the use of aromatic Indian spices. There is even a Plum Soup in this collection, perfect for using up autumn gluts, which deliciously combines dessert plums, wine and cinnamon.

The starters and light dishes in this chapter are a wonderful microcosm of the best Britain has to offer in terms of using fresh ingredients – vegetables from kitchen gardens, fish from our seas and shorelines, and cheese and egg dishes that suit breakfasts, brunches and lunches, as well as some old-style savouries for formal dinner menus.

## 001 Garden fresh tomato soup

**PREPARATION TIME** 15 minutes **COOKING TIME** 30 minutes

1 onion, chopped
1 carrot, chopped
1 celery stick, chopped
2 tbsp vegetable oil
750g (1lb 9oz) ripe tomatoes, cored,
   skinned and chopped
1 large sprig of marjoram or rosemary

1 large sprig of thyme
850ml (1½ pints, 3⅓ cups) vegetable stock
sea salt and freshly ground black pepper
4 tbsp single cream, half-fat crème fraîche
   or natural yogurt, to swirl
2 tbsp chopped chives or spring onion
   tops (optional), to sprinkle

1   Gently sauté the onion, carrot and celery in the oil in a large pan for 5 minutes.
    Add the chopped tomatoes, herbs and seasoning. Cover and sweat for a
    further 5 minutes.
2   Add the stock, bring to the boil then simmer for 20 minutes. Strain off and reserve
    the liquid. Blitz the vegetables in a liquidizer or food processor until smooth,
    gradually pouring in the liquid.
3   Return to the pan, check the seasoning and reheat. Ladle into warmed bowls.
    Swirl with the cream and sprinkle with the chives, if using.

## 002 Chilled cucumber soup

**PREPARATION TIME** 15 minutes **COOKING TIME** 25 minutes

1 large cucumber
2 shallots, chopped
2 tbsp vegetable oil
25g (1 oz) butter
2 tsp cider or wine vinegar
1 tbsp chopped dill or fennel
1 tbsp chopped mint

2 tbsp semolina
1 litre (1¾ pints, 4 cups) vegetable
   stock or water
3 tbsp half-fat crème fraîche or
   single cream
sea salt and freshly ground black pepper

1   Top and tail the cucumber, then cut off 12 thin slices and reserve for the garnish.
    Quarter the rest lengthways and chop roughly. Sauté gently in a large pan with the
    shallots, oil and butter for 5 minutes.
2   Add the vinegar, cook for 1 minute then stir in the herbs, semolina and stock or
    water. Season, bring to the boil, stirring briskly to blend the semolina, then simmer
    for 20 minutes. Strain off and reserve the liquid. Blend the vegetables in a liquidizer
    or food processor until smooth, gradually pouring in the reserved liquid, together
    with the crème fraîche.
3   To serve cold, cool, check the seasoning (cold soups need extra) and chill until
    required. To serve hot, pour back into the pan, reheat and check the seasoning.
    Top each serving with the reserved cucumber and a light grinding of pepper.

## 003 Split pea and bacon soup

**PREPARATION TIME** 5 minutes plus soaking **COOKING TIME** 1 hour

1 onion, chopped
1 carrot, chopped
150g (5oz, ¾ cup) split peas or green lentils,
   soaked overnight and drained
125g (4oz) smoked streaky bacon, chopped

1 litre (1¾ pints, 4 cups) vegetable stock
1 bay leaf
2 sprigs of thyme
sea salt and freshly ground black pepper

1   Put all the ingredients in a large pan and season to taste. Bring to the boil, stirring,
    then simmer, partially covered, for about 1 hour or until the pulses have softened
    and broken down.
2   Remove the bay and thyme to serve.

## 004 Watercress and potato soup

**PREPARATION TIME** 5 minutes  **COOKING TIME** 20 minutes

1 large floury potato, peeled and finely diced
4 spring onions, chopped
3 tbsp vegetable oil
800ml (1½ pints, 3⅓ cups) vegetable stock
200g (7oz) watercress, washed and roughly
   chopped

sea salt and freshly ground black pepper
single cream, to swirl
2 tbsp chopped chives, to sprinkle

1  Gently sauté the potato and onions in the oil in a large pan for about 5 minutes
   then pour in the stock and add seasoning to taste.
2  Bring to the boil, partially cover and simmer for 10 minutes until the potato starts
   to break down. Press down several times with a masher.
3  Drop in the watercress, return to a simmer and cook for 2–3 minutes. Check the
   seasoning. To serve hot, swirl with a little cream and sprinkle with chives.
   To serve cool, blend in a liquidizer or food processor until smooth and chill.
   Serve with the cream and chives.

## 005 Cream of mushroom soup

**PREPARATION TIME** 12 minutes  **COOKING TIME** 30 minutes

3–4 shallots or 1 onion, finely chopped
2 cloves garlic, crushed
1 stick celery, chopped
3 tbsp vegetable oil
40g (1½oz) butter
250g (9oz) chestnut or brown mushrooms,
   stalks chopped, caps sliced
4 tbsp dry sherry (optional)

800ml (1½ pints, 3⅓ cups) chicken or
   vegetable stock
1 bay leaf
2 sprigs of thyme
sea salt and freshly ground black pepper
3–4 tbsp double cream, to swirl
chopped parsley, to sprinkle

1  Sauté the shallots, garlic and celery in the oil in a large pan for about 5 minutes
   until softened. Remove from the pan with a slotted spoon and set aside.
2  Melt the butter in the pan and sauté the mushroom stalks and two-thirds of the
   caps over a high heat. Deglaze with the sherry, if using, for 1 minute then return
   the vegetables and add the stock. Season well, add the herbs and bring to the boil
   then simmer, partially covered, for 15 minutes.
3  Discard the bay and thyme stalks and blend the soup in a liquidizer or food
   processor until smooth then return to the pan. Bring back to the boil, add the
   remaining mushrooms and simmer for 5 minutes. Check the seasoning and serve
   with a swirl of cream and a little chopped parsley.

## 006 Chicken noodle soup

**PREPARATION TIME** 3 minutes  **COOKING TIME** 10 minutes

1 litre (1¾ pints, 4 cups) Chicken stock
   (see page 16)
2 tsp vegetable bouillon powder or 1 chicken
   stock cube
125g (4oz) cooked chicken breast, pulled
   into fine shreds

4 tbsp sweetcorn kernels
1 nest thin egg noodles or vermicelli pasta
sea salt and freshly ground black pepper
1 spring onion, finely shredded, to sprinkle

1  Put the chicken stock in a pan and bring to the boil. Whisk in the bouillon powder
   to incorporate. Drop in the shredded chicken and sweetcorn then add the noodles,
   broken into small lengths.
2  Simmer for about 5 minutes, check the seasoning and serve sprinkled with the
   shredded spring onion.

## 007 Chicken consommé

**PREPARATION TIME** 10 minutes **COOKING TIME** 50–60 minutes

2 fresh chicken carcasses, roughly chopped,
    or about 1kg (2lb 4oz) wings
vegetable oil, for frying
3 shallots or 1 onion, roughly sliced
2 carrots, 1 roughly chopped, 1 cut in long
    thin sticks
1 stick celery, roughly chopped
1 leek, chopped
2 cloves garlic, roughly crushed

2 sprigs of thyme
1 tbsp tomato purée
1 small skinless, boneless chicken
    breast, chopped
1 tsp black or white peppercorns
2 egg whites
sea salt
½ small courgette, cut in long thin sticks and
    1 tbsp finely chopped chives, to garnish

1. Brown the chopped carcasses or wings in a little hot oil in a large pan, then remove and drain. Wipe out the pan and return the bones or wings. Add the shallots, chopped carrot, celery, leek, garlic, thyme, tomato purée, chopped chicken and peppercorns. Pour in 2 litres (3½ pints, 8 cups) water.

2. Bring to the boil then lower the heat to cook at a very gentle simmer for 30–40 minutes until reduced by half. Season with salt to taste. Remove from the heat and stand for 10 minutes, then strain through a sieve lined with wet muslin or a clean J-cloth. Leave to cool.

3. Wash out the pan and return the cooled liquid. Roughly whip the egg whites and stir in. Bring the liquid slowly back to the boil, whisking all the time. A grey crust will form that filters the liquid until clear.

4. Stop whisking when boiling, simmer for 2 minutes so the liquid boils through the egg crust then remove from the heat. Spoon the crust into the lined sieve and carefully pour through the liquid. By now it should be crystal clear. Blanch the carrot and courgette sticks in boiling water for 1–2 minutes. Reheat the consommé and serve garnished with the vegetable sticks and chives.

## 008 Beef tea

**PREPARATION TIME** 5 minutes **COOKING TIME** 4 hours–overnight

500g (1lb 2oz) lean shin of beef, trimmed of
    all fat and cut in large chunks
2 slices of onion
1 small carrot, roughly chopped
1 stick celery, roughly chopped

1 bay leaf
1 sprig of thyme
1 tsp black or white peppercorns
1 tsp sea salt
a little dry sherry, to serve (optional)

1. Put all the ingredients except the sherry into a large cast-iron casserole. Preheat the oven to 150°C (300°F, Gas Mark 2) if cooking overnight.

2. Cover with 1 litre (1¾ pints, 4 cups) boiling water. Bring slowly to the point of boiling, skimming off any scum. Cover with a tight-fitting lid. If cooking in the oven allow 8–10 hours; if cooking on the hob, turn the heat to the lowest setting and poach the liquid for at least 4 hours. The meat should be very tender.

3. Allow the contents to settle off the heat without stirring for 30 minutes, then carefully pour off the clear liquid into a jug. Discard the meat and vegetables. Reheat in cups with a splash of sherry, if liked. It can be frozen in single portions.

## 009 Beetroot, apple and cumin seed soup

**PREPARATION TIME** 10–12 minutes **COOKING TIME** 30 minutes

1 red onion, finely chopped
1 stick celery, finely chopped
500g (1lb 2oz) raw beetroot, peeled and
  finely chopped
1 small cooking apple, peeled, cored and
  chopped
3 tbsp vegetable oil

1 tsp cumin seeds
1 tbsp cider vinegar (optional)
1 litre (1¾ pints, 4 cups) vegetable stock
sea salt and freshly ground black pepper
natural yogurt, to swirl
sprigs of coriander or flat leaf parsley
  (optional), to garnish

1   Put all the chopped vegetables and apple in a large pan with the oil. Heat until
    sizzling then lower the heat, cover and sweat for about 10 minutes, shaking
    the pan occasionally to prevent any sticking.
2   Stir in the cumin seeds and vinegar and cook for 1–2 minutes then add the stock
    and seasoning. Reheat until boiling, then simmer gently, uncovered, for 15 minutes
    until vegetables are tender.
3   If you wish, blend the soup in a food processor or liquidizer until smooth. Check the
    seasoning. To serve hot, swirl yogurt over each bowl and add a sprig of coriander,
    if using. To serve cold, chill until required, adding a little extra seasoning.

## 010 Spicy parsnip soup with prawns

**PREPARATION TIME** 15 minutes   **COOKING TIME** 30 minutes

1 onion, chopped
500g (1lb 2oz) young parsnips, peeled
  and chopped
4 tbsp vegetable oil
1 tsp mild curry powder plus extra pinches
1 litre (1¾ pints, 4 cups) vegetable or
  fish stock

large knob of butter or 3 tbsp double cream
8–12 cooked, peeled langoustines or Dublin
  Bay prawns, peeled (tiger prawns can be
  substituted)
squeeze of fresh lemon juice
sea salt and freshly ground black pepper

1 Sauté the onions and parsnips in 3 tbsp of the oil in a large pan for about
  10 minutes until softened and lightly brown. Mix in the 1 tsp curry powder and
  cook for a further minute.
2 Add the stock and seasoning and bring to the boil. Partially cover and simmer for
  20 minutes until the parsnips are softened. Blend the soup in a liquidizer or food
  processor until creamy. Return to the pan and stir in the butter or cream.
3 Heat the remaining oil in a small frying pan and when hot, fry the prawns until
  lightly browned and firm. Season and squeeze over a little lemon juice.
4 Ladle the soup into four warmed bowls and drop in the prawns. Serve with a light
  sprinkling of curry powder.

## 011 Partan Bree

**PREPARATION TIME** 10 minutes   **COOKING TIME** 20 minutes

50g (2oz, ¼ cup) long grain white rice or
  basmati (not easy-cook)
400ml (14fl oz, 1¾ cups) fish stock
300ml (10fl oz, 1¼ cups) milk
250ml (9fl oz, 1 cup) single cream
300g (10oz) brown and white crab meat from
  1–2 dressed crabs

few drops of hot pepper sauce (optional)
squeeze of fresh lemon juice
sea salt and freshly ground white or
  black pepper
2 tbsp chopped chives or spring
  onion tops, to sprinkle

1 Simmer the rice in the stock in a covered pan for 15 minutes until soft. Blend until
  smooth in a liquidizer or food processor, then return to the pan.
2 Stir in the milk, cream, crab meat and seasoning. Bring to the boil then simmer
  gently for 5 minutes. Add the pepper sauce, if using, and lemon juice to taste.
  Serve sprinkled with chives.

## 012 Smoked haddock and potato soup

**PREPARATION TIME** 10 minutes   **COOKING TIME** 25 minutes

1 large baking potato, peeled and diced small
1 large leek, green ends trimmed, thinly sliced
2 tbsp vegetable oil
good knob of butter (optional)
½ tsp mild curry powder
600ml (1 pint, 2½ cups) fish stock or water
300ml (10fl oz, 1¼ cups) milk

300g (10oz) smoked haddock fillet, skinned
  and diced small
4 tbsp frozen peas
sea salt and freshly ground white or
  black pepper
2 tbsp chopped parsley, to sprinkle

1 Put the potato and leek in a large pan with the oil and butter, if using. Heat, then
  cover and sweat gently for 5 minutes. Stir in the curry powder, then add the stock.
  Bring to the boil, then simmer for 10 minutes until the potato is soft.
2 Add the milk, return to a simmer and drop in the diced fish. Season with pepper only
  (the haddock will be salty). Cook for 5 minutes, then add the peas and simmer for
  3 minutes. Check the soup for salt (it may not need much) and serve sprinkled with
  parsley and extra pepper.

## 013 Mulligatawny

**PREPARATION TIME** 15 minutes plus soaking    **COOKING TIME** 1 hour

200g (7oz, 1 cup) brown lentils, soaked
    overnight, or red lentils, washed
1 large onion, chopped
1 large fresh red chilli, seeded and chopped
2 cloves garlic, crushed
1 small green dessert apple, cored, peeled
    and chopped
40g (1½oz) butter
1 tbsp vegetable oil

1 tbsp mild curry powder
4 tomatoes, roughly chopped
1 tbsp tomato purée
1.25 litres (2 pints, 5 cups) vegetable or
    chicken or lamb stock
3 cloves
4 tbsp raisins
sea salt and freshly ground black pepper
1 lemon, quartered, to serve

1   Drain the lentils. Put the onion, chilli, garlic and apple into a large pan and add the
    butter and oil. Heat until sizzling then cook gently for 5 minutes.
2   Mix in the curry powder and cook for 1 minute, then stir in the lentils, tomatoes
    and tomato purée. Pour in the stock, season and add the cloves. Bring to the boil,
    partially cover and simmer 40–50 minutes until the lentils are very soft.
3   Blend in a liquidizer or food processor if liked and return to the pan. Add the raisins
    and cook for a further 5 minutes, then serve with a wedge of lemon.

## 014 Broccoli and Stilton soup

**PREPARATION TIME** 5 minutes    **COOKING TIME** 15 minutes

4 heads broccoli, stalks trimmed and
    finely chopped
125ml (4fl oz, ½ cup) double cream

100g (3½oz) Stilton cheese, crumbled
2 tsp sea salt
freshly ground white or black pepper

1   Put the broccoli into a pan with 1 litre (1¾ pints, 4 cups) water and the salt. Bring
    to the boil then simmer for 10 minutes.
2   Strain the water but reserve. Place the broccoli in a liquidizer or food processor and
    blend for 2 minutes, scraping down the sides once or twice, until very smooth. Then
    add the cream and the pepper.
3   With the blades running, slowly add the reserved water. Return to the pan and reheat
    gently. Serve in warmed soup bowls with the Stilton cheese crumbled over.

## 015 Hotch potch

**PREPARATION TIME** 10 minutes    **COOKING TIME** 1 hour 20 minutes

1 kg (2lb 4oz) neck of lamb, roughly chopped
2 carrots, chopped small
1 small onion, chopped
150g (5oz) swede or turnip, chopped
100g (3½oz) frozen broad beans

½ small cauliflower, cut in small florets
1 Little Gem lettuce, shredded
100g (3½oz, 1 cup) frozen peas
sea salt and freshly ground black pepper
2 tbsp chopped parsley, to sprinkle

1   Put the lamb with 2 litres (3½ pints, 8 cups) water and 1 tsp salt in a large pan.
    Bring to the boil then simmer for about 50 minutes until tender and the liquid is
    reduced by half. Skim off any scum during cooking. Strain the broth and reserve.
    Pull the meat from the bones and chop.
2   Return the liquid to the pan with the carrots, onion, swede and meat. Return to the
    boil then simmer for 15 minutes. Stir in the broad beans and cauliflower and simmer
    for 5 minutes then add the lettuce and peas. Simmer for a further 5 minutes and
    check the seasoning. Serve sprinkled with parsley.

## 016 Welsh cawl

**PREPARATION TIME** 10 minutes    **COOKING TIME** 1 hour 20 minutes

1kg (2lb 4oz) stewing lamb, pork or
    shin of beef, diced small
1 small sprig of rosemary
2 leeks, trimmed and chopped
1 potato, peeled and chopped

1 carrot, chopped
1 turnip or parsnip, chopped
100g (3½oz, 1 cup) frozen peas
sea salt and freshly ground black pepper

1   Put the lamb with 2 litres (3½ pints, 8 cups) water and the rosemary in a large pan.
    Bring to the boil then simmer for about 50 minutes until tender and the liquid is
    reduced by half. Skim off any scum during cooking. Strain the broth and reserve.
    Pick off the meat and chop.
2   Add the vegetables except the peas to the broth and cook for 15–20 minutes
    until softened, then add the peas and the chopped meat and cook for a further
    10 minutes. Check the seasoning and serve.

## 017 Pumpkin soup with scallops

**PREPARATION TIME** 15 minutes    **COOKING TIME** 30 minutes

500g (1lb 2oz) prepared weight pumpkin,
  chopped small
1 small onion, chopped
2 tbsp vegetable oil plus a little extra for
  cooking the scallops
good knob of butter
2 sprigs of thyme
1 litre (1¾ pints, 4 cups) vegetable or
  fish stock

3 tbsp freshly grated Parmesan cheese
  (optional)
125ml (4fl oz, ½ cup) single cream
6 large scallops, corals discarded
few pinches of mild curry powder
sea salt and freshly ground black pepper

1   Sauté the pumpkin and onion in 2 tbsp of the oil with the butter for about 5 minutes
    until softened. Add the thyme and stock. Season lightly and bring to the boil then
    simmer gently for 15 minutes until very soft.
2   Strain the liquid and reserve. Discard the thyme stalks and blend the pumpkin in a
    liquidizer or food processor until smooth and creamy. Whiz in the Parmesan cheese,
    if using, with the strained liquid and cream. Return to the pan, reheat gently and
    check the seasoning.
3   Season and dust the scallops lightly with the curry powder. Heat a little extra oil
    and pan-fry the scallops for 1 minute on each side (no more or they will become
    unpleasantly hard). Remove, leave to stand 2–3 minutes, then slice each scallop
    in half. Ladle the soup into 4 warmed shallow bowls and place 3 halves of
    scallop in each. Grind over more pepper and serve.

## 018 Cock-a-leekie

**PREPARATION TIME** 10 minutes    **COOKING TIME** about 30 minutes

50g (2oz) streaky smoked bacon, chopped
good knob of butter
2 large skinless, boneless chicken thighs,
  chopped small
2 leeks, trimmed and thinly sliced

1.25 litres (2 pints, 5 cups) chicken stock
8 small no-soak prunes or 50g
  (2oz, ⅓ cup) raisins
4 tbsp single cream (optional)
sea salt and freshly ground black pepper

1   Sauté the bacon in the butter for 2 minutes until browned, then add the chicken and
    seasoning and cook a further 2 minutes, stirring. Add the leeks, cook for 2 minutes,
    then pour in the stock.
2   Bring to the boil, stirring, and simmer for 20 minutes until slightly reduced. Add
    the prunes or raisins and cook for 5 minutes. Stir in the cream, if using, check the
    seasoning and serve.

## 019 Plum soup

**PREPARATION TIME** 5 minutes    **COOKING TIME** 10 minutes

500g (1lb 2oz) ripe red dessert plums
150ml (5fl oz, scant ⅔ cup) red wine
125g (4oz, ⅔ cup) caster sugar

1 tbsp red wine vinegar
½ tsp ground cinnamon, plus extra to dust
soured cream or half-fat crème fraîche

1   Cut about a quarter of the plums into wedges and set aside. Stone and roughly
    chop the remainder.
2   Place the wine, sugar and vinegar into a pan with 200ml (7fl oz, ¾ cup) water.
    Bring to the boil, stirring until the sugar dissolves. Add the chopped plums and
    cinnamon. Simmer for 3 minutes. Blend to a thin purée in a liquidizer or food
    processor. If wished, rub the purée through a sieve with the back of a ladle.
3   Chill and serve in dessert bowls with swirls of cream, the reserved plum wedges
    and dust with a little cinnamon.

## 020 Cream of celery soup

**PREPARATION TIME** 5 minutes    **COOKING TIME** 35 minutes

1 large head celery, trimmed, some leaves
  reserved, sticks chopped
1 onion, chopped
2 tbsp vegetable oil
large knob of butter

1.2 litres (2 pints, 5 cups) vegetable or
  chicken stock
250ml (9fl oz, 1 cup) single cream
sea salt and freshly ground black pepper

1   Put the celery, onion, oil and butter into a large saucepan and heat until sizzling.
    Partially cover and cook for 10 minutes until softened, stirring once or twice, then
    pour in the stock and season.
2   Bring to the boil then simmer, uncovered, for 20 minutes until the celery is very soft.
    Strain off and reserve the stock. Purée the vegetables in a liquidizer or food processor
    until smooth and creamy.
3   Return to the pan and mix in the stock and cream. Reheat gently, then simmer for
    2 minutes before serving.

## 021 Palestine soup

**PREPARATION TIME** 10 minutes    **COOKING TIME** 25 minutes

500g (1lb 2oz) large Jerusalem artichokes,
  scrubbed well and chopped small
1 onion, chopped
2 cloves garlic, crushed
1 large sprig of thyme
3 tbsp vegetable oil

500ml (18fl oz, 2 cups) vegetable
  or chicken stock
500ml (18fl oz, 2 cups) skimmed milk
juice of ½ lemon
sea salt and freshly ground black pepper
2 tbsp chopped parsley, to sprinkle

1   Gently sauté the artichokes, onion, garlic and thyme in the oil in a large pan for
    10 minutes, stirring once.
2   Add the stock and season to taste. Bring to the boil and simmer, uncovered, for
    a further 10 minutes until softened. Press the artichokes using a potato masher to
    a rough purée.
3   Pour in the milk and simmer for a further 5 minutes. Check the seasoning and add
    the lemon juice but do not allow to boil. Serve sprinkled with parsley.

## 022 Snaffles mousse

**PREPARATION TIME** 5 minutes plus chilling    **COOKING TIME** nil

200ml (7fl oz, ¾ cup) consommé, canned
200g (7oz) cream cheese, softened at
  room temperature
1 clove garlic, crushed

½ tsp mild curry powder
squeeze of fresh lemon juice
sea salt and freshly ground black pepper

1   Whisk the consommé into the cream cheese until smooth. Add the garlic, curry
    powder and lemon juice to taste. Whisk again and check the seasoning.
2   Pour into 4 ramekins or small glass dishes and chill until firm. Serve with fingers
    of hot toast, lemon wedges and watercress salad.

# 023 Morecambe Bay potted shrimps

**PREPARATION TIME** 2 minutes   **COOKING TIME** nil

200g (7oz) peeled and cooked brown shrimps
pinches of ground ginger
100g (3½oz) unsalted butter, melted

1   Divide the shrimps between 4 ramekin dishes, or small glass or plastic pots. Sprinkle lightly with ground ginger. Pour over the melted butter, stir to mix, then chill until firm.
2   To serve, if using plastic pots, run a table knife around the rims and demould onto small plates. Serve with hot toast fingers.

## 024 Smoked salmon with honey mustard dressing

**PREPARATION TIME** 5 minutes   **COOKING TIME** nil

selection of baby salad leaves or sprigs of
   watercress, washed
some cucumber, thinly sliced
300–400g (10–14oz) smoked salmon
freshly ground black pepper
slices of brown bread or soda bread,
   buttered, to serve

DRESSING
125ml (4fl oz, ½ cup) Vinaigrette, preferably
   homemade (see page 19)
2 tsp honey
2 tsp coarse grain mustard
1 tbsp chopped parsley
2 tsp chopped dill or chives

1   Whisk together the dressing ingredients. Arrange the salad leaves and cucumber on
    4 plates and place the salmon on top, scrunching into rosettes. Grind over pepper.
2   Drizzle with the dressing and serve with the bread.

## 025 Roasted baby beetroots with crumbly Lancashire cheese

**PREPARATION TIME** 7 minutes plus cooling   **COOKING TIME** 45 minutes

500g (1lb 2oz) raw baby beetroots
1 onion, peeled and cut into
   thin wedges
½ tsp cumin or fennel or dill seeds
2 tbsp olive or sunflower oil

2 tbsp cider vinegar or balsamic vinegar
200g (7oz) Lancashire cheese
sea salt and freshly ground black pepper
chopped parsley or chives, to sprinkle

1   Preheat the oven to 190°C (375°F, Gas Mark 5). Trim the stalks and roots of the
    beets and wash well. Place in the centre of a large sheet of foil with the onion
    wedges, spice seeds, oil, vinegar and seasoning. Wrap loosely.
2   Bake the parcel in a roasting pan for 45 minutes or until the beets are tender when
    pierced. Remove and cool for 30 minutes, then divide between 4 plates, drizzle over
    the baking juices and crumble over the cheese. Sprinkle with herbs and a little more
    pepper and serve.

## 026 Egg and watercress mousse

**PREPARATION TIME** 15 minutes plus setting   **COOKING TIME** 2–3 minutes

200ml (7fl oz, ¾ cup) chicken consommé,
   canned
1 tbsp dry sherry or Worcestershire sauce
1 sheet leaf gelatine, soaked in cold water
   and squeezed, or 1 tsp gelatine crystals,
   soaked in 1 tbsp cold water

5 large eggs, hard-boiled
100g (3½ oz) watercress or rocket, roughly
   chopped, plus extra sprigs to garnish
225ml (8fl oz, 1 cup) double cream,
   softly whipped
sea salt and freshly ground black pepper

1   Heat the consommé with the sherry or sauce. Stir the gelatine into the hot consommé
    until dissolved. Cool until on the point of setting.
2   Slice one of the eggs. Pour 4 tbsp consommé into the base of a medium soufflé dish
    or 4 ramekins. Arrange the egg slices in the dish or dishes, with a few tiny leaves of
    cress or rocket and chill to set.
3   Finely chop the remaining eggs and mix into the cooled consommé with the cress.
    Chill until almost setting, then fold the cream into the egg mixture.
4   Season well and spoon on top of the set egg slices. Chill until firm, then demould
    by dipping the dish or dishes in hot water for a few seconds. Garnish with cress.

## 027 Tomato en gelée

**PREPARATION TIME** 20 minutes plus draining and chilling  **COOKING TIME** 10 minutes

1kg (2lb 4oz) vine-ripened tomatoes
1 stick celery, chopped
2 tbsp chopped onion
2 bay leaves
2 good pinches of ground paprika
1 tbsp tarragon vinegar

1 tbsp lemon juice
4 sheets leaf gelatine, soaked in cold water to
cover and squeezed, or 1 sachet gelatine
crystals, soaked in a little cold water
sea salt and freshly ground black pepper

1   Dip half the tomatoes in boiling water for 5 seconds, then drain and skin. Slice the
    flesh finely and layer in a colander placed over a bowl. Lightly sprinkle with salt and
    leave to drain for 30 minutes.
2   Roughly chop the remaining tomatoes and place in a pan with the celery, onion,
    bay leaves, 1 tsp salt and paprika. Simmer for 10 minutes then strain through a
    fine sieve into a bowl.
3   Stir the soaked gelatine into the hot tomato liquid. Add any juices from the slices,
    along with the lemon juice and vinegar. Check the seasoning and cool. Arrange
    the tomato slices in 4 small dishes, pour over the tomato liquid and chill until firm.

## 028 Chicken and liver pâté

**SERVES** 6–8   **PREPARATION TIME** 10 minutes plus chilling   **COOKING TIME** 15 minutes

1 onion, chopped
1 fat clove garlic, crushed
1 tbsp vegetable oil
125g (4oz) butter plus 75g (3oz), melted
    (optional)
250g (9oz) chicken livers, thawed if frozen

2 skinless, boneless chicken breasts, diced
1 sprig of thyme or rosemary
2–3 tbsp dry sherry (optional)
6 tbsp cream or half-fat crème fraîche
2–3 bay leaves (optional)
sea salt and freshly ground black pepper

1   Gently sauté the onion and garlic in the oil in a large frying pan for 5 minutes.
    Remove with a slotted spoon. Melt the butter in the pan and when hot stir in the
    livers and chicken plus the herbs and seasoning.
2   Stir until lightly browned then mix in the sherry, if using. Cook for a further minute
    then return the onions and garlic and cook on a gentle heat for 10 minutes until firm.
3   Blend to a purée with the cream in a liquidizer or food processor. Check the
    seasoning again and pour into a non-stick loaf tin or dish (base-lined with
    non-stick baking parchment), cool and chill until set. If liked, pour over the melted
    butter. Press the bay leaves, if using, onto the surface then chill again. To serve,
    demould and cut in slices.

## 029 Gratin of queen scallops

**PREPARATION TIME** 5 minutes   **COOKING TIME** 10–12 minutes plus browning

400g (14oz) shelled queen scallops
2 spring onions, chopped
200ml (7fl oz, ¾ cup) half-fat crème fraîche
2 tbsp mayonnaise

4 tbsp grated Gruyère cheese
1 tbsp dried breadcrumbs
sea salt and freshly ground black pepper

1   Preheat the oven to 190°C (375°F, Gas Mark 5). Mix together the scallops, onions,
    crème fraîche and mayonnaise. Season well and divide between 4 small shallow
    ovenproof dishes.
2   Sprinkle the tops with the cheese and crumbs and bake for 10–12 minutes until hot
    and bubbling.
3   Meanwhile, preheat the grill and brown the tops of the dishes until golden. Serve hot.

## 030 Essex oysters with shallot vinegar

**PREPARATION TIME** about 20 minutes   **COOKING TIME** nil

2 dozen fresh oysters, rock or the more
   creamy 'natives'
crushed ice or Maldon salt flakes

2 shallots, finely chopped
1 tsp finely chopped red chilli (optional)
125ml (4fl oz, ½ cup) wine or cider vinegar

1   To shuck the oysters, wrap your left hand tightly in a tea towel to protect it (right hand if you are left-handed). Place an oyster on a board, holding it with your wrapped hand, hinge side exposed. Use the tip of an oyster knife to push firmly into the hinge, wiggling the knife until you break the hinge and the oyster relaxes the shell. Slide the knife in at the side, cutting through the muscle inside. Hold the oyster over a bowl to catch the juice. Flip open the flat half of the shell and discard. Use the knife to cut under the oyster in the other half to loosen it. Repeat with remaining oysters. Wash the oysters in the reserved juice if necessary.

2   Sit the oyster half shells on plates of crushed ice or salt flakes. Mix the shallots and chilli, if using, in vinegar and spoon over the oysters just before serving.

## 031 Scotch woodcock

**PREPARATION TIME** 5 minutes    **COOKING TIME** 10 minutes

50g (2oz) can anchovy fillets, rinsed
  and drained
2 large slices of white or brown bread
good knob of butter, plus extra for spreading

6 large eggs, beaten
2 tbsp single cream or whole milk
sea salt and freshly ground black pepper
chopped parsley, to sprinkle

1   Pat the anchovies on kitchen paper, then halve each fillet lengthways.
2   Toast the bread, butter lightly, remove the crusts then halve diagonally. Keep warm.
3   Melt the knob of butter in a non-stick pan. Beat the eggs with the cream, season, and scramble until lightly set.
4   Place the toast halves on 4 small warmed plates, top with egg, arrange the anchovy fillets criss-cross fashion, sprinkle with parsley and serve.

## 032 Portabella mushrooms with bacon stuffing au gratin

**PREPARATION TIME** 10 minutes    **COOKING TIME** 20–22 minutes

4 large Portabella or field mushrooms, peeled
  if necessary
vegetable oil, for brushing and frying
1 small onion, chopped
1 fat clove garlic, crushed
knob of butter

100g (3½oz) smoked streaky bacon, chopped
100g (3½oz, 1½ cups) fresh white
  breadcrumbs
2 tbsp chopped parsley
50g (2oz) Cheddar cheese, grated
sea salt and freshly ground black pepper

1   Preheat the oven to 180°C (350°F, Gas Mark 4). Remove the mushroom stalks and chop finely. Brush the caps with oil and place in a shallow ovenproof dish. Cover loosely with foil and bake for 10 minutes.
2   Meanwhile, sauté the onion, garlic and mushroom stalks in a little more oil and the butter for 3 minutes until softened. Add the bacon and cook, stirring, for 3 minutes. Mix in the breadcrumbs, parsley and seasoning.
3   Spoon into the upturned mushrooms, sprinkle with cheese and return to the oven for 10–12 minutes until golden on top. Serve hot.

## 033 Oyster patties

**MAKES** 12    **PREPARATION TIME** 15 minutes plus oyster shucking    **COOKING TIME** 15 minutes

12 bite-sized frozen vol-au-vent cases
1 egg yolk beaten with 1 tsp water
12 shucked oysters
2–3 tbsp crème fraîche

dashes of Tabasco or Worcestershire sauce
a little chopped parsley
sea salt and freshly ground black pepper

1   Preheat the oven to 200°C (400°F, Gas Mark 6). Glaze the pastry cases with the yolk and bake for 10–12 minutes until risen and golden. Remove the puffed-up tops and scoop out the insides, then return to the oven for a further 3 minutes to crisp the cases. Remove and allow to cool.
2   Chop the shucked oysters (see page 34 for how to remove them from the shells) and mix with the crème fraîche, pepper and sauce to taste. Check for salt; the mixture may not need any. Mix in the parsley and spoon into the cases. Serve immediately.

## 034 Omelette Arnold Bennett

**SERVES** 6　**PREPARATION TIME** 5 minutes　**COOKING TIME** 15–20 minutes

250g (9oz) smoked haddock, poached
　and flaked
2 tbsp double cream
2 tbsp chopped chives or spring onions
5 eggs, beaten

50g (2oz) Cheddar cheese, grated
knob of butter
handful of crisp croûtons (optional)
sea salt and freshly ground black pepper

1　Mix together the flaked fish, cream, chives, eggs and cheese.
2　Heat the butter in a medium non-stick frying pan until foaming. Pour in the mixture.
3　Cook over a low heat, drawing the edges to the middle. When it is semi-cooked
　scatter over the croûtons, if using, and seasoning (you may not need salt). Continue
　cooking until completely set.
4　Serve from the pan or slide out onto a board, and cut into wedges.

## 035 Roes on toast

**PREPARATION TIME** 5 minutes   **COOKING TIME** 5 minutes

flour, for coating
pinch of mustard powder
200g (7oz) sole or herring roes, hard or soft
vegetable oil, for frying

small knob of butter
juice of 1/2 lemon
4 slices of hot buttered toast
sea salt and freshly ground black pepper

1   Mix the flour, mustard and seasoning then toss in the roes. Heat some oil in a frying pan and fry the roes for about 2–3 minutes until golden on all sides.
2   Add the butter and lemon to the pan, pile the roes onto the hot toasts and serve.

## 036 Sardine toasties

**PREPARATION TIME** 3 minutes   **COOKING TIME** 2 minutes

2 x 100g (3 1/2oz) cans sardines
juice of 1/2 large lemon
4 slices of hot buttered toast

1/2 small red onion, sliced thinly (optional)
sea salt and freshly ground black pepper

1   Drain the sardines and tip into a bowl. Mash roughly with a fork (including the soft bones, which are a good source of calcium). Season and mix in the lemon juice.
2   Spoon the sardines onto the toast, spreading to the edges. Top with red onion slices, if liked, season with extra pepper and serve.

## 037 Veal and ham pie

**SERVES** 6   **PREPARATION TIME** 40 minutes   **COOKING TIME** 2 hours plus cooling

350g (12oz) unsmoked collar bacon,
   diced small
350g (12oz) casserole veal, diced small
1 tsp dried mixed herbs or dried
   sage, crumbled
1/2 tsp sea salt
freshly ground white pepper
3 eggs, hard-boiled and peeled
300ml (10fl oz, 1 1/4 cups) veal or
   chicken stock
1 tbsp gelatine crystals, soaked in
   a little cold water

**PASTRY**
350g (12oz, 2 1/3 cups) plain flour
1/4 tsp sea salt
125g (4oz) lard
about 150ml (5fl oz, 2/3 cup) water

1   Mix together the meats, herbs and seasoning. Chill.
2   Make the pastry. Mix the flour and salt in a bowl. Heat the lard and water in a pan and when on the point of boiling pour onto the flour and mix with a wooden spoon to form a dough. Cool for 5 minutes then turn out onto a floured board and knead until smooth.
3   Cut off a quarter of the dough. Shape the remainder into a ball and roll out to a circle about 5mm (1/4in) thick, large enough to line a 17cm (7in) deep loose-bottomed cake tin. Press evenly into the tin, bringing the edges up over the top. Use your hands to mould the dough.
4   Push in the meats and arrange the eggs in the centre. Roll out the remaining pastry to form a lid. Brush the edges with water and press the edges together to seal. Cut a small round hole in the centre. Leave to rest while you preheat the oven to 180°C (350°F, Gas Mark 4).
5   Bake for about 2 hours until the pastry is golden brown and crisp. Cool for 30 minutes. Boil the stock and pour onto the soaked gelatine, stirring until dissolved, then pour into the pie through the hole using a thin pie funnel. Cool to room temperature then chill overnight. Serve in wedges.

## 038  Double Gloucester and wild garlic tart

**PREPARATION TIME** 10 minutes plus resting   **COOKING TIME** 55 minutes

1 recipe quantity Shortcrust pastry (see
   page 18), or 300g (10oz) ready-made
2 eggs plus 2 yolks
300ml (10fl oz, 1¼ cups) single cream
a little freshly grated nutmeg

good handful of wild garlic leaves, washed
   and patted dry
150g (5oz) mature Double Gloucester
   cheese, grated
sea salt and freshly ground black pepper

1 Preheat the oven to 190°C (375°F, Gas Mark 5). Roll out the pastry thinly and use
to line a 20cm (8in) tart tin at least 2cm (1in) deep, leaving the edges overhanging.
Press well into the sides and prick the base. Rest for 20 minutes then line with
baking parchment and beans and bake blind on a flat baking sheet for 15 minutes.
2 Remove the parchment and beans and return to the oven for a further 5 minutes.
Lower the temperature to 150°C (325°F, Gas Mark 3). Remove the case and trim off
the overhanging pastry with a sharp knife.
3 Beat the eggs, yolks, cream, nutmeg and seasoning to taste. Shred the wild garlic
then scatter over the base of the case with the cheese. Carefully pour in the custard,
return to the oven and bake for 30 minutes until lightly set and golden. Cool for
10 minutes then demould and cut to serve.

## 039  Country house tomato and watercress tart

**PREPARATION TIME** 10 minutes plus resting   **COOKING TIME** 55 minutes

1 recipe quantity Shortcrust pastry
   (see page 18), or 300g (10oz) ready-made
2 eggs plus 2 yolks
300ml (10fl oz, 1¼ cups) single cream
a little freshly grated nutmeg
4 spring onions, trimmed and shredded

1 sprig of thyme
100g (3½oz) watercress, roughly chopped
125g (4oz) mature Cheddar cheese, grated
2 tomatoes, sliced
sea salt and freshly ground black pepper

1 Preheat the oven to 190°C (375°F, Gas Mark 5). Roll out the pastry thinly and use
to line a 20cm (8in) tart tin at least 2cm (¾in) deep, leaving the edges overhanging.
Press well into the sides and prick the base. Rest for 20 minutes then line with
baking parchment and beans and bake blind on a flat baking sheet for 15 minutes.
2 Remove the parchment and beans and return to the oven for a further 5 minutes.
Lower the temperature to 150°C (325°F, Gas Mark 3). Remove the case and trim off
the overhanging pastry with a sharp knife.
3 Beat together the eggs, yolks, cream, nutmeg and seasoning to taste. Scatter the
shredded onion, thyme and watercress into the tart base, along with the cheese.
4 Arrange the tomato slices on top and pour in the custard and bake for 30–35 minutes
until lightly set and golden. Cool for 10 minutes before serving.

## 040  Tarts of smoked eel and scrambled eggs

**PREPARATION TIME** 5 minutes   **COOKING TIME** 5 minutes

4 ready-made thin tartlet cases made with filo
   or puff pastry, about 10cm (4in) diameter
   (see page 39)
6–8 eggs, beaten

good knob of butter
150g (5oz) smoked eel fillet, broken in chunks
sea salt and freshly ground black pepper
chopped parsley, to sprinkle

1 Reheat the pastry cases in a low oven. Season the eggs and melt the butter gently in
a non-stick pan.
2 Gently stir the eggs in the pan until lightly set. Spoon into the tart cases and fork
through the eel fillets. Sprinkle with parsley and serve.

## 041 Goat's cheese tartlets

**PREPARATION TIME** 20 minutes plus resting   **COOKING TIME** 25 minutes

about 300g (10oz) puff pastry,
  thawed if frozen
1 red onion, thinly sliced
2 tbsp vegetable oil

small head broccoli, trimmed to small florets
100g (3½oz) soft goat's cheese
50g (2oz) grated Cheddar, preferably goat's
sea salt and freshly ground black pepper

1   Cut the pastry into 4, roll each quarter out thinly and use to line 4 tartlet cases, about
    10cm (4in) diameter, 2cm (¾in) deep. Chill for 15 minutes. Preheat the oven to
    190°C (375°F, Gas Mark 5). Prick the bases then line with baking parchment and
    beans. Bake blind on a flat baking sheet for 15 minutes. Remove the parchment and
    beans and return the cases to the oven for a further 5 minutes.
2   Meanwhile, sauté the onion in oil for 5 minutes. Boil the broccoli for 3 minutes until
    tender. Drain well and mix with the soft cheese. Spoon the onion into the pastry
    cases, top with the creamy broccoli and scatter with the grated cheese. Return to the
    oven for 5 minutes. Cool for 10 minutes then serve.

## 042 Lancashire cheese and chutney on toast

**PREPARATION TIME** 5 minutes   **COOKING TIME** 5–10 minutes

4 slices of farmhouse brown bread, toasted, or
  2 large brown baps, split and toasted
4 tbsp tomato or apple chutney or tangy pickle

200g (7oz) Lancashire cheese, grated
pinch or two of dried thyme
freshly ground black pepper

1  Spread the toast or baps with chutney and top with grated cheese. Season and
sprinkle with thyme, then grill until hot and bubbling.


## 043 Cheese and bacon croûtes

**PREPARATION TIME** 2 minutes   **COOKING TIME** 10 minutes

8 thin slices of white bread
vegetable oil, for frying
4 rashers streaky bacon, chopped

75g (3oz) butter, softened
75g (3oz) freshly grated Parmesan cheese
freshly ground black pepper

1  Preheat the oven to 180°C (350°F, Gas Mark 4). Using a small saucer as a template,
cut the bread into rounds. Fry gently in hot oil on each side until crisp and light
golden. Drain on kitchen paper.
2  Fry the bacon until crisp and drain also. Mix together the butter, Parmesan and
bacon and use to make sandwiches with the bread. Reheat in the oven for
5 minutes to melt the cheese, then serve.


## 044 Macaroni cheese and chicken bake

**PREPARATION TIME** 20 minutes   **COOKING TIME** 35 minutes

250g (9oz) macaroni
1 red onion, chopped
1 recipe quantity Béchamel sauce
  (see page 17)
100g (3½oz) grated Cheddar or similar
  hard cheese, plus 3 tbsp for topping
2 cooked chicken breasts, skinned
  and chopped

125g (4oz) whole green beans, blanched and
  chopped
2 tbsp freshly grated Parmesan cheese
3 tbsp dried breadcrumbs
1 tomato, sliced
sea salt and freshly ground pepper

1  Boil the macaroni and chopped onion in salted water for 10–12 minutes, according
to the packet instructions. Drain and rinse.
2  Meanwhile, make the Béchamel sauce. Mix in the macaroni and onion together with
the cheese, chopped chicken and beans. Tip into a large, shallow, heatproof dish.
3  Preheat the oven to 190°C (375°F, Gas Mark 5). Mix together the extra grated
Cheddar and Parmesan plus breadcrumbs and scatter over the dish, top with
sliced tomato and bake for 20–25 minutes until hot, bubbling and crisp. Cool for
10 minutes, then serve.

# 045 Sausage and egg plait

**SERVES** 6–8   **PREPARATION TIME** 15 minutes   **COOKING TIME** 45–50 minutes

1 x 375g (13oz) sheet ready-rolled puff pastry,
   or 1 x 425g (15oz) pack of 2 sheets
2–3 tbsp chutney or brown sauce
500g (1lb 2oz) premium-quality sausagemeat

3 large eggs, hard-boiled
flour, to coat
1 egg yolk, beaten with 1 tsp cold water

1   Preheat the oven to 375°C (190°F, Gas Mark 5). Lay the pastry on a non-stick baking sheet. Spread chutney or sauce lengthways down the centre in a line. (If using a double sheet pack, lay out one sheet and spread chutney over the entire sheet.)

2   Pat out the sausagemeat to an oblong about 12cm (5in) wide and place on the chutney. Trim the ends of the eggs, toss in a little flour to coat and place down the sausagemeat, butted up to each other. Shape the sausagemeat around them.

3   Slash the pastry at 2cm (¾in) intervals down both sides of the pastry up to the sausagemeat, then fold over each side alternately as a plait. Press the ends together. (If using a double sheet pack, slash the second sheet down the centre and press on top of the sausagemeat.) Brush egg yolk all over the pastry.

4   Bake for 45–50 minutes, turning if necessary, until evenly golden brown and crisp. Cool for 10–15 minutes before cutting.

## 046 Scotch eggs

**PREPARATION TIME** 10 minutes plus chilling     **COOKING TIME** 10–15 minutes

4 eggs, hard-boiled
flour, to coat
500g (1lb 2oz) premium-quality sausagemeat
1 egg, beaten

100g (3½oz, 1 cup) dried, natural colour
    breadcrumbs
vegetable oil, for deep-frying

1   Toss the eggs in flour to coat then wrap each in some sausagemeat, pressing well to seal. Dip first in beaten egg then toss in the breadcrumbs and shake off the excess. Chill for 1 hour to set the crumbs.

2   Heat enough oil to a depth of 4cm (1½in) in a wok to around 180°C (350°F) and deep-fry the eggs for around 5 minutes, making sure they don't over-brown. Drain well, cool then cut in half.


## 047 Cocotte eggs

**PREPARATION TIME** 3 minutes     **COOKING TIME** 15 minutes

125g (4oz) mushrooms, sliced
50g (2oz) butter
a little chopped parsley
4 eggs

4 tbsp double cream
50g (2oz) Cheddar cheese, grated
sea salt and freshly ground black pepper

1   Preheat the oven to 190°C (375°F, Gas Mark 5). Sauté the mushrooms in butter, season and spoon into 4 ramekins. Sprinkle with parsley.

2   Crack in the eggs, season again, and spoon 1 tbsp cream over each egg. Sprinkle with cheese and bake for 15 minutes until lightly set. Serve with toast.


## 048 Asparagus and salmon quiche

**PREPARATION TIME** 15 minutes plus resting     **COOKING TIME** 50–55 minutes

1 recipe quantity Shortcrust pastry (see page
    18) or 300g (10oz) ready-made
250g (9oz) asparagus spears, trimmed, tips
    reserved and stems chopped

2 eggs plus 2 yolks
300ml (10fl oz, 1¼ cups) single cream
125g (4oz) smoked salmon slices
sea salt and freshly ground black pepper

1   Preheat the oven to 190°C (375°F, Gas Mark 5). Roll out the pastry thinly and use to line a 20cm (8in) tart tin at least 2cm (¾in) deep, leaving the edges overhanging. Press well into the sides and prick the base. Rest for 20 minutes then line with baking parchment and beans and bake blind on a baking sheet for 15 minutes.

2   Meanwhile, set aside the asparagus tips and simmer the chopped stalks for 5 minutes in boiling salted water. Remove with a slotted spoon and purée in a liquidizer, then mix in the eggs, yolks, cream and seasoning.

3   Blanch the asparagus tips for 2 minutes and drain.

4   Remove the parchment and beans and return to the oven for a further 5 minutes. Lower the temperature to 150°C (325°F, Gas Mark 3). Remove the case and trim off the overhanging pastry with a sharp knife, taking care not to crack the pastry.

5   Snip the salmon into pieces and scatter in the pastry case along with the asparagus tips. Pour over the custard and return to the oven for 30–35 minutes until lightly set and golden. Cool for 10 minutes before serving.

## 049 Egg and asparagus mousse

**PREPARATION TIME** 15 minutes plus boiling eggs and overnight chilling   **COOKING TIME** 5 minutes

1 sheet leaf gelatine, soaked in cold water
   and squeezed, or 1 tsp gelatine crystals,
   soaked in 1 tbsp cold water
200ml (7fl oz, ¾ cup) chicken consommé
1 tbsp dry sherry or Worcestershire sauce
150g (5oz) asparagus spears, trimmed

4 large eggs, hard-boiled and
   finely chopped
150ml (5fl oz, ⅔ cup) double cream,
   lightly whipped
sea salt and freshly ground black pepper

1   Heat the consommé until almost boiling, Remove from the heat, mix in the sherry or
    sauce then stir through the gelatine until dissolved. Cool, then pour about 4 tbsp into
    the base of a 600ml (1 pint, 2½ cup) mould or 4 ramekins.
2   Chop the asparagus, reserving the tips. Blanch the tips for 2 minutes then drain and
    scatter over the consommé in the moulds. Chill until set.
3   Blanch the remaining asparagus for 2–3 minutes, drain and cool. Mix with the
    chopped egg, remaining consommé and seasoning to taste. Chill until on the point
    of setting then fold in the lightly whipped cream. Spoon over the asparagus tips and
    chill overnight until set.
4   To demould, dip the mould or ramekins briefly in hot water. Run a round-bladed
    knife round the sides to loosen the mousse and shake out onto a serving plate or
    individual plates.

## 050 Cheese and herb omelette

**SERVES** 1   **PREPARATION TIME** 10 minutes   **COOKING TIME** 5–7 minutes

½ slice of white bread, crusts removed,
   cut into cubes
vegetable oil, for frying
2 tbsp chopped herbs (chives, thyme,
   rosemary, sage, marjoram)
2 large eggs, beaten

knob of butter
40g (1½oz) British cheese (Cheddar,
   Red Leicester, Cheshire, Double Gloucester,
   Lancashire) grated
sea salt and freshly ground black pepper

1   Gently fry the bread cubes in a little oil, turning frequently until crisp and golden on
    all sides, then drain on kitchen paper.
2   Mix the herbs with the beaten eggs and season to taste. Melt the butter in a
    non-stick omelette pan and pour in the eggs. Cook, drawing the edges to the
    centre until lightly set.
3   Scatter in the cheese, cook for about 1 minute longer until it starts to melt then
    scatter over the croûtons. Fold in three and slide onto a warm plate.

## 051 Stuffed anchovy eggs

**PREPARATION TIME** 10 minutes   **COOKING TIME** 8–10 minutes for the eggs

4 eggs, hard-boiled and peeled
1 tbsp mayonnaise
1 tsp anchovy paste or anchovies
   in oil, mashed

1 tsp capers
8 canned anchovy fillets, slit lengthways
freshly ground black pepper
cress, to sprinkle

1   Halve the eggs, scoop out the yolks and mash with the mayonnaise, anchovy paste
    and capers. Spoon into the white 'shells', mounding the mixture up.
2   To serve, arrange the anchovy strips over each egg half to form a cross and sprinkle
    with a little cress and ground black pepper.

## 052 Welsh rarebit

**PREPARATION TIME** 5 minutes  **COOKING TIME** 10–12 minutes

200g (7oz) mature Cheddar cheese, grated
good knob of butter
1 tsp dry mustard powder
4 tbsp milk or brown ale

4 slices of farmhouse brown bread
freshly ground black pepper
1 tomato, cut into wedges, to garnish
torn coriander leaves, to sprinkle

1 Put the cheese, butter, mustard and milk into a heavy-based pan and heat slowly, stirring until melted and creamy. Season lightly.
2 Heat the grill until hot. Toast one side of each bread slice then spread the cheese on the other side. Grill until golden and bubbling. Top with tomato and coriander.

### VARIATIONS

Use Double Gloucester cheese instead of Cheddar cheese or use Stilton for a blue cheese rarebit. For a Buck rarebit, top with a poached egg.

## 053 Hot Madras eggs with basmati rice

**PREPARATION TIME** 10 minutes **COOKING TIME** 15 minutes

1 large onion, sliced
1 fat clove garlic, crushed
1 tbsp grated or chopped fresh ginger root
1 fresh green chilli, split, seeded and chopped
2 tbsp vegetable oil
1–2 tsp chilli powder, to taste
2 tomatoes, chopped finely or half a
    400g (14oz) can chopped tomatoes

6 large eggs, hard-boiled
    and quartered
200g (7oz, 1¼ cups) basmati rice
good knob of butter
2 tbsp chopped coriander or parsley
sea salt and freshly ground
    black pepper
natural yogurt, to serve

1   Sauté the onion, garlic, ginger and fresh chilli in the oil in a large pan for 5 minutes. Stir in the chilli powder to taste, then mix in the tomatoes and 125ml (4fl oz, ½ cup) water. Season, bring to the boil then simmer for 5 minutes and add the eggs. Reheat until piping hot, check the seasoning and set aside.
2   Meanwhile, boil the rice in plenty of lightly salted water for about 10 minutes then drain and let stand for 5 minutes. Stir through the butter and herbs and serve with the eggs and some yogurt.

## 054 Spinach soufflé

**PREPARATION TIME** 15 minutes **COOKING TIME** 30 minutes

250g (9oz) leaf spinach, washed
a little melted butter and some dried
    breadcrumbs, to dust the dish
1 small onion, chopped
1 tbsp vegetable oil
25g (1oz) butter
2 tbsp flour
1 tsp dry mustard powder

½ tsp ground cumin or mild curry powder
200ml (7fl oz, ¾ cup) hot milk
125g (4oz) mature grated Cheddar,
    Red Leicester or Double Gloucester cheese
2–3 tbsp grated Parmesan cheese
4 large eggs, separated, plus 1 extra white
sea salt and freshly ground black pepper

1   Cook the spinach in just the water clinging to its leaves until wilted. Drain, squeeze dry and chop finely. Preheat the oven to 180°C (375°F, Gas Mark 4). Butter a 1 litre (1¾ pint, 4 cup) soufflé dish and dust with breadcrumbs.
2   Sauté the onion in the oil in a large non-stick pan for 3 minutes then add the butter, allow to melt then stir in the flour and spices. Cook for 1 minute and then gradually beat in the hot milk until smooth and thickened. Cook for a further minute and remove from the heat.
3   Stir in the two cheeses (but reserve 2 tbsp of the Cheddar), then beat in the yolks. Season well.
4   Whisk the 5 egg whites until stiff but not dry. Fold into the mixture, spoon into the dish, level the top and scatter with the remaining cheese. Bake for 20–25 minutes until risen and slightly wobbly in the middle. Serve immediately.

### VARIATION

#### Asparagus and leek soufflé
Substitute a 250g (9oz) bunch of asparagus spears for the spinach and 1 leek, cleaned and chopped, for the onion. Trim the woody ends from the asparagus (they should snap easily where they are tender), then chop the stems finely and the tips roughly. Sauté the asparagus and leeks in 2 tbsp oil and proceed with the recipe from step 2 above.

# CHAPTER 2

# FISH & SHELLFISH

Our island nation has a long and proud association with the sea. British waters are rich in fish and shellfish species. Two thousand years ago, the Romans enjoyed our plump native oysters and established oyster beds that still provide for our tables. Today, sea fishermen brave treacherous waters to bring home a bountiful catch to salt, smoke or sell freshly landed, and many countrymen cast their lines into rivers and freshwater lakes for delicious salmon, trout, perch and pike.

Fish and chips may be our most famous dish but our fishy heritage also includes crisp fishcakes, creamy fish pies, soused cockles and whelks, Arbroath smokies, spicy whitebait, fresh lobster and, of course, some of the finest smoked salmon in the world.

The big challenge we currently face is to conserve stocks of popular fish such as cod and haddock by adapting our traditional recipes to use our equally delicious but lesser-known native species, including hake, coley, gurnard, whiting and pollock. With that reason in mind, many of the white fish varieties in recipes in this chapter are interchangeable – see what your fishmonger has to offer.

## 055 Tomato soused herrings

**PREPARATION TIME** 10 minutes   **COOKING TIME** 20 minutes

4 fresh herrings, each about 180g (6oz),
   or 8 sardines, gutted and heads removed
1 tomato, chopped
125ml (4fl oz, ½ cup) wine vinegar
125ml (4fl oz, ½ cup) tomato juice

2 cloves garlic, sliced
1 bay leaf
1 sprig of thyme
1 tbsp Worcestershire sauce
sea salt and freshly ground black pepper

1 Preheat the oven to 180°C (350°F, Gas Mark 4). Slit each fish down to the tail
and open out, skin side up. Press down with the heel of your hand or thumb
on the backbone, then turn over and pull out the skeleton from the top end.
Season the flesh.

2 Divide the tomato between the fish and roll up from the wide end, leaving the
tails sticking up. Place join side down in a small ovenproof dish.

3 Boil together the vinegar, tomato juice and 125ml (4fl oz, ½ cup) water with the
garlic, herbs and Worcestershire sauce for 2 minutes then pour over the fish.
Cover with a sheet of foil and bake for 20 minutes.

4 Remove from the oven, cool then chill in the pickle. Serve cold with bread and butter.

## 056 Herrings in oatmeal

**PREPARATION TIME** 10 minutes   **COOKING TIME** 10 minutes

4 fresh herrings, each about 250g (9oz),
   gutted and heads removed
125g (4oz, ¾ cup) fine oatmeal
   (not oatflakes)
vegetable oil, for frying

knob of butter
sea salt and freshly ground black pepper
chopped parsley, to sprinkle
lemon wedges, to serve

1 Prepare and bone the fish as in the previous recipe. If there are any roes inside,
remove these and fry also.

2 Toss well in the oatmeal (using a plastic food bag is the best), shaking off the excess.
Toss in any roes too.

3 Heat a thin film of oil in a large frying pan. Season the fish and fry flesh side down
first for about 3 minutes then flip over and cook the skin side for 2 minutes until
crisp. Add the butter and, when melted, swirl to coat the fish.

4 Transfer to warmed plates, sprinkle with parsley and a squeeze of lemon.

## 057 Kipper salad

**PREPARATION TIME** 10 minutes plus marinating   **COOKING TIME** 20–22 minutes

4 kipper fillets
1 small red onion, thinly sliced
2 tbsp white wine or cider vinegar
2 tbsp lemon juice
3 tbsp light olive oil

1 tsp coriander seeds, roughly crushed
½ tsp dry mustard powder
1 small fennel bulb
3 tbsp roughly chopped parsley
sea salt and freshly ground black pepper

1 Pull the skin and bones from the kippers, then roughly break up the fillets into
chunks. Place in a small non-metallic bowl with the sliced onion. Whisk together the
vinegar, lemon juice, oil, crushed seeds and mustard powder. Pour over the kipper
chunks, cover and marinate in the fridge overnight.

2 Meanwhile, cut the fennel lengthways into wafer thin slices using a mandolin or
Japanese slicer and place in a bowl of iced water for 30 minutes until crisp and curly.
Drain, pat dry and chill.

3 To serve, drain off the marinade and the seeds and toss the kippers, onion and
fennel with the chopped parsley. Serve with sliced tomatoes and brown bread
and butter.

## 058 Stuffed sole rolls

**PREPARATION TIME** 15 minutes   **COOKING TIME** 15 minutes

4 lemon or Dover sole fillets, or plaice fillets,
 each about 170g (5½oz), skinned
3 shallots, chopped
1 rasher smoked streaky bacon, chopped
50g (2oz) butter
1 small glass (175ml, 6fl oz, ¾ cup) dry
 cider or white wine plus 3 tbsp
50g (2oz, 1 cup) fresh white breadcrumbs

3 tbsp chopped mixed herbs
 (parsley, thyme, tarragon)
grated zest and juice of 1 lemon
1 egg yolk
sea salt and freshly ground white or
 black pepper
sprigs of parsley, to garnish

1  Preheat the oven to 180°C (350°F, Gas Mark 4). Trim the fillets of any side 'frills'.
2  Sauté 2 of the shallots and the bacon with half the butter for 5 minutes, add the
   3 tbsp cider and cook for a further minute. Remove from the heat and mix in the
   breadcrumbs, herbs, lemon zest, juice, yolk and seasoning.
3  Spread over the skinned side of the sole fillets and roll up from the wide end.
   Place join side down in an ovenproof dish, cover loosely with greased foil and
   bake for 12–15 minutes until just firm.
4  Meanwhile, simmer the remaining shallot in the glass of cider for about 5 minutes
   until reduced by half. Tip in any baking juices, then whisk in the remaining butter.
   Season and spoon over the sole rolls. Garnish with the parsley and serve.

## 059 Poached skate wings with capers

**PREPARATION TIME** 10 minutes   **COOKING TIME** 10 minutes

2 lemons, 1 sliced, 1 juiced
2 tbsp white wine vinegar
1 small onion, sliced
1 bay leaf
½ tsp black or white peppercorns
4 skate wing portions, each about 180g
 (6oz), skinned

100g (3½oz) butter
1 tbsp small capers
good pinch of mild curry powder
sea salt and freshly ground black or
 white pepper

1  Put the sliced lemon, vinegar, onion, bay leaf, peppercorns and 1.5 litres
   (2½ pints, 6 cups) water into a large shallow pan. Bring to the boil then lower
   the heat to a simmer for 10 minutes.
2  Add the skate portions and poach for 5–10 minutes until just firm. Remove from
   the liquid, pat dry and place on a serving dish.
3  Heat the butter in a small pan until it begins to turn a golden, nutty brown. Stir in
   the capers and curry powder, cook for a few seconds then mix in the lemon juice.
   Season, pour over the skate and serve.

## 060 Poached smoked haddock and egg

**PREPARATION TIME** 2 minutes    **COOKING TIME** 10 minutes

1 large smoked haddock fillet, about 700g
    (1lb 9oz), skinned
4 eggs

good knob of butter
a little cider or wine vinegar
sea salt and freshly ground black pepper

1   Check the fish for bones then cut into 4 portions. Bring a large shallow frying pan
    of water to the boil and slide in the fish. Poach gently for around 5 minutes until the
    flesh feels just firm. Transfer to warmed plates and top with a little butter.
2   Wipe out the pan and refill with boiling water. Add the vinegar and seasoning. Crack
    in the eggs, one at a time and poach gently for 3–5 minutes until the yolks are lightly
    set. Remove with a slotted spoon to kitchen paper, trim to neat rounds and place on
    the fish. Season with pepper and a little salt and serve.

## 061 Cod mornay

**PREPARATION TIME** 10 minutes plus making the sauce    **COOKING TIME** 20 minutes

700–800g (1lb 9oz–1lb 12oz) cod
    fillet, skinned
2 tsp coarse grain mustard
125g (4oz) grated Cheddar cheese
1 recipe quantity Béchamel or Quick
    white sauce (see page 17)

2 tbsp dried breadcrumbs
1 large tomato, sliced
sea salt and freshly ground black pepper

1   Preheat the oven to 190°C (375°F, Gas Mark 5). Check the fish for bones then cut
    into 4 portions. Lay in a shallow ovenproof dish.
2   Mix the mustard and two-thirds of the cheese into the sauce and pour over the fish.
    Mix the remaining cheese with the breadcrumbs.
3   Dot the tomato slices on top and sprinkle lightly with the cheesy crumbs. Bake for
    20 minutes until golden. Stand for 5 minutes before serving.

## 062 Dover sole on the bone

**PREPARATION TIME** 5 minutes    **COOKING TIME** 10–12 minutes

2 whole Dover soles, each about 600g
    (1lb 5oz), skinned and heads removed
100g (3½oz) butter

juice of 1 lemon
sea salt and freshly ground black pepper
chopped parsley, to sprinkle

1   Preheat the grill to high. Trim the fish of the side 'frills'.
2   Heat the butter in a pan until it starts to turn a pale brown then remove immediately
    from the heat and mix in the lemon juice. Keep warm.
3   Season and grill the fish on a sheet of foil for 2–3 minutes on each side, turning
    carefully. Remove from the heat, let stand for 2 minutes before cutting the fillets
    from the bone, to give 8 fillets in total.
4   Arrange 2 fillets per person on warmed plates, pour over the butter and lemon,
    season again and sprinkle with the parsley.

## 063 Fresh fish cakes

**PREPARATION TIME** 15 minutes plus chilling **COOKING TIME** 5–8 minutes

500g (1lb 2oz) old floury potatoes, peeled
and chopped
large knob of butter or margarine
1 tbsp mayonnaise
2–3 tbsp chopped herbs (chives, dill
and parsley)
300g (10oz) fresh and smoked salmon, cod or
haddock fillet, skinned (or use flaked crab)

flour, for coating
1 egg, beaten
6 tbsp dried, natural colour breadcrumbs
vegetable oil, for frying
sea salt and freshly ground black pepper
lemon wedges, to serve
tomato ketchup, to serve (optional)

1   Bring the potatoes to the boil in a large pan of salted water and cook until tender,
about 10 minutes. Drain, return to the pan to dry, then mash well. Mix in the
seasoning, butter and mayonnaise, then the herbs.
2   Meanwhile, grill the fish lightly under a preheated grill for 5 minutes. Flake into
chunks, removing any bones, and stir into the potato. Spoon onto a large flat plate,
flatten and allow to cool. Then divide into 4 equal portions and shape into neat
rounds about 1.5cm (¾in) thick.
3   Dip the cakes first into the flour, shaking off the excess, then into the egg and finally
the breadcrumbs. Place on another plate and chill for 1–2 hours to firm.
4   Heat about 5mm (¼in) oil in a large frying pan. Shallow-fry the fish cakes for
2–3 minutes on each side until golden and crisp. Drain on kitchen paper and serve
hot with a squeeze of lemon and ketchup, if liked.

## 064 Kedgeree

**PREPARATION TIME** 10 minutes    **COOKING TIME** 20 minutes

300g (10oz) smoked haddock fillet
1 bay leaf or 6 cardamom pods
200g (7oz, 1¼ cups) basmati rice
good knob of butter
1 tsp mild or medium curry paste
2 spring onions, chopped

3 tbsp chopped parsley
a little double or whipping cream
  (optional)
3 eggs, hard-boiled and quartered
sea salt and freshly ground black pepper

1   Check the fish for bones, then place in a shallow pan with about 400ml (14fl oz,
    1²/₃ cups) hot water – just enough to cover the fillets. Add the bay leaf and black
    pepper to taste (no salt at this stage, as the fish is salty).
2   Bring to a simmer then cover and poach for 5–7 minutes until the flesh is just firm.
    Strain the stock into a large pan. Skin and flake the fish.
3   Bring the strained liquid to the boil, stir in the rice, then cover and reduce the
    heat to a simmer. Cook for 10 minutes. Remove the pan from the heat and let
    stand for 5 minutes, then fork through the butter, curry paste, spring onions and
    chopped parsley.
4   Fork through the flaked fish (try not to break it up too much), season to taste, then
    reheat gently. Stir in some cream, if using, check the seasoning and serve piping
    hot topped with egg quarters.

### VARIATION

### Ambassador's kedgeree

Make the kedgeree as above and spoon into a shallow ovenproof dish. Make up a
recipe quantity of Béchamel sauce (see page 17). Mix in 75g (3oz) grated Gruyère
or mature Cheddar cheese and pour over the kedgeree. Sprinkle with a further 50g
(2oz) grated cheese mixed with 2 tbsp dried breadcrumbs. Bake at 190°C (375°F,
Gas Mark 5) for 15 minutes until the top is golden brown and crisp.

## 065 Poached lobster

**PREPARATION TIME** 10 minutes plus chilling and cooling    **COOKING TIME** 20 minutes

2 live lobsters, each about 1kg (2lb 4oz)
Court bouillon, see page 16

1   Check that the lobsters' claws are tied with rubber bands. Place them in the freezer
    for a couple of hours so they become very sleepy.
2   Remove the dormant lobsters and place them belly side down on a large chopping
    board. Cover the tails with a thick clean cloth and find a cross on the head. Push
    the tip of a large heavy knife firmly through the shell at this point in order to kill
    each one humanely and quickly.
3   Bring the bouillon to the boil in a pan large enough to accommodate both lobsters
    and lower them in. Cover and simmer for 15–20 minutes until the shells turn bright
    pink. Remove from the pan and allow to cool.
4   Pull off the two large claws and crack through the shell. Cut each lobster in half
    lengthways and remove the small sac and intestine from the body plus any coral
    sac. You can remove all meat and chop it neatly, then replace in the cleaned shell.
    Serve half a lobster and a large claw per person.

# 066 Rye Bay scallops gratin

**PREPARATION TIME** 10 minutes    **COOKING TIME** 15 minutes

12 large scallops, with corals, off the shell
200g (7oz) fresh baby leaf spinach
vegetable oil, for frying
pinches of mild curry powder
3 tbsp dry white wine

200ml (7fl oz, ¾ cup) single cream
3 tbsp grated Cheddar or Gruyère cheese
3 tbsp fresh white breadcrumbs
sea salt and freshly ground black pepper

1    Remove the dark threads from the scallops and the small hard muscles on the side. Wash well and pat dry. Preheat the grill.
2    Sauté the spinach in a frying pan with a little oil until wilted. Season and drain, pressing down well to remove the liquid. Chop roughly and spread into the base of a large, shallow, ovenproof dish.
3    Heat a little more oil in a frying pan and fry the scallops for just 2 minutes on each side. Do not overcook or they will become rubbery. Dust with a little curry powder and seasoning. Swirl in the wine, cook until reduced down, then spoon the scallops and the cooking juices on top of the spinach. Pour over the cream, sprinkle with the cheese and crumbs and grill for 3–5 minutes until golden brown and bubbling. Serve immediately.

# 067 Fish jalousie

**PREPARATION TIME** 15 minutes    **COOKING TIME** 30–35 minutes

250g (9oz) smoked haddock or salmon
    fillet, skinned
150g (5oz) button mushrooms, sliced
50g (2oz) butter
2 tbsp dry sherry or vermouth
200g (7oz) half-fat crème fraîche
125g (4oz) peeled prawns, thawed if frozen

1 tbsp chopped dill
1 tbsp chopped chives or spring
    onion tops
500g (1lb 2oz) puff pastry, thawed if frozen
1 egg yolk, beaten with 1 tsp cold water
sea salt and freshly ground black pepper

1    Check the fish for bones and cut into small cubes. Sauté the mushrooms in the butter for 5 minutes, then add the sherry and cook for 1–2 minutes.
2    Remove from the heat and allow to cool. Mix in the crème fraîche, prawns, herbs and fish. Season lightly and cool completely.
3    Cut the pastry in half and roll out 2 equal oblongs about 3mm (¼in) thick, measuring approximately 30 x 23cm (12 x 9in). Place one sheet on a non-stick baking sheet. Spoon the cooled filling in the centre and spread out evenly, leaving a small gap around the edges.
4    Brush round the edges with egg yolk. Top with the remaining pastry sheet and press the edges well together, then trim neatly and 'knock up' the edges with the back of a knife and crimp or pinch firmly together.
5    Make 3 slashes across the top with a sharp knife and brush evenly all over with the remaining yolk to glaze. Place in the fridge to chill while you preheat the oven to 190°C (375°F, Gas Mark 5). Bake for 30–35 minutes until golden brown and crisp. Let stand for 5 minutes then serve.

## 068 Poached party salmon

**SERVES** 6–8  **PREPARATION TIME** 10 minutes plus cooling and decorating  **COOKING TIME** 30 minutes

1 whole salmon, about 1.5kg (3lb 5oz),
   gutted and washed
Court bouillon (see page 16)
2 lemons, 1 sliced, 1 cut in wedges
2 tsp sea salt
2 sheets leaf gelatine, soaked in cold water to
   cover and squeezed, or 2 tsp gelatine
   crystals, soaked in 2 tbsp cold water

½ cucumber
dill, flat leaf parsley or coriander sprigs
   or watercress, to garnish

1   Place the fish into a fish kettle and pour over the court bouillon. Add the lemon slices and salt and bring slowly to the boil. Reduce the heat to a very gentle simmer and cook for 30 minutes.
2   Remove from the heat, measure off 250ml (9fl oz, 1 cup) hot bouillon and stir in the soaked gelatine until dissolved. Cool the fish in the remaining bouillon for 1 hour.
3   Slice the cucumber wafer thin using a mandolin or Japanese food slicer. Drain the fish and peel off the skin. Scrape off the brown flesh with the back of a spoon.
4   Dip the cucumber slices into the setting bouillon and arrange in overlapping lines on the top of the fish. Chill until ready to serve and garnish with herbs or cress and lemon wedges. This is nice with thick homemade Mayonnaise (see page 210).

## 069 Christmas Eve baked salmon with hot beetroot dressing

**SERVES** 6   **PREPARATION TIME** 15 minutes   **COOKING TIME** 20 minutes

1 side fresh salmon fillet, about 1kg
    (2lb 4oz), skin on
olive or vegetable oil, to coat
3 tbsp soy sauce
1 tbsp freshly grated ginger
2 tbsp lemon juice
freshly ground white or black pepper
2 bunches of watercress or large bag
    wild rocket or baby spinach leaves
1 lemon, cut in 6 wedges, to serve

**RELISH**
250g (9oz) cooked whole beetroot
    (not pickled), diced small
4 tbsp coarse grain mustard
2 tbsp sugar
2 tbsp balsamic or red wine vinegar

1  Preheat the oven to 190°C (375°F, Gas Mark 5). Brush the skin and flesh of the salmon with a little oil and place in a non-stick roasting pan.
2  Mix together the soy, ginger and lemon juice and pour over the salmon. Grind over some pepper. Marinate for 5 minutes while the oven is heating then bake the fish for about 15 minutes, basting once with the pan juices, until the flesh feels just firm. Do not overcook. Remove and let stand for 10 minutes.
3  Meanwhile, mix together the diced beetroot, mustard, sugar and vinegar. Arrange the watercress, rocket or spinach on a large platter and place the salmon on top. Spoon over the beetroot and serve with the lemon wedges.

## 070 Crab and ginger tart

**PREPARATION TIME** 25 minutes   **COOKING TIME** 50 minutes

1 recipe quantity Shortcrust pastry
    (see page 18), or 300g (10oz) ready-made
4 spring onions, chopped
2 tsp grated fresh ginger root
½ large fresh red chilli, seeded and chopped
140g (5oz) dressed crab, white and
    brown meat

1 egg plus 1 egg yolk
150ml (5fl oz, ⅔ cup) single cream
150ml (5fl oz, ⅔ cup) milk
25g (1oz) grated Cheddar cheese
sea salt and freshly ground black pepper

1  Preheat the oven to 190°C (375°F, Gas Mark 5). Roll out the pastry thinly and use to line a 20cm (8in) round loose-bottomed tart tin, about 2.5cm (1in) deep, leaving the edges overhanging slightly. Rest for 20 minutes then line with baking parchment and beans and bake blind on a flat baking sheet for 15 minutes.
2  Remove the parchment and beans and return to the oven for a further 5 minutes. Lower the temperature to 150°C (325°F, Gas Mark 3). Remove the tart from the oven.
3  Sprinkle the onions into the pastry case. Beat together the ginger, chilli, crab meat, egg, yolk, cream and milk, adding seasoning to taste.
4  Pour the custard into the case and sprinkle in the cheese. Return to the oven for about 30 minutes until golden and lightly set. Cool for 5 minutes and trim off the excess pastry using a very sharp knife. Serve warm.

## 071 Abroath smokies mousse

PREPARATION TIME 15 minutes   COOKING TIME nil

1 pair small–medium Abroath smokies
200g (7oz) crème fraîche or cream cheese
1 tbsp horseradish sauce
2 tsp small capers in brine, rinsed
   and drained

1 tbsp chopped chives
1 tbsp chopped parsley
grated zest and juice of 1 lime
freshly ground black pepper

1  Skin, fillet and flake the smokies. Beat together the crème fraîche with the remaining ingredients then fork though the fish.

2  Spoon into a small terrine and chill. Serve scooped from the dish or spoon into quenelles using two dessert spoons. Good with hot toast or crackers.


## 072 Hake with cockle sauce

PREPARATION TIME 5 minutes   COOKING TIME 10–12 minutes

half recipe quantity Béchamel sauce
   (see page 17)
200g (7oz) cockles, freshly steamed, or in
   brine and rinsed
2 tbsp laverbread or 2 sheets nori seaweed,
   crumbled

4 hake, cod or haddock steaks, each about
   125g (4oz)
vegetable oil, for frying
knob of butter
sea salt and freshly ground black pepper

1  Reheat the sauce, adding a little fish stock or water to thin if necessary. Stir in the cockles and laverbread or nori. Check the seasoning and simmer for 2 minutes. Cover and keep warm.

2  Season the fish and heat a little oil in a large frying pan. Pan-fry the fish for about 3 minutes on each side, then add a little butter to the pan and swirl the fish in it. Serve with the sauce.


## 073 Cornish mackerel with gooseberry and rhubarb sauce

PREPARATION TIME 5 minutes   COOKING TIME 15–20 minutes

4 whole fresh mackerel, gutted and
   heads removed
sea salt and freshly ground black pepper

SAUCE
2 sticks rhubarb, chopped
150g (5oz) fresh or frozen gooseberries
1–2 tbsp sugar
25g (1oz) butter

1  Put the fruits and sugar into a small pan and heat until juices start to run. Mash with a fork until softened. Mix in the butter and some seasoning. Set aside.

2  Heat a grill until hot. Slash the mackerel skin twice on each side and season. Grill for 3–5 minutes on each side until the skin crisps and the flesh is cooked. Remove and let stand for 5 minutes then serve with the sauce. The rich and tart flavours of this dish go well with boiled new potatoes.

## 074 Fish in beer batter

**PREPARATION TIME** 5 minutes  **COOKING TIME** 15 minutes

100g (3½oz, ⅔ cup) self-raising flour
150ml (5fl oz, ⅔ cup) beer or lager
250g (9oz) frozen garden peas
4 pieces cod fillet, each about 125g
　(4oz), skinned

vegetable oil, for deep-frying
sea salt and freshly ground black pepper
sprigs of mint, to garnish (optional)
malt vinegar, to sprinkle

1　Blend the flour, beer and 1 tsp salt in a food processor or liquidizer until smooth.
　Pour into a shallow bowl.
2　Boil the peas for 3 minutes in salted water. Drain and crush with a fork or potato
　masher. Keep warm.
3　Heat about 3cm (1¼in) oil in a deep-sided frying pan to around 170°C (325°F).
4　Season the fish. Dip into the batter then lay carefully in the hot oil. Deep fry in 2
　batches for 3–4 minutes until golden brown and crisp. Drain on kitchen paper and
　serve with the peas (minted if liked), sprinkled with vinegar and some chunky chips.

## 075 Old Hastings hot dab baps

**PREPARATION TIME** 5 minutes   **COOKING TIME** 10 minutes

4 dabs (small plaice), filleted
plain flour, to coat
1 tsp ground paprika or mild chilli
   powder, optional

light olive oil
4 fresh baps, warmed, split and buttered
sea salt and freshly ground black pepper
mayonnaise, ketchup or brown sauce, to serve

1   Check the dab fillets for stray bones and trim any side 'frills'. Mix together the flour, spices and seasoning.
2   Heat a thin layer of oil in a non-stick pan. Dip the fillets into the flour, shaking off the excess. Fry for 1–2 minutes on each side in the hot oil until lightly crisp. Remove and place 2 fillets in each bap. Serve immediately with mayonnaise or sauce.


## 076 Mussels with crispy garlic crumbs

**PREPARATION TIME** 12 minutes   **COOKING TIME** 10 minutes

24 large fresh mussels, washed
125g (4oz, 2 cups) fresh white breadcrumbs
2 fat cloves garlic, finely chopped
2 tbsp chopped parsley

grated lemon zest
50g (2oz) butter, melted
sea salt and freshly ground black pepper
Maldon salt flakes, to serve

1   Tip the mussels into a large bowl of cold water. Pull off the beards and discard any mussels that remain open when tapped. Drain the rest in a colander. Steam over a pan of simmering water for 3–5 minutes until they open. Cool slightly then snap off the top shells, leaving the meat in the other half. Lay out flesh side up on a grill rack. Preheat the grill to medium.
2   Mix together the crumbs, garlic, parsley, zest and some seasoning. Divide the mixture between the mussels, drizzle with the butter and grill until lightly browned and crisp. Serve on a bed of Maldon salt flakes.


## 077 Stewed eels and parsley sauce

**PREPARATION TIME** 5 minutes   **COOKING TIME** 20 minutes

1 eel, about 675g (1lb 8oz), skinned, gutted
   and cut in chunks
1 onion, chopped
600ml (1 pint, 2½ cups) fish stock
   (see page 16)

25g (1oz) butter
25g (1oz) flour
150ml (5fl oz, ⅔ cup) single cream
4 tbsp chopped parsley
sea salt and freshly ground black pepper

1   Simmer the eel and the onion in the stock for about 10–15 minutes until tender. Remove the eel with a slooted spoon and transfer to a serving dish and keep warm. Boil the stock to reduce by two-thirds and strain.
2   Melt the butter in another pan and stir in the flour. Cook for 1 minute then gradually whisk in the hot stock until smooth. Mix in the cream, return to the boil and simmer for 2 minutes. Stir in the parsley, check the seasoning and serve with the eel. Good with mashed potatoes.

## 078 Dublin Bay prawns with whiskey sauce

**PREPARATION TIME** 15 minutes  **COOKING TIME** 20 minutes

1 recipe quantity Court bouillon (see page 16)
24 Dublin Bay prawns (langoustines)
1 small glass (175ml, 6fl oz, $^2/_3$ cup) dry
 white wine
150ml (5fl oz, $^2/_3$ cup) double or
 whipping cream

3–4 tbsp Irish whiskey
200g (7oz) baby leaf spinach
knob of butter
sea salt and freshly ground black pepper
chives, to garnish
pinches of paprika or cayenne, to sprinkle

1  Bring the court bouillon to the boil in a deep pot, and add the prawns. You may have to do this in batches. Cover and simmer for 5 minutes then remove the shellfish with a slotted spoon or tongs. Cool and shell but keep 4 whole as garnish.

2  Ladle a small cupful of bouillon into a shallow pan and add the wine. Simmer to reduce by a quarter, then stir in the cream and seasoning to taste. Simmer for 1–2 minutes, then add the whiskey and cook for a further minute. Keep warm.

3  Stir-fry the spinach in a frying pan with the butter and seasoning until wilted. Drain and squeeze out the excess liquid then press gently into a small bowl. Turn out onto serving plates and tease out a few leaves. Arrange the prawns on the side. Garnish each plate with the reserved prawns and a few chives and sprinkle with paprika. Serve with the sauce for dipping.

## 079 Whelks with vinegar

PREPARATION TIME 1 minute   COOKING TIME nil

600ml (1 pint, 2½ cups) boiled whelks
malt vinegar or mustard Vinaigrette
    (see page 19), for dipping

1   Divide the whelks between 4 plates and provide a long pin to extract the flesh from
    the shells. Pour vinegar or dressing into small bowls for dipping.

## 080 John Dory with thyme butter

PREPARATION TIME 15 minutes   COOKING TIME 5–7 minutes

100g (3½oz) butter, softened
1 tbsp chopped parsley
2 large sprigs of thyme, leaves only
4 John Dory, each about 175g (6oz)

seasoned flour, to coat
olive oil, for frying
sea salt and freshly ground black pepper
1 lemon, quartered, to serve

1   Mix the butter with the parsley and thyme. Shape into a roll in a sheet of foil then
    chill until firm and cut into four pats.
2   Toss the John Dory in the seasoned flour to coat, shaking off the excess. Shallow-fry
    in hot olive oil for 2 minutes on each side. Drain on kitchen paper. Serve topped with
    a pat of butter and the lemon wedges.

## 081 Cod and prawn soufflé

PREPARATION TIME 10 minutes   COOKING TIME 30–40 minutes

25g (1oz) butter, plus extra for greasing
250g (9oz) fresh cod fillet, skinned
250ml (9fl oz, 1 cup) milk
1 small onion, chopped
2½ tbsp flour
½ tsp curry powder
75g (3oz) grated Gruyère cheese

25g (1oz) grated fresh Parmesan cheese
100g (3½oz) peeled prawns, thawed if
    frozen, patted dry and chopped
2 large eggs, separated
4 large Pancakes, about 23cm (9in) diameter,
    (see page 17)
sea salt and freshly ground black pepper

1   Preheat the oven to 190°C (375°F, Gas Mark 5). Lightly butter a large shallow
    ovenproof dish.
2   Poach the cod in the milk with seasoning for 5 minutes until firm. Strain the milk
    into a jug. Skin and finely flake the fish, checking for and removing any bones
    with your fingers.
3   Wipe out the pan and sauté the onion with the butter for 3 minutes. Stir in the flour
    and curry powder. Cook for a few seconds then gradually mix in the hot milk until
    smooth and thickened.
4   Simmer for 2 minutes then remove from the heat and stir in three-quarters of the
    cheese and the prawns. Cool for 5 minutes then beat in the egg yolks and
    lightly mix in the cod.
5   Whisk the egg whites until they form firm peaks and fold gently into the fish mixture.
    Place a pancake in the dish and spoon a quarter of the filling down the centre.
    Loosely fold over the sides. Repeat with the remaining pancakes and filling.
    Sprinkle with the remaining cheese, then bake for 15–20 minutes until risen and
    golden brown. Serve immediately.

## 082 Fish, leek and bacon lasagne

**PREPARATION TIME** 10 minutes **COOKING TIME** 45 minutes

300g (10oz) white fish fillets (coley, whiting
  or pollock), skinned
600ml (1 pint, 2½ cups) milk
1 bay leaf
75g (3oz) lean smoked bacon, chopped
1 large leek, thinly sliced
40g (1½oz) butter
40g (1½oz, ¼ cup) flour

100g (3½oz) smoked Cheddar or Double
  Gloucester, grated
125g (4oz, 1 cup) frozen peas
6 sheets no-cook lasagne
2–3 tbsp freshly grated Parmesan
2 tbsp dried breadcrumbs
1 tomato, chopped
sea salt and freshly ground black pepper

1  Poach the fish in the milk with the bay leaf and seasoning for 5 minutes. Strain the
   milk into a jug. Skin and flake the fish, removing any bones with your fingers.
2  Sauté the bacon and leek in the butter for 5 minutes then mix in the flour. Cook for
   1 minute then gradually stir in the hot milk until smooth and thickened. Simmer
   for a further minute.
3  Remove from the heat and mix in the grated Cheddar and peas then gently mix in
   the flaked fish. Preheat the oven to 190°C (375°F, Gas Mark 5). Lightly grease a
   medium, shallow, ovenproof dish.
4  Layer the fish and pasta, ensuring the pasta does not overlap. Finish with a layer of
   sauce, sprinkle over the Parmesan, crumbs and tomato and bake for 30–35 minutes
   until the pasta is soft. Let stand for 5 minutes before serving.

## 083 Plaice baked in cream

**PREPARATION TIME** 7 minutes **COOKING TIME** 10 minutes

good knob of butter, for greasing
4 plaice fillets, skinned and side
  'frills' trimmed
1 tbsp each chopped parsley, dill
  and chives

2 tbsp dry sherry or white wine
150ml (5fl oz, ⅔ cup) single cream
sea salt and freshly ground black pepper

1  Preheat the oven to 180°C (350°F, Gas Mark 4). Lightly grease a shallow ovenproof
   dish with the butter.
2  Check the fish for any pin bones and pull them out with your fingernails. Season the
   fish on its skinned side and divide the chopped herbs between the fillets. Fold each
   in half and place in the dish.
3  Sprinkle with the sherry, pour over the cream, season again and cover loosely with a
   butter paper or a sheet of foil. Bake for 10 minutes then let stand, covered, for
   5 minutes before serving.

## 084 Smoked haddock in cream and wild garlic sauce

**PREPARATION TIME** 10–12 minutes **COOKING TIME** 15–20 minutes

400g (14oz) undyed smoked haddock
  fillet, skinned
6–8 large wild garlic leaves, shredded
  freshly ground black pepper

300ml (10fl oz, 1¼ cups) half-fat crème
  fraîche or single cream

1  Preheat the oven to 190°C (375°F, Gas Mark 5). Cut the fish into 4 portions. Place in
   an ovenproof dish, top with the garlic leaves and spoon over the crème fraîche.
2  Season with pepper only and bake for 15–20 minutes until bubbling and just cooked.
   Let stand for 5 minutes then serve.

## 085 Scallops with black pudding on tattie scones

**PREPARATION TIME** 15 minutes   **COOKING TIME** 15–20 minutes

200g (7oz) hot mashed floury potato
25g (1oz) butter, plus extra for frying
50g (2oz, ⅓ cup) plain flour
½ tsp sea salt
¼ tsp baking powder

4 slices of black pudding
4 large scallops, cleaned, corals removed
olive oil, for frying
sea salt and freshly ground black pepper
chopped parsley, to sprinkle

1 Beat the potato with the butter. Sift together the flour, salt and baking powder then work into the potato as a smooth dough.

2 Shape into four round scones the diameter of the black pudding slices. Melt a little butter in a hot non-stick frying pan and cook the scones for 3–4 minutes on each side on a medium heat. Keep warm.

3 Fry the black pudding for 1–2 minutes on each side and keep warm.

4 Wipe out the pan, heat a little oil, season the scallops and fry these for no more than 1–2 minutes on each side until lightly browned but still springy. Rest for 2 minutes then slice each in half.

5 Place a slice of pudding on each scone and top with 2 scallop halves. Sprinkle with the chopped parsley and serve.

## 086 Smoked trout mousse with pickled beetroot

**PREPARATION TIME** 10 minutes plus chilling    **COOKING TIME** nil

200g (7oz) smoked trout fillets, skinned
200ml (7fl oz, ¾ cup) double cream
1 tbsp horseradish relish
grated zest and juice of ½ lime
2 tbsp chopped parsley

2 tbsp capers
freshly ground black pepper
1 tbsp chopped chives, to sprinkle
6 tbsp chopped pickled beetroot, to serve

1    Check the fish for any pin bones, then flake and mash lightly with a fork. Lightly whip
the cream and mix in the horseradish, lime zest and juice and pepper (no need to
add any salt as the fish is already salted).
2    Stir in the fish, the herbs and capers. Chill until ready to serve then form into
quenelles using 2 dessert spoons to mould an oval shape. Transfer to plates, sprinkle
with chives and serve with the beetroot. Nice with toast.

## 087 Devilled whitebait

**PREPARATION TIME** 7 minutes    **COOKING TIME** about 12 minutes

5 tbsp plain flour
1 tsp cayenne pepper or paprika
1 tsp mustard powder
1 tsp sea salt, plus extra for serving

500g (1lb 2oz) fresh whitebait
vegetable oil, for deep-frying
freshly ground white or black pepper
1 lemon, cut in wedges, to serve

1    Sift together the flour, cayenne, mustard and salt and tip into a shallow bowl.
Sprinkle with pepper.
2    Pick over the whitebait, discarding any that are broken. Pour enough oil to a depth
of about 4cm (1½in) in a deep-sided pan and heat to 180°C (350°F).
3    Toss a quarter of the whitebait in the seasoned flour, shake off the excess and lower
into the hot oil using a frying basket. Fry for 2 minutes until golden and crisp. Drain
on kitchen paper. Repeat with the remaining fish, reheating the oil between batches.
Serve sprinkled with salt, with lemon wedges to squeeze.

## 088 Hake with garlic sausage and green sauce

**PREPARATION TIME** 10 minutes    **COOKING TIME** 20 minutes

4 hake fillets, each about 125g (4oz), skinned
vegetable oil or melted butter, to coat
4 fresh garlicky chipolata sausages
sea salt and freshly ground black pepper
1 lemon, cut into wedges, to serve

**SAUCE**
2 tbsp each chopped parsley, chives, dill
and sorrel (if available)
2 tbsp mayonnaise
2 tbsp milk
sea salt and freshly ground black pepper

1    Preheat the grill. Brush the fish with oil or butter, season and cook for 3–5 minutes
on each side until just firm. Remove and keep warm.
2    Grill the chipolatas, turning regularly, until cooked.
3    Beat the herbs with the mayonnaise, milk and seasoning. Serve the sauce with the
fish, sausages and wedges of lemon.

## 089 Monkfish roasted with rosemary

**PREPARATION TIME** 10 minutes    **COOKING TIME** 25 minutes

1 large monkfish tail, about 800g (1lb 12oz)
   on the bone, grey membrane removed
2 fat garlic cloves, cut in spikes
2 sprigs of rosemary, snipped in 4

2 tbsp olive oil
50g (2oz) butter
juice of 1 lemon
sea salt and freshly ground black pepper

1    Preheat the oven to 190°C (375°F, Gas Mark 5).
2    Stab the fish with the tip of the knife and insert spikes of garlic and rosemary alternately on one side of the fish. Place in a roasting pan, trickle with the oil, dot with butter and season.
3    Cover loosely with a sheet of foil and roast for 25 minutes, uncovering for the last 10 minutes. Let stand for 5 minutes then cut from the bone and trickle the pan juices with the lemon juice over the fish before serving.

# 090 Tweed kettle

**PREPARATION TIME** 10 minutes plus cooling  **COOKING TIME** 20 minutes

1 whole fresh salmon, about 800g–1kg
  (1lb 12oz–2lb 4oz), gutted, head removed
1 bay leaf
1 large shallot, chopped
150ml (5fl oz, ⅔ cup) dry white wine
1 blade mace or ½ tsp ground mace

200g (7oz) mushrooms, sliced
good knob of butter
vegetable oil, for frying
sea salt and freshly ground white or
  black pepper
chopped parsley, to sprinkle

1 Put the fish into a large pan (cut in half if necessary). Cover with water, add the bay leaf and 1 tsp salt. Bring to the boil then simmer for 5 minutes. Remove the pan from the heat and cool for 15 minutes.

2 Remove the salmon, peel the skin and pull the flesh off the bones in bite-sized chunks. Place these in a warmed shallow dish.

3 Return the skin and bones to the cooking liquid and boil down until reduced to 300ml (10fl oz, 1¼ cups). Strain and return the liquid to the pan with the shallot, wine and mace. Boil again until reduced by a third.

4 Meanwhile, sauté the mushrooms in a little butter and oil for 5 minutes until softened. Season and sprinkle over the salmon. Strain over the sauce and serve sprinkled with parsley.

# 091 Mussels in cider cream sauce

**PREPARATION TIME** 12 minutes  **COOKING TIME** 10–12 minutes

2 x 1kg (2lb 4oz) bags fresh mussels
1 shallot or small onion, sliced
1 bay leaf
handful of parsley stalks
2 sprigs of thyme

400ml (14fl oz, 1⅔ cups) dry cider
150ml (5fl oz, ⅔ cup) single cream
squeeze of fresh lemon juice
sea salt and freshly ground black pepper
chopped parsley, to sprinkle

1 Tip the mussels into a large bowl of cold water. Pull off the beards and discard any mussels that remain open when tapped. Drain the rest in a colander.

2 Put the shallot, bay, parsley stalks, thyme and cider into a large pan with some seasoning. Bring to the boil, simmer for 3 minutes then tip in the mussels. Clamp on the lid and cook for 5 minutes.

3 Uncover and discard any mussels that have not opened. Use a slotted spoon to divide the mussels between 4 warmed soup bowls. (If you prefer, you can pull the flesh from the shells first.)

4 Reheat the pan juices with the cream, stirring for 1–2 minutes, then remove from the heat, mix in the lemon juice and check the seasoning. Pour over the mussels and serve immediately, sprinkled with parsley.

# CHAPTER 3

# MEAT, GAME & POULTRY

Lush pastures, a mild climate and fine livestock breeding have blessed Britain with excellent beef, lamb and pork. So it's no wonder many traditional recipes are simple roasts, grills or stews. Our signature dishes, Roast Beef with Yorkshire Pudding and Horseradish Sauce, or Lamb with Mint Sauce, provided leftovers for two or three week-day meals with a potato-topped pie, rissoles and cold meat sandwiches. Cheaper cuts, along with offal, provided an equally tempting choice of pasties and pies (hot and cold), sausages and stews, many with evocative regional names.

Game has long been a tradition, served at the best country tables or quietly poached to eke out meagre peasant fare. While the gentry enjoyed venison and game birds shot for sport, pigeons, hares and rabbits were popped into pots 'below stairs' or cooked over open-hearth fires. Chicken was a real treat before intensive rearing made it a cheap meat of indifferent quality. Happily, old standards return with organic, traditionally raised poultry back on our meat counters.

## 092 Christmas spiced silverside of beef

**SERVES** 8–10   **PREPARATION TIME** 20 minutes plus 7-9 days marinating   **COOKING TIME** 2 hours plus cooling

2kg (4lb 8oz) joint of beef (silverside or aitchbone)
150g (5½oz, ½ cup) coarse sea salt or sea salt flakes
1 tbsp black peppercorns
1 tbsp red (Sichuan) or green peppercorns
2 tsp coriander berries
1 tsp fennel seeds
1 tsp allspice berries

1 tsp juniper berries
12 cloves
1 tsp freshly grated nutmeg or 2 blades mace
½ stick cinnamon
4½ tsp saltpetre* (optional)
75g (3oz, ½ cup) soft brown sugar
3 large dried bay leaves, broken
1 tsp dried thyme leaves

1   Stab the beef several times with a thin-bladed knife, then place in a large non-metallic dish and sprinkle with the salt, rubbing in well. Cover and refrigerate for 24 hours, then drain off any juices and scrape off and discard much of the salt.

2   Crush the spices (use all of them or a choice of at least 4–5) using a pestle and mortar or a spice grinder, then mix with the saltpetre, if using, and the sugar. Sprinkle all over the beef, rubbing in well, then replace in the dish and scatter with the bay and thyme.

3   Cover and return to the fridge for at least 7 days, turning every day or so and basting it with the juices. For a more spicy flavour, marinate for 9 days.

4   When ready to cook, place the joint and juices in a large pan and cover with cold water. Bring to the boil then cover and simmer gently for about 2 hours, checking the water once or twice to see the meat is still submerged and topping up with boiling water as necessary. Allow to cool in the water for 20 minutes, then remove and carve in thin slices. Good hot or cold.

**Note** Saltpetre (potassium nitrate) is used commercially in cured meats, sausages, etc. to keep the meat pink. Without it the meat will turn grey, although still be perfectly edible. Buy saltpetre from a speciality sausage maker or on the Internet at www.sausagemaking.org

## 093 Boiled beef with carrots and dumplings

**SERVES** 6   **PREPARATION TIME** 25 minutes including dumplings   **COOKING TIME** 1 hour 25 minutes

1kg (2lb 4oz) salt beef joint (brisket or silverside)
4–6 carrots, scrubbed, topped and tailed
2 onions, quartered
2 sticks celery, cut in chunks
2 bay leaves
2 sprigs of thyme
a few parsley stalks

1 star anise
½ tsp black peppercorns
½ recipe quantity Suet pastry (see page 19)
sea salt and freshly ground black pepper
2 tbsp chopped parsley, to sprinkle

1   Place the beef in a large pan and cover with cold water. Bring to the boil and skim off any scum that rises. Simmer for 30 minutes then add the vegetables, herbs, star anise and peppercorns. Continue cooking for a further 30–40 minutes until the meat feels tender when pierced with a thin knife.

2   Transfer the meat and vegetables to a warm dish with a slotted spoon and scoop out the herbs and peppercorns. Shape the suet crust into 6–8 small balls.

3   Reheat the stock to a gentle simmer and drop in the balls, cover and cook on a gentle heat for 15 minutes until risen and fluffy.

4   Cut the meat into thick slices and serve with the vegetables, dumplings and some of the stock, sprinkled with parsley.

## 094 Rare beef and egg salad

**PREPARATION TIME** 15 minutes plus soaking  **COOKING TIME** 30 minutes

1 fillet of beef joint, about 700g (1lb 9oz),
  trimmed
vegetable oil, for brushing
1 red onion, thinly sliced
1 bunch of watercress
1 head chicory, leaves separated and halved
2 spring onions, shredded

⅓ –½ recipe quantity Vinaigrette dressing
  (see page 19)
2 tsp coarse grain mustard
1 tbsp balsamic vinegar
2 eggs, hard-boiled and quartered
2–3 tbsp roughly chopped walnuts
sea salt and freshly ground black pepper

1  Preheat the oven to 200°C (400°F, Gas Mark 6). Brush the beef with oil, season
   and roast for 25 minutes for medium-rare, 30 minutes for well-done. Remove, cool,
   wrap in clingfilm and chill.
2  Soak the onion in a bowl of cold water for 1 hour, then drain and pat dry. Separate
   out the cress and toss with the chicory and both onions. Place in a shallow dish.
3  Slice the beef thinly and arrange over the leaves, seasoning to taste. Mix any meat
   juices into the dressing along with the grain mustard and balsamic vinegar.
4  Scatter over the eggs, drizzle with dressing, sprinkle with nuts and serve.

## 095 Beef olives

**PREPARATION TIME** 20 minutes  **COOKING TIME** 1 hour 30 minutes

800g (1lb 12oz) lean stewing beef (bavette,
  skirt or topside)
vegetable oil, for frying
2 shallots, thinly sliced
2 tbsp flour
400ml (14fl oz, 1⅔ cups) beef stock
2 tbsp tomato purée
4 tbsp soured cream
sea salt and freshly ground black pepper

**STUFFING**
125g (4oz, 2 cups) fresh white breadcrumbs
50g (2oz) lean ham, finely chopped
zest of 1 lemon
50g (2oz) butter, melted
large sprig of thyme, leaves only
2 tbsp chopped flat-leaf parsley, plus
  sprigs to garnish

1  Preheat the oven to 170°C (325°F, Gas Mark 3). Make up the stuffing by mixing
   together all the ingredients and season.
2  Cut the beef into 8 even slices then use a steak mallet to bat out each one thinly
   between sheets of non-stick baking parchment. Divide the stuffing between the
   slices, press down to firm and roll up neatly to form an 'olive'. Tie up each olive at
   both ends using thin kitchen twine.
3  Heat a smear of oil in a large frying pan. When hot, brown the olives all over, starting
   join side down. Place in a shallow, cast-iron casserole, join side down.
4  Add a little more oil to the pan and sauté the shallots for 5 minutes. Sprinkle in
   the flour, stir well then mix in the stock. Bring to the boil, stirring constantly, then
   add the tomato purée and seasoning. Allow to bubble for 1–2 minutes then pour
   over the olives.
5  Cover tightly with foil or a lid and bake for approximately 1 hour –1 hour 15 minutes
   until the meat is tender. Remove the olives to a serving platter, cover and keep warm.
   Place the casserole on the hob and boil the cooking liquid rapidly until it has reduced
   by half.
6  Snip and remove the kitchen twine from the olives (they should hold their shape).
   Strain over the sauce and serve with a dollop of soured cream and sprigs of parsley.
   Creamy celeriac and potato mash would be perfect to accompany.

## 096 Steak and kidney suet pudding

**SERVES** 4–6  **PREPARATION TIME** 20 minutes plus making pastry  **COOKING TIME** 2 hours 15 minutes plus overnight

750g (1lb 10oz) braising beef, cubed
250g (9oz) ox, pig's or lamb's kidney,
  cored and chopped
vegetable oil, for frying
1 red onion, roughly chopped
2 cloves garlic, crushed
250ml (9fl oz, 1 cup) beer or ale

250ml (9fl oz, 1 cup) Beef stock (see page 16)
2 tbsp flour
1 bay leaf
2 sprigs of thyme
2 tbsp Worcestershire or Harvey's sauce
1 recipe quantity Suet pastry (see page 19)
sea salt and freshly ground black pepper

1 Fry the beef and kidney in batches in hot oil until nicely browned. Spoon into a heavy-based pan or cast-iron casserole.
2 Add the onion and garlic to the pan and sauté gently for 10 minutes then pour in the beer or ale and the stock. Bring to the boil and simmer for 5 minutes.
3 Mix the flour to a smooth paste with 125ml (4fl oz, ½ cup) cold water and whisk into the simmering stock until thickened and smooth.
4 Pour over the meat, add the herbs, sauce and seasoning. Bring back to the boil then cover and turn right down to a gentle simmer and cook for about 1 hour 15 minutes, stirring once or twice, until tender. Remove from the heat, cool and chill overnight.
5 Line the base of a 1 litre (1¾ pint, 4 cup) heatproof pudding basin with a small disc of non-stick baking parchment. Lightly grease the sides. Roll out the suet pastry to a 30cm (12in) round. Cut out a quarter and roll into a small ball. Curl the remainder into a cone and press into the base and sides of the basin. Wet the edges.
6 Spoon in the chilled meat filling. Roll out the small suet ball to a round to fit the basin top and press down, pinching the edges to seal.
7 Bring a large pan a third full of water to the boil. Fit in a shallow collapsible steamer basket, sit the pudding on top, then cover and simmer gently for up to 1 hour, topping the water level up once or twice with more boiling water. Let stand for 10 minutes before serving.

## 097  Steak and kidney pie

**SERVES** 4–6  **PREPARATION TIME** 20 minutes plus making pastry  **COOKING TIME** 2 hours 15 minutes plus overnight

1 recipe quantity Steak and kidney filling
(see page 70)
1 recipe quantity Rough puff pastry
(see page 18)

1 egg yolk, beaten with 1 tsp cold water

1   Follow the recipe opposite for making the Steak and kidney pie filling. After chilling, spoon into a medium pie dish. Preheat the oven to 190°C (375°F, Gas Mark 5).
2   Roll out the pastry into a rectangle (or oval) large enough to cover the top with a slight overhang. Cut some lengths from the edge and use to line the rim of the pie dish, sealing with water. Cover the top with the pastry, knock back and crimp the edges, make a cross on the top and decorate with small leaves of pastry rolled and cut from any scraps. Glaze evenly with the egg yolk and bake for 40 minutes until crisp and golden all over.

## 098  Beef wellington

**SERVES** 6  **PREPARATION TIME** 30 minutes plus chilling and resting  **COOKING TIME** 55–60 minutes cooking

1 beef fillet, about 1kg (2lb 4oz), trimmed
vegetable oil or melted butter, to coat
250g (9oz) mushrooms, chopped finely
50g (2oz) butter
large sprig of thyme, leaves only
100ml (3½fl oz, ⅓ cup) red wine
2 large Pancakes (see page 17), or 6
slices Parma ham

500g (1lb 2oz) puff pastry or 1 recipe quantity
Rough puff pastry (see page 18)
2 egg yolks, beaten with 1 tsp cold water
sea salt and freshly ground black pepper

1   Preheat the oven to 220°C (450°F, Gas Mark 7). Brush the beef with oil and season well. Place in a roasting pan and roast for 15 minutes for rare, 20 minutes for medium-rare. Remove, cool and chill.
2   Heat a little more oil in a large frying pan and stir-fry the mushrooms over a high heat, adding the butter as they soften. Season and add the thyme and wine. Cook for approximately 10 minutes until softened. Remove, cool and chill.
3   Lay a large sheet of clingfilm on a board and spread out the pancakes or the ham in a rectangle. Spread with the mushroom mix, then place the beef at one end and roll up firmly in the clingfilm, twisting the ends. Chill again for 20 minutes.
4   Preheat the oven to 200°C (400°F, Gas Mark 6). Roll out the pastry to a thin rectangle about 28 x 35cm (11 x 14in). Unwrap the beef, place in the centre and wrap the pastry around it, pressing well to the sides and trimming the ends to fit neatly. Seal with egg glaze then glaze all over. Use the pastry trimmings to make pastry leaves if liked, sealing with more glaze.
5   Slash the top 2–3 times with a small knife, place on a baking sheet and bake for 25 minutes for medium-rare, 30 minutes for well-done. Let stand for 10 minutes before cutting in slices.

## 099 Irish steak sandwich

**SERVES** 2 **PREPARATION TIME** 5 minutes **COOKING TIME** 20 minutes

1 onion, thinly sliced
vegetable oil, for frying
few dashes of Worcestershire sauce
2 large crusty baps, slit, or 4 slices of
white crusty bread

butter, softened, for spreading
English or French mustard, for spreading
1 rump steak, about 250g (9oz)
handful of watercress sprigs or rocket leaves
sea salt and freshly ground black pepper

1   Sauté the onion in the oil for about 15 minutes, stirring slowly until softened and
slightly caramelized. Season and add Worcestershire sauce to taste.
2   Butter the baps and spread with mustard to taste. Heat a heavy non-stick frying pan
and smear with a little oil. Season the steak and fry for 3–4 minutes on each side or
until medium-rare. Press with the back of a fork to check: it will be slightly bouncy.
3   Transfer to a board and rest for 5 minutes. Trim off any fat and slice the steak into
strips. Pile the strips onto half the bread and season again. Top with some watercress
and sandwich together. Serve wrapped in paper napkins.

## 100 Steak Diane

**SERVES** 2 **PREPARATION TIME** 5 minutes **COOKING TIME** 5 minutes

2 fillets steaks, each about 170g (7oz)
olive oil, for frying
about 2 tbsp of butter
3–4 tbsp Worcestershire sauce

a little lemon juice
large pinch of English mustard powder
sea salt and freshly ground black pepper

1   Bat out the steaks between two large sheets of non-stick baking parchment to about
5mm (¼in) thick. Heat a frying pan until hot, smear with a little olive oil and cook
the steaks as you like them, rare or medium, about 1–2 minutes on each side. Press
with the back of a fork to check: cooked rare, the steak will be quite bouncy. Season
and transfer to a plate.
2   Melt the butter in the pan. Mix in the Worcestershire sauce to taste, lemon juice and
mustard. Return the steaks, coat in the juices then serve immediately with skinny
chips and some watercress.

## 101 Carpetbagger's rump steak

**SERVES** 2 **PREPARATION TIME** 10 minutes **COOKING TIME** 20 minutes

1 rump or sirloin steak about 3–4 cm
(1¼–1½in) thick, about 350–400g
(12–14oz)
200g (7oz) chestnut mushrooms, sliced
50g (2oz) butter
vegetable oil, for frying

1 tbsp dry sherry
good pinch of dried sage or thyme
½ glass (85ml, 3fl oz, ⅓ cup) dry white
wine or stock
2 tbsp double cream or crème fraîche
sea salt and freshly ground black pepper

1   Trim the steak of any fat, then carefully slit it almost in half and open up.
2   Stir-fry the mushrooms in the butter with a little oil and seasoning until they start
to wilt, about 7 minutes. Stir in the sherry, herbs and seasoning and cook for a
further 2 minutes.
3   Spoon onto the opened steak then fold back over like a sandwich. Secure the edges
with toothpicks or simply press firmly.
4   Heat some oil in a large, heavy-based, non-stick pan. Fry the steak for 3–4 minutes
on each side for medium-rare, or for a further 2 minutes if you prefer it well-done,
seasoning well on both sides.
5   Transfer to a platter and pour the wine into the pan and bubble up for a minute or so.
Mix in the cream, add some seasoning and any meat juices.
6   Cut the steak in half, pour over the juices and serve.

## 102 Roast beef, Yorkshire puddings and horseradish sauce

**SERVES** 6   **PREPARATION TIME** 15 minutes plus resting   **COOKING TIME** 1 hour 45 minutes

1.25kg (2lb 12oz) prime roasting joint of beef (wing rib or sirloin), ideally bone-in
1 tbsp dry mustard powder
vegetable oil or beef dripping, to coat
1 recipe quantity Batter (see page 17)
1 tbsp flour
150ml (5fl oz, scant ²/₃ cup) red wine

300ml (10fl oz, 1¼ cups) beef stock
½ beef stock cube or 1 tsp gravy powder (optional)
3–4 tbsp horseradish relish
3–4 tbsp crème fraîche or whipped double cream
sea salt and freshly ground black pepper

1   Bring the joint to room temperature if chilled. Preheat the oven to 200°C (400°F, Gas Mark 6).

2   Rub the beef fat layer with mustard powder and season well. Place in a roasting pan and brush the sides with oil.

3   Roast for 20 minutes, baste with the pan juices, then reduce the temperature to 180°C (350°F, Gas Mark 4). Cook the meat for 25 minutes for rare, 35–40 minutes for medium-rare to well-done. Transfer the meat to a warm serving dish. Cover the joint loosely with foil and let stand for about 30 minutes.

4   To make the puddings, pour dribbles of oil or melted dripping into a 12-hole bun tin. Increase the oven temperature to 200°C (400°F, Gas Mark 6) and heat the tin for 5 minutes. Remove, pour in the batter and return to the oven and cook for 15–20 minutes until risen and golden.

5   To make the gravy, place the roasting pan on the hob. Heat the meat juices and stir in the flour. Cook for 1 minute on a low heat, then mix in the red wine, stock and stock cube. Bring to the boil and boil for 5 minutes until slightly reduced. Check the seasoning, strain the gravy into a jug and keep warm. Pour in any extra juices from the joint after it has stood before carving.

6   Mix the horseradish with the crème fraîche. Carve the beef thinly with a long sharp knife and serve with the mini Yorkshire puddings, pan gravy and horseradish.

## 103 Sunday lunch beef curry

PREPARATION TIME 30 minutes    COOKING TIME 1 hour

600–700g (1lb 5–9oz) lean braising
    beef, cubed
vegetable oil or ghee, for frying
1 large onion, thinly sliced
1–2 large fresh green chillies, split, seeded
    then chopped
2 tbsp grated fresh root ginger
3 fat cloves garlic, crushed
3 tbsp desiccated coconut
2–3 tbsp curry powder, mild, medium or
    hot, to taste
1 tbsp tomato purée
sea salt and freshly ground black pepper

natural yogurt, to serve
2 tbsp chopped coriander, to sprinkle

**TRIMMINGS**
2 eggs, hard-boiled, peeled and chopped
1 banana, sliced and dipped in lemon juice
¼ cucumber, chopped
1 large tomato, chopped
3 tbsp desiccated coconut, lightly toasted
hot Indian pickle or mango chutney
4–8 grilled poppadums

1  Brown the meat in two or more batches in hot oil in a frying pan and transfer to
a large casserole. Sauté the onion, chillies, ginger and garlic in a little more oil for
approximately 10 minutes.

2  Meanwhile, pour 500ml (18fl oz, 2 cups) boiling water over the coconut and steep
for 15 minutes then strain into a jug, pressing down on the coconut.

3  Stir the curry powder into the vegetables and cook for 1–2 minutes then mix in the
hot coconut water (discarding the desiccated coconut) and tomato purée. Bring to
the boil and pour over the meat, adding seasoning to taste. Cover and simmer gently
for 45–50 minutes until the meat is tender. (The dish can be cooled and chilled
ahead at this point then reheated until boiling. It will taste better for this.)

4  Lay out the trimmings in small dishes and serve the curry hot, with yogurt spooned
on top and sprinkled with coriander. Serve with hot basmati rice or naan bread.

## 104 Scottish mince 'n' tatties

PREPARATION TIME 10 minutes    COOKING TIME 25–30 minutes

800g–1kg (1lb 12oz–2lb 4oz) old potatoes
    (Maris Piper, Desirée or King Edward)
good knob of butter
600g (1lb 5oz) lean beef mince
vegetable oil or beef dripping, for frying
1 onion, finely chopped
1 tbsp flour

500ml (18fl oz, 2 cups) Beef or chicken stock
    (see page 16)
1 sprig of thyme
1 bay leaf
Worcestershire or Harvey's sauce, to taste
sea salt and freshly ground black pepper
2 tbsp chopped parsley, to sprinkle

1  Peel and cut the potatoes into chunks, then boil until just tender, about 12–15
minutes. Drain and return to the pan off the heat with a good knob of butter and
seasoning. Cover and keep warm.

2  Meanwhile, fry the mince in a little oil in a heavy-based casserole over a high heat
until browned and crumbly. Stir in the onion and cook for a further 5 minutes, then
mix in the flour and cook for 1 minute.

3  Gradually mix in the stock until it becomes smooth and thickened, then add the
herbs and season. Simmer, uncovered, for about 15 minutes, stirring occasionally.
Add dashes of sauce to taste. Serve hot with the potatoes, sprinkled with the parsley.

## 105 Irish corned beef and cabbage

**SERVES** 6 **PREPARATION TIME** 10 minutes **COOKING TIME** 1 hour 15 minutes–1 hour 30 minutes

1kg (2lb 2oz) salted brisket or silverside beef
2 carrots, chopped in chunks
1 large onion, cut in wedges
1 bay leaf
1 large sprig of thyme

a few parsley stalks
2 cloves
1 tsp black peppercorns
250ml (9fl oz, 1 cup) dry cider
1 small green cabbage, quartered

1 Put the beef, carrots, onion, herbs, cloves and peppercorns into a large pan. Add the cider and enough cold water just to cover the beef.
2 Bring slowly to the boil, then lower the heat, cover and simmer gently for about 1 hour–1 hour 15 minutes.
3 If your pan is large enough, add the cabbage and cook for a further 15 minutes so the cabbage is just cooked (longer if you like it softer). Otherwise, place the cabbage in a separate pan, pour some of the cooking liquor to cover and cook for 15 minutes until tender.
4 Slice the beef to serve; drizzle with cooking liquor and serve with the cabbage.

## 106 Spaghetti bolognese

**PREPARATION TIME** 15 minutes **COOKING TIME** 40 minutes

500g (1lb 2oz) lean minced beef
olive oil, for frying
2 rashers smoked streaky bacon, finely sliced
1 onion, finely chopped
1 carrot, finely chopped
1 small stick celery, finely chopped
2 fat cloves garlic, crushed
1 x 400g (14oz) can chopped tomatoes

2 tbsp tomato purée
½ tsp dried oregano or mixed herbs
350–400g (12–14oz) spaghetti
good knob of butter
freshly grated nutmeg (optional)
sea salt and freshly ground black pepper
freshly grated Parmesan, to sprinkle

1 Heat a large, deep-sided pan until hot, then fry the mince in a little olive oil until browned and crumbly. Add the bacon and cook until sealed. Stir in the vegetables and garlic, adding extra oil if necessary. Cook for about 5 minutes longer.
2 Add the tomatoes and purée plus about ½ can of water and the herbs. Season well, stir and bring to the boil.
3 Cover and simmer for 15–20 minutes until the meat is cooked and the sauce thickened. Keep warm. The sauce can be made ahead and chilled until required. In fact, this improves the flavour.
4 Meanwhile, cook the spaghetti according to the packet instructions, or for about 10–12 minutes. Drain well, rinse in hot running water and return to the pan with some butter or more oil. Grate over a little nutmeg, if liked. Serve the sauce on the spaghetti with Parmesan to sprinkle.

### VARIATION

#### Lentil and Mushroom 'Spag Bol'

Omit the mince and bacon. Add 250g (9oz) mushrooms, finely chopped, and sauté with the vegetables and garlic in oil until softened, about 5 minutes. Then add a 400g (14oz) can lentils, rinsed and drained, in step 2. Cover and simmer for just 10 minutes. Serve with vegetarian Parmesan.

## 107 Cornish pasties

**PREPARATION TIME** 30 minutes    **COOKING TIME** 45 minutes plus cooling

500g (1lb 2oz) Shortcrust pastry
(see page 18)
1 small onion, finely chopped
250g (9oz) chopped swede, turnip or carrot
400g (14oz) lean braising steak (skirt or
chuck), diced small

500g (1lb 2oz) potatoes, finely sliced
1 egg yolk, beaten with 1 tsp cold water
sea salt and freshly ground white pepper

1   Divide the pastry into 4 rounds. Roll each of these into circles, about 23cm (9in), and
    cut out using a small dinner plate as a template.
2   Lay one on a board and arrange a quarter of the onion and swede down the centre.
    Top with a quarter of the diced meat, season well and top with a quarter of the
    potato. Season again.
3   Dampen the edges with water and gather two sides of the pastry together, pressing
    firmly to seal. Crimp by folding the pastry over in waves and tuck the ends in to seal.
    Place on a non-stick baking sheet.
4   Repeat with the remaining pastry and filling. Chill and rest for 20 minutes while
    you preheat the oven to 200°C (400°F, Gas Mark 6). Glaze the pasties evenly and
    make a small nick in each for a steam hole. Bake for 15 minutes, then reduce the
    temperature to 160°C (325°F, Gas Mark 3) and cook a further 25–30 minutes.
    Remove and cool for 20 minutes before eating, although they do keep warm for
    a long time.

## 108 Homemade beef burgers

**SERVES** 6 **PREPARATION TIME** 10 minutes **COOKING TIME** 20–25 minutes

600g (1lb 5oz) lean steak mince
1 tbsp HP brown sauce
½ tsp dried mixed herbs (optional)
1 tsp English mustard powder

1 large onion
vegetable oil, for frying and brushing
sea salt and freshly ground black pepper

1 Place the mince in a bowl with 1 tsp salt, some pepper, the sauce, herbs and mustard powder. Grate in about 1 tbsp of the onion and mix well, then shape into 4 neat round patties. Chill for 20 minutes.
2 Slice the remaining onion thinly into rings and sauté gently in a little of the oil for 10 minutes until softened. Add seasoning.
3 Brush the burgers with some oil while you preheat a grill, then cook the burgers for 3–4 minutes on each side for medium-rare, 5–6 minutes for well-done. Tuck into warmed baps with onions and some salad.

## 109 Corned beef hash cakes

**PREPARATION TIME** 20 minutes **COOKING TIME** 20 minutes

2 baking potatoes, each about 250g (9oz), peeled and diced
1 onion, finely chopped
vegetable oil, for frying
1 x 340g (11oz) can corned beef, chilled
1 tbsp chopped parsley

1 tbsp Worcestershire or Harvey's sauce
1 tsp English mustard powder
1 egg, beaten
flour, to coat
sea salt and freshly ground black pepper

1 Boil the potatoes for about 7 minutes until just tender, then drain. Sauté the onion with a little oil for 5 minutes until softened then mix in the potatoes and cook for a further 2–3 minutes. Tip into a bowl, cool and mash slightly with a fork.
2 Cut the corned beef into small dice and mix into the bowl with the parsley, sauce, mustard powder, egg and seasoning. Chill then shape into 4 round cakes and toss in a little flour to coat.
3 Heat more oil in a shallow pan and fry the cakes for 2–3 minutes on each side until golden and crisp. Drain and serve hot topped with poached eggs and steamed green beans.

## 110 Forfar bridies (Scottish pasties)

**PREPARATION TIME** 20 minutes plus chilling **COOKING TIME** 40 minutes

500g (1lb 2oz) rump steak (or venison), roughly cubed
1 small onion, roughly chopped
3 tbsp shredded suet
1 recipe quantity Shortcrust pastry (see page 18) or 1 x 500g (1lb 2oz) pack, thawed if frozen

1 egg yolk, beaten with 1 tsp cold water
sea salt and freshly ground black pepper

1 Pulse the meat in a food processor with the onion until coarsely minced. Tip into a bowl and mix with the suet and seasoning.
2 Knead the pastry into 4 balls then roll each one into rounds about 5mm (¼in) thick. Brush the edges with water and spoon the filling on half of each pastry round. Fold to enclose, press to seal and crimp, then mould slightly into half moons.
3 Chill for 30 minutes on a non-stick baking sheet while you preheat the oven to 200°C (400°F, Gas Mark 6). Brush evenly with the egg yolk, slash once on top and bake for 35–40 minutes until golden.

## 111 Hot salted tongue with port and orange sauce

SERVES 6    PREPARATION TIME 10 minutes    COOKING TIME 1 hour 15 minutes

1 salted tongue, about 1kg (2lb 4oz)
1 small onion, roughly sliced
1 carrot, roughly chopped
1 large bay leaf
2 star anise
2 tsp coriander seeds
1 tsp black peppercorns

SAUCE
2 shallots, finely chopped
a little vegetable oil
a knob of butter
300ml (10fl oz, 1¼ cups) red wine
150ml (5fl oz, ⅔ cup) ruby port
300ml (10fl oz, 1¼ cups) Chicken
    stock (see page 16)
zest and juice of 1 orange
2 sprigs of thyme
sea salt and freshly ground black pepper

1   Place the tongue in a large pan and cover with cold water. Bring to the boil and skim off any scum that rises. Reduce the heat to a simmer and stir in the onion, carrot, bay leaf, 1 star anise, 1 tsp coriander and the peppercorns.
2   Cover and cook gently for 1 hour–1 hour 15 minutes until the meat feels tender when pierced. Cool for 20 minutes in the stock then transfer to a board and peel off the skin. Remove any small bones and carve into thin slices. Place on a platter and spoon over a little of the cooking liquor to keep moist. Cover and keep warm.
3   Meanwhile, make the sauce. Put all the ingredients into a pan, including the remaining star anise and coriander seeds, and bring to the boil. Simmer until reduced by half, then strain and serve hot with the tongue slices.

## 112 Roast loin of veal

PREPARATION TIME 10 minutes    COOKING TIME 1 hour 30 minutes

1 boned and rolled loin of veal, about 1.5kg
    (3lb 5oz)
2–3 sprigs of thyme or rosemary
4–6 rashers streaky bacon
1 glass (175ml, 6fl oz, ⅔ cup) white wine
250ml (9fl oz, 1 cup) Veal or chicken stock
    (see page 16)

1 tsp soft brown sugar
juice of ½ lemon
good knob of butter
sea salt and freshly ground black pepper

1   Season the top of the joint, lay on top of the herb sprigs in a roasting pan and cover with the bacon rashers. Rest while you preheat the oven to 180°C (350°F, Gas Mark 4). Cook the joint for about 1 hour 30 minutes. Remove and rest for 10 minutes then transfer the meat to a plate and keep warm.
2   Place the roasting pan on the hob. Pour in the wine and heat gently, stirring for about 2–3 minutes, then stir in the stock. Bring to the boil, add the sugar and simmer for 5 minutes until reduced by a third. Mix in the lemon juice, then whisk in the butter and check the seasoning.
3   Slice the veal and arrange on 4 warmed plates. Pour the sauce over the slices and serve with new potatoes tossed in butter and parsley, green or runner beans, or cauliflower florets and young whole carrots.

## 113 Veal fricassée

**PREPARATION TIME** 15 minutes    **COOKING TIME** 1 hour 30 minutes

650g (1lb 6oz) pie veal, cubed
200g (7oz) gammon, cubed
vegetable oil, for frying
1 large onion, halved and sliced
1 sprig of marjoram or thyme
good knob of butter
150g (5oz) large button mushrooms,
   thinly sliced
2 tbsp dry sherry

1 tbsp flour
400ml (14fl oz, 1¾ cups) Veal or chicken
   stock (see page 16)
150ml (5fl oz, ⅔ cup) double cream
1 egg yolk
squeeze of fresh lemon juice
sea salt and freshly ground black pepper
chopped parsley, to sprinkle

1  Brown the veal and gammon cubes in some hot oil in a large heavy-based pan for about 10 minutes. Cook in batches and remove to a plate while you brown the rest.
2  Add the onion to the pan with the herbs and cook for 5 minutes, then stir in the butter and, when melted, add the mushrooms and mix in. Cook for a further 5 minutes, then add the sherry and cook until absorbed.
3  Sprinkle and stir in the flour, then gradually add the stock, stirring over a low heat until absorbed.
4  Return the meat, season well, cover and simmer gently for 45 minutes or until the meat is tender.
5  Beat the cream with the egg yolk and stir into the pan. Reheat very gently without boiling, then remove from the heat and stir in the lemon juice. Check the seasoning and serve hot, sprinkled with the parsley.

## 114 Calf's liver and bacon

**PREPARATION TIME** 5 minutes    **COOKING TIME** 20 minutes

1 red onion, thinly sliced
olive oil, for frying
1 sprig of thyme or rosemary
2 tbsp double cream or crème fraîche
4 rashers smoked back bacon

4 slices calf's liver, each about 100g (3½oz),
   cut not too thinly
knob of butter
sea salt and freshly ground black pepper

1  Sauté the onion in some oil in a pan with the herbs and seasoning for about 15 minutes, stirring frequently until softened. Then mix in the cream. Set aside.
2  When ready to serve, fry the bacon in a little more oil until crisp, then remove and set aside. Add a little extra oil to the pan and fry the liver for 2–3 minutes on each side depending on thickness. The insides should be pink and juicy.
3  Slide in a knob of butter and turn the liver slices as it melts. Remove and serve with the bacon on top and onions alongside. Best with creamy mash or chips.

## 115 Tripe and onions

**PREPARATION TIME** 10 minutes    **COOKING TIME** 30 minutes

2 large onions, thinly sliced
400ml (14fl oz, 1⅔ cups) milk
1 packet parsley sauce mix

500g (1lb 2oz) pre-cooked tripe
sea salt and freshly ground white pepper
chopped parsley, to sprinkle

1  Put the onions with the milk in a non-stick pan and simmer, stirring frequently so the base doesn't burn, until the onions are soft – about 15 minutes. Strain off the milk, blend with the sauce mix, then return the sauce to the onions.
2  Cut the tripe into small squares, about 2.5cm (1in), and mix into the pan. Season with salt and pepper and cook for about 10 minutes until hot. Sprinkle with parsley and serve immediately with mashed potatoes.

## 116 Roast leg of lamb with two sauces

**PREPARATION TIME** 20 minutes    **COOKING TIME** 1 hour 30 minutes plus resting

1 leg of lamb, bone in, about 1.5kg (3lb 5oz)
2 fat cloves garlic, sliced into spikes
vegetable oil, for rubbing
1–2 sprigs of rosemary
sea salt and freshly ground black pepper

**ONION SAUCE**
1 large onion, halved then thinly sliced
vegetable oil, for frying

½ recipe quantity Béchamel sauce
   (see page 17)
a little freshly grated nutmeg

**MINT SAUCE**
10 sprigs of mint, leaves only
2–3 tbsp white wine or cider vinegar
1 tsp sugar

1   Preheat the oven to 180°C (350°F, Gas Mark 4). Stab the meat several times with a thin sharp knife and insert the garlic spikes. Rub with a little oil, season well and place on top of the rosemary in a roasting pan. Roast for about 1 hour 30 minutes, basting once or twice with a little more oil.

2   Meanwhile, gently sauté the onion slices in some oil for about 10 minutes until soft and tender. Make up the Béchamel sauce and mix in the onion. Season with a little nutmeg and keep warm.

3   For the mint sauce, blanch the mint leaves in a small pan of boiling water for a few seconds. Drain, run under cold water then pat dry and chop finely. Mix with the vinegar and sugar.

4   Check that the lamb is cooked by inserting a thin skewer: the juices will be slightly pink for medium-rare. Remove and stand, loosely covered, for 15 minutes then carve by cutting at right angles to the bone. Serve with any meat juices poured over and the sauces on the side.

## 117 Slow roast aromatic lamb shoulder

**PREPARATION TIME** 10 minutes    **COOKING TIME** 2 hours plus resting

1 lamb shoulder, about 1.5kg (3lb 5oz)
1 tsp sea salt
1 tsp mild curry powder
1 large red onion, thinly sliced

vegetable oil, for brushing
freshly ground black pepper
2 bunches watercress, washed, to serve

1   Preheat the oven to 150°C (300°F, Gas Mark 2). Mix together the salt and curry powder. Place the onions slices in the centre of a roasting pan. Brush the lamb with oil, place on the onions, sprinkle with the spicy salt and grind over some pepper.

2   Cover the top loosely with a butter paper or foil and cook about 2 hours, uncovering for the last hour. Remove and stand for 15 minutes then cut the meat from the bone in chunks and pull into shreds with 2 forks.

3   Tip out any fat from the pan and place on the hob with 250ml (9fl oz, 1 cup) water. Heat until boiling, stirring up the onion, then season and mix into the meat.

4   Place the watercress on a serving platter and arrange the meat on top. Serve hot.

# 118 Guard of honour

**SERVES** 6 **PREPARATION TIME** 20 minutes **COOKING TIME** 50–55 minutes plus resting

1 doubled-sided best end neck of lamb,
   about 2kg (4lb 8 oz)
2 tbsp dry sherry
2 tsp flour
250ml (9fl oz, 1 cup) Lamb stock
   (see page 17)
sea salt and freshly ground black pepper

**STUFFING**
1 small onion, finely chopped

25g (1oz) butter
vegetable oil, for frying
50g (2oz) fresh brown breadcrumbs
50g (2oz) walnuts, finely chopped
50g (2oz) apricots, chopped
1 sprig of thyme and 1 sprig of
   marjoram, leaves stripped
small bunch of parsley, chopped
grated zest of 1 lemon
1 egg, beaten

1    Ask the butcher to chine the rib bones about 5cm (2in) up and to bone out the central back bone, taking care not to nick the skin. Also, ask for the rib bone tips to be 'French trimmed'. (Use the bones and scraps to make the lamb stock.) Score both fat sides criss-cross fashion.

2    To make the stuffing, gently fry the onion in the butter and oil for 5 minutes until softened then stir in the remaining ingredients and seasoning. Cool until firm.

3    Preheat the oven to 190°C (375°F, Gas Mark 5). Mound the stuffing in the centre of the lamb and fold up, pressing the bones together so that they interlock, and tie in 3 or 4 places with kitchen twine. Place in a roasting pan and cover the bone tips with bits of foil. Roast for 40–45 minutes until the meat is medium and the stuffing cooked. Remove and stand for 10 minutes then transfer the lamb to a warm platter.

4    Place the roasting pan on the hob on a medium heat and stir in the sherry then the flour. Heat for 1 minute, then gradually mix in the stock and bubble up until thickened. Season. Cut the lamb into double chops and serve with the gravy.

## 119 Welsh lamb roast with laverbread sauce

**PREPARATION TIME** 10 minutes **COOKING TIME** 45–50 minutes plus resting

1 boned and rolled lamb loin, about 750g
  (1lb 10oz)
vegetable oil, for rubbing
1 sprig of rosemary, leaves stripped
  and chopped
1 glass (175ml, 6fl oz, ⅔ cup) dry
  white wine

250ml (9fl oz, 1 cup) Lamb stock
  (see page 16)
1 x 175g (6oz) can laverbread
grated zest and juice of 1 orange
knob of butter
a little chopped parsley
sea salt and freshly ground black pepper

1 Preheat the oven to 190°C (375°F, Gas Mark 5). If there is no fat layer on the loin, rub with some oil. Season, sprinkle with the rosemary and roast in a small roasting pan for about 35–40 minutes until nicely pink. Remove the meat to a serving platter and stand for 10 minutes.

2 Tip any meat juices into the roasting pan, place on the hob on a medium heat and stir in the wine. Bubble up until reduced by half then add the stock and bring back to the boil. Simmer for 2 minutes then stir in the laverbread and orange zest and juice. Check the seasoning, beat in the butter and parsley and serve alongside thick slices of meat.

## 120 Kay's roast hearts and mushy peas

**SERVES** 2 **PREPARATION TIME** 10 minutes **COOKING TIME** 50 minutes plus resting

2 large lamb's hearts
3 tbsp fresh white breadcrumbs
1 tbsp shredded suet
1 tsp grated onion
grated zest of ½ lemon
2 tbsp chopped parsley

a little beaten egg, to bind
Beef stock or gravy (see page 16)
1 x 400g (14oz) can mushy peas
sea salt and freshly ground black pepper

1 Preheat the oven to 150°C (300°F, Gas Mark 2). Snip open the hearts with kitchen scissor to form pockets. Mix together the breadcrumbs, suet, onion, lemon, parsley and some seasoning, then bind with a little egg.

2 Spoon the mixture into the hearts, pressing down with the back of a spoon. Secure the openings with a toothpick or simply press together.

3 Place in a small, shallow, ovenproof dish with some stock or gravy on the bottom. Season and cover loosely with foil.

4 Bake for 45–50 minutes until tender. Remove, stand for 10 minutes then slice each heart in 3 or 4. Heat the peas and serve with the hearts and pan juices poured over.

## 121 Braised lamb chops and stovies

**PREPARATION TIME** 20 minutes **COOKING TIME** 1 hour 10 minutes

4 lamb shoulder chops or 8 cutlets
vegetable oil, for frying and brushing
1 large onion, thinly sliced
750–1kg (1lb 10oz–2lb 4oz) potatoes,
  peeled and thinly sliced

1 sprig of rosemary or thyme, leaves
  stripped and chopped
400ml (14fl oz, 1⅔ cups) Lamb stock
  (see page 16) or gravy
sea salt and freshly ground black pepper

1 Preheat the oven to 180°C (350°F, Gas Mark 4). Brown the chops in a little hot oil for 2 minutes on each side then place in a shallow casserole dish.

2 Sauté the onion in a little more oil for 5 minutes until softened. Spread on top of the lamb, alternating with the potatoes and sprinkling herbs and seasoning between the layers.

3 Brush the top with a little more oil. Pour over the stock or gravy, cover loosely with a butter paper or foil and bake for 1 hour, uncovering for the last 30 minutes.

## 122 Mrs Leech's lamb stew with dumplings

**PREPARATION TIME** 20 minutes  **COOKING TIME** 1 hour 20 minutes

750g (1lb 10oz) lean breast or shoulder
   of lamb, diced
vegetable oil, for frying
1 onion, sliced
2 carrots, thinly sliced
2 tbsp flour
500ml (18fl oz, 2 cups) Lamb stock
   (see page 16)

2 bay leaves
1 x 225g (8oz) can butter beans, drained
sea salt and freshly ground black pepper

**DUMPLINGS**
150g (5oz, 1 cup) self-raising flour
75g (2½oz, ½ cup) shredded suet
1 tsp dried mixed herbs

1   Brown the meat in a large heavy-based pan in hot oil, then remove. Add the vegetables and fry gently until softened, about 10 minutes.
2   Stir in the flour then add the stock and bring to the boil, stirring until thickened. Add the bay leaves and seasoning and return the meat. Cover and simmer gently for 40 minutes then stir in the butter beans.
3   Mix together the dumpling ingredients. Add just enough cold water to make a firm dough and shape into 8 small balls. Drop into the pot, cover and simmer gently for 20 minutes.

## 123 Lamb's liver, onions and gravy

**PREPARATION TIME** 10 minutes  **COOKING TIME** 20 minutes

1 large red onion, thinly sliced
1 sprig of thyme or rosemary
vegetable oil, for frying
1 tbsp balsamic or red wine vinegar
pinch of sugar
2 tbsp chopped parsley
350–400g (12–14oz) lamb's liver,
   thinly sliced

a little seasoned flour (1 tbsp reserved
   for gravy), to coat
good knob of butter
300ml (10fl oz, 1¼ cups) hot Chicken, beef
   or lamb stock (see page 16)
2 tbsp half-fat crème fraîche
1–2 dashes of Worcestershire sauce
sea salt and freshly ground black pepper

1   Sauté the onion in a frying pan with the thyme or rosemary in a little vegetable oil for around 10 minutes until softened. Stir in the vinegar, sugar, salt and pepper and cook for a further 2 minutes. Remove the herb sprig and mix in the parsley. Set the pan aside and keep warm.
2   Toss the liver in the seasoned flour. Heat a little more oil in a second frying pan with the butter, lay in the floured liver and cook for 3 minutes or so on each side – do not overcook. Season in the pan then transfer the liver to serving plates.
3   Sprinkle the remaining flour into the pan, stir up then gradually mix in the stock. Bring to the boil then bubble until reduced by half. Stir in the crème fraîche and seasoning to taste, then serve with the liver and onions.

PREPARATION TIME 10 minutes    COOKING TIME about 35 minutes

500g (1lb 2oz) lean minced lamb
1 onion, chopped
1 carrot, coarsely grated
vegetable oil, for frying
1 tbsp flour
1 sprig of rosemary or thyme, leaves
   stripped and chopped
500ml (18fl oz, 2 cups) Lamb stock
   (see page 16)

dash of Worcestershire sauce
2 large floury potatoes (Desirée or King
   Edward), peeled and diced
1 swede or celeriac, about 500g (1lb 2oz),
   peeled and diced
good knob of butter
2 tbsp grated Cheddar cheese or breadcrumbs
sea salt and freshly ground black pepper

1   Brown the mince in a heated large frying pan, stirring until browned and crumbly.
    Remove with a slotted spoon to a plate.
2   Sauté the onion and carrot in the pan juices with a little oil, if necessary, for about
    5 minutes until softened. Sprinkle in the flour and cook for 1 minute, then add the
    herbs and stock, stirring as it comes to the boil.
3   Season and mix in Worcestershire sauce to taste then return the lamb and simmer
    for 15 minutes. Tip into individual pie dishes and keep warm.
4   Meanwhile, boil the potato and swede until tender, about 12–15 minutes. Drain well
    and return to the pan. Mash until smooth and lump-free, mixing in the butter and
    seasoning.
5   Preheat the grill to medium. Spoon the mash over the mince, spreading with the
    back of a fork. Sprinkle with cheese or breadcrumbs and grill until lightly golden
    and crispy.

## 125 Old country faggots

**PREPARATION TIME** 15 minutes **COOKING TIME** 30 minutes

250g (9oz) lamb's or pig's liver
1 onion, grated or finely chopped
lard or vegetable oil, for frying
250g (9oz) minced pork
1 tsp chopped sage
freshly grated nutmeg

100g (3½oz, 1⅔ cups) fresh white
  breadcrumbs
1 egg, beaten
150ml (5fl oz, ⅔ cup) Lamb or chicken stock
  (see page 16)
sea salt and freshly ground white pepper

1  Whiz the liver and onion in a food processor to a coarse purée.
2  Heat a little lard in a frying pan and fry the liver and onion purée with the pork mince, the sage, nutmeg and some seasoning. Cook gently for about 5 minutes.
3  Cool the mince and mix in a bowl with the breadcrumbs and egg, moistening with a little water if necessary. Wet your hands and shape the mixture into 8 balls. Place in an ovenproof dish.
4  Preheat the oven to 180°C (350°F, Gas Mark 4). Pour over the stock and loosely cover the dish with foil. Bake the faggots for about 20 minutes, basting once or twice, until dark brown and glossy.

## 126 Haggis 'n' neeps

**SERVES** 4–6 **PREPARATION TIME** 20 minutes **COOKING TIME** 50 minutes

1 haggis, about 600g (1lb 5oz)
1kg (1lb 2oz) floury potatoes (Desirée or King
  Edward), peeled and chopped
100g (3½oz) butter
100ml (3½fl oz, ⅓ cup) hot creamy milk

2 spring onions, finely chopped
1 small swede or turnip, about 600g (1lb 5oz),
  peeled and chopped
a little freshly grated nutmeg
sea salt and freshly ground white pepper

1  Preheat the oven to 180°C (350°F, Gas Mark 4). Wrap the haggis in foil and bake for 45–50 minutes or according to instructions.
2  Meanwhile, boil the potatoes until tender, about 12–15 minutes. Drain well, return to the pan over a low heat to dry off, then mash until smooth. Beat in half the butter and the milk. Season and mix in the onions.
3  At the same time, boil the swede until tender, drain and mash in the same way as the potato, adding the remaining butter, seasoning and nutmeg.
4  Cut open the haggis on a large plate and spoon out to serve alongside the mashed 'neeps n' tatties'. Serve with shots of whisky.

## 127 Lancashire hot pot with black pudding

**PREPARATION TIME** 15 minutes **COOKING TIME** 1 hour 40 minutes plus resting

8 lamb neck chops, trimmed of excess fat
125g (4oz) roll black pudding or 3
  lamb's kidneys
1 onion, sliced thickly
1kg (2lb 4oz) potatoes, peeled and
  thinly sliced

500ml (18fl oz, 2 cups) Lamb or chicken stock
  (see page 16)
knob of butter, melted
sea salt and freshly ground white pepper

1  Preheat the oven to 180°C (350°F, Gas Mark 4). Place the chops in the base of a large casserole dish.
2  Cut the black pudding in chunks or if using kidneys cut in chunks around the cores. Add to the casserole with the onion and arrange the potatoes neatly on top, seasoning between the layers.
3  Pour in the stock and brush the potatoes with butter. Cover and bake for 1 hour, then uncover and bake for a further 30–40 minutes until nicely browned on top. Let stand 15 minutes before serving.

## 128 Lamb neck kebabs with lemony lentils

**PREPARATION TIME** 20 minutes plus marinating    **COOKING TIME** 35 minutes

4 lamb neck fillets, about 125g (4oz) each
1 tbsp chopped rosemary leaves
2 tbsp vegetable oil
1 tbsp wine vinegar
200g (7oz, 1 cup) green or small brown
    lentils, presoaked and rinsed

good knob of butter
juice of 1 lemon
2 tbsp chopped parsley
sea salt and freshly ground black pepper

1   Trim the fillets of excess fat then cut into 2cm (³/₄in) thick rounds. Pop into a food
    bag with the rosemary, oil, vinegar and seasoning. Rub well together and marinate for
    15 minutes.
2   Cook the lentils according to the packet instructions then drain and return to the pan.
    Season well and mix in the butter, lemon, seasoning and parsley.
3   Drain and spear the lamb on 4 wooden skewers then grill or barbecue for 12–15
    minutes on a medium heat until just cooked. Serve with the lentils and some boiled
    long-grain rice.

## 129 Breaded lamb cutlets with reform sauce

**PREPARATION TIME** 20 minutes    **COOKING TIME** 25 minutes

8 loin of lamb cutlets, trimmed
1 egg, beaten
100g (3½oz, 1 cup) dried breadcrumbs
vegetable oil, for frying
sea salt and freshly ground black pepper

**REFORM SAUCE**
1 small onion, finely chopped
1 small carrot, finely chopped
50g (2oz) lean ham or cooked tongue,
    finely chopped
½ tsp juniper berries or black peppercorns,
    crushed

1 bay leaf
2 cloves
1 sprig of thyme
good knob of butter
4 tbsp red wine vinegar
3 tbsp red port or redcurrant jelly
400ml (14fl oz/1²/₃ cups) Lamb or chicken
    stock (see page 16)
1 tbsp cornflour blended with a little
    cold water

1   First make the sauce. Sauté the onion, carrot, ham, juniper or peppercorns, bay leaf,
    cloves and thyme in the butter for about 5 minutes. Add the vinegar and port and
    cook a further 2 minutes.
2   Add the stock, bring to the boil then cook until reduced by half, about 10 minutes.
    Pour some of the hot sauce into the blended cornflour, mix well then stir back into
    the sauce, heating until thickened. Set aside and keep warm.
3   Meanwhile, dip the cutlets into the beaten egg then into the crumbs, shaking off the
    excess. Heat about 1cm (½in) oil in a heavy-based frying pan until hot and fry the
    chops over a medium heat for about 3 minutes on each side. Drain on kitchen paper
    and serve with the sauce.

# 130 Irish stew

**PREPARATION TIME** 15 minutes   **COOKING TIME** 1 hour 30 minutes –2 hours

750g (1lb 10oz) lamb neck chops
1 large onion, sliced
1kg (2lb 4oz) potatoes, peeled and quartered

1–2 sprigs of thyme
sea salt and freshly ground black pepper
3 tbsp roughly chopped parsley, to sprinkle

1   Preheat the oven to 150°C (300°F, Gas Mark 2). Trim the chops of excess fat but
leave on a little on. Place in a casserole with a well-fitting lid. Lay the onion and
potatoes on top with the thyme.

2   Pour in enough boiling water just to cover the ingredients and season well. Cover
with the lid and simmer very gently for 1 hour 30 minutes–2 hours until the meat falls
from the bones. Serve in large shallow soup bowls sprinkled with the parsley with
crusty bread to mop up the broth.

## 131 Lamb leg steaks with wow wow sauce

PREPARATION TIME 10 minutes   COOKING TIME 12–15 minutes

4 lamb leg steaks, each about 150g (5oz)
vegetable oil, to coat
sea salt and freshly ground black pepper

**WOW WOW SAUCE**
50g (2oz) butter
2 tbsp flour
1 tsp English mustard powder

250ml (9fl oz, 1 cup) hot Lamb or chicken
   stock (see page 16)
4 pickled walnuts, chopped
1 tbsp red wine vinegar
1 tbsp mushroom ketchup, if available
1 tbsp port
2 tbsp chopped parsley

1   First make the sauce. Melt the butter in a pan and stir in the flour and mustard powder. Cook for 1 minute then gradually stir in the stock until smooth. Simmer for 1–2 minutes then mix in the remaining ingredients and cook for a further minute. Check seasoning and keep warm.
2   Meanwhile, preheat the grill until hot, brush the chops lightly on each side with oil and season. Cook for 2–3 minutes on each side, rest for 5 minutes then serve with the hot sauce spooned over

## 132 Old-fashioned lamb rissoles

PREPARATION TIME 30 minutes plus chilling   COOKING TIME 10 minutes plus reheating

1 onion, chopped
1 fat clove garlic, crushed
1 large fresh red chilli, seeded and chopped
   (optional)
2 tbsp vegetable oil or dripping from the roast
a little leftover gravy, if available
1 tsp dried thyme or winter savory
1 tbsp Worcestershire sauce

250g–350g (9–12oz) cold roast lamb
50g (2oz, ½ cup) fresh breadcrumbs
1 large egg, beaten
100g (3½oz, 1 cup) dried, natural
   colour breadcrumbs
vegetable oil, for frying
sea salt and freshly ground white pepper

1   Sauté the onion, garlic and chilli, if using, in the oil for 5 minutes. Add the gravy if you have any, herbs and Worcestershire sauce and cook for a further 2 minutes.
2   Tip into a big bowl and cool for 10 minutes while you mince the lamb (or pulse in a food processor) until crumbly. Add to the bowl with the fresh breadcrumbs, 1 tsp salt and pepper to taste.
3   Chill the mixture until firm then shape into 8 patties. Dip into egg then into the dried crumbs, shaking off the excess. Chill for 30 minutes to set the crust.
4   Preheat the oven to 150°C (300°F, Gas Mark 2). Heat about 5mm (¼in) oil in a large frying pan until hot, and fry the rissoles in two batches for about 2 minutes on each side over a medium heat. Transfer to the warm oven for a further 10–15 minutes to heat right through.

# 133 Crown roast of pork with prune and sausage stuffing

**SERVES** 6–8  **PREPARATION TIME** 15 minutes  **COOKING TIME** 1 hour 35 minutes plus resting

2 pork loins, chined and rind removed,
  2kg (4lb 8oz) total weight
vegetable oil or pork dripping, for roasting
1–2 tbsp flour
150ml (5fl oz, $2/3$ cup) red or white wine
250ml (9fl oz, 1 cup) hot Chicken or veal stock
  (see page 16)
1 sprig of sage
4 tbsp port or 2 tbsp redcurrant jelly
sea salt and freshly ground black pepper

**STUFFING**
4 thick premium-quality sausages
8 no-soak stoned prunes, chopped
100g ($3^{1}/_{2}$oz, $1^{2}/_{3}$ cups) fresh white
  breadcrumbs
1 small red onion, grated
a little freshly grated nutmeg
2–3 tbsp chopped parsley

1   Trim as much fat as possible from the loins and also trim off any meat inside the loins so they are even. Ask the butcher to nick the flesh between the base of the bones and to stitch the loin ends together into a round, to form a crown.

2   To make the stuffing, work together all the ingredients using wet hands. Press half into the centre of the pork 'crown', mounding up in the centre. Shape the remaining stuffing into 6–8 balls and set aside.

3   Preheat the oven to 190°C (375°F, Gas Mark 5). Transfer the pork to a roasting pan and wrap the bone tips with foil. Roast the joint for up to 1 hour 30 minutes, basting the meat 2–3 times with oil during cooking. Cover the stuffing when the top begins to brown.

4   Half an hour before the end of roasting time, surround the crown with the stuffing balls, rolling in the pan to coat in the juices, and cook until firm. When cooked, remove the crown and cover loosely with a tent of foil. Let stand for 20 minutes.

5   Strain any juices back into the pan. Sprinkle in the flour and mix to thicken. Gradually mix in the wine and then the hot stock. Add the sage, bubble up, season and simmer for 2–3 minutes. Pour in the port and cook for a further 2 minutes then strain into a warmed gravy boat.

6   Cut the joint between the chops to serve with some stuffing and gravy.

# 134 Slow roast pork shoulder with orange honey glaze

**PREPARATION TIME** 15 minutes  **COOKING TIME** 1 hour 40 minutes plus resting

1 rindless, boned and rolled pork shoulder
  joint, about 1.5kg (3lb 5oz)
1 sprig of dried sage, crushed
grated zest and juice of 1 large orange

juice of $1/2$ lemon
2 tbsp clear honey
1 tbsp coarse grain mustard
sea salt and freshly ground black pepper

1   Preheat the oven to 190°C (375°F, Gas Mark 5). Mix the sage with 1 tsp salt and rub all over the meat. Place in a roasting pan, sprinkle with pepper and roast for 30 minutes. Reduce the temperature to 170°C (325°F, Gas Mark 3) and continue cooking for a further 30 minutes.

2   Mix together the orange zest and juice, lemon juice, honey and mustard and spoon over the pork. Continue roasting for a further 40 minutes, basting 2–3 times.

3   Remove the joint and let stand for 10 minutes before carving into thick slices. Pour a small glass of water (about 150ml, 5fl oz, $2/3$ cup) into the pan, place it on the hob on a medium heat and cook until bubbling, stirring up the meaty deposits. Strain over the sliced meat and serve.

## 135 Chipstead churdles

**PREPARATION TIME** 25 minutes   **COOKING TIME** 35 minutes

200g (7oz) lean bacon, chopped roughly
200g (7oz) pig's or lamb's liver, chopped
1 onion, chopped
vegetable oil or dripping, for frying
½ tsp dried mixed herbs
2 large button mushrooms, chopped
½ Bramley apple, peeled and chopped

2 tbsp chopped parsley
1 recipe quantity Shortcrust pastry
  (see page 18)
1 egg yolk mixed with 1 tsp cold water
1 tbsp dried breadcrumbs
2 tbsp grated mild Cheddar cheese
sea salt and freshly ground white pepper

1   Stir-fry together the bacon, liver and onion in a little hot oil for about 5 minutes until
    lightly browned. Add the herbs and seasoning. Set aside to cool.
2   Pulse the mixture in a food processor until coarsely minced, then tip into a bowl and
    mix in the mushrooms, apple and parsley. Chill lightly while you make the tarts.
3   Cut the pastry into 4 and roll each quarter to a round about 15cm (6in) in diameter.
4   Lightly brush round the edges with the egg and spoon the filling in the centre. Draw
    up the edges like a three-cornered hat and pinch together, leaving the centre open.
    Mix together the breadcrumbs and cheese and scatter on top.
5   Rest the churdles while you preheat the oven to 190°C (375°F, Gas Mark 5) then
    bake on a non-stick baking sheet for about 30 minutes until golden brown and crisp.
    Serve with creamy wholegrain mustard and a salad.

## 136 Demerara and mustard glazed ham

**PREPARATION TIME** 30 minutes   **COOKING TIME** 1 hour 40 minutes

1 half gammon joint, about 2.5kg (5lb 8oz),
   green or smoked
1 stick cinnamon
1 tsp peppercorns
1 tsp coriander seeds
2 bay leaves
10–12 whole cloves

**GLAZE**

125g (4oz, ½ cup) demerara sugar
1 tbsp coarse grain mustard
1 tbsp Worcestershire sauce

1   Put the gammon in a large pan and cover with cold water. Add the cinnamon, peppercorns, coriander and bay leaves. Bring to the boil then simmer for 50 minutes, checking the water level and topping up with boiling water if necessary. Skim off any scum that rises to the top.

2   Preheat the oven to 190°C (375°F, Gas Mark 5). Transfer the joint to a large roasting pan, peel off the rind and score the fat criss-cross fashion. Stud with the cloves.

3   Mix the glaze ingredients and spoon half over the studded fat. Roast for 15 minutes, then spoon over the remaining glaze and return to the oven for a further 25 minutes glazing with the juices 2–3 times. Turn the pan at least once so the meat doesn't burn. Stand for 10–15 minutes before carving. This can also be served cold.

## 137 Black pudding with bacon and pan-roasted apples

**PREPARATION TIME** 5 minutes   **COOKING TIME** 15–20 minutes

1 large Cox's apple, cored and cut in wedges
vegetable oil, for frying
knob of butter

8 rashers lean dry-cure back bacon
8 slices black pudding, about 1.5cm
   (⅝in) thick

1   Heat a heavy-based frying pan, add a smear of oil and sauté the apple slices for about 10 minutes, turning once or twice, until softened. Slide in a knob of butter as the slices soften. Remove and wipe out the pan.

2   Add a little more oil to the pan, and fry the bacon until crispy. Remove and cook the black pudding on a medium heat for about 2 minutes on each side until dark and crispy. Serve the bacon, pudding and apple together.

## 138 Boiled collar of bacon with pease pudding

**PREPARATION TIME** 15 minutes plus soaking   **COOKING TIME** 1 hour plus cooling

1 collar of bacon joint, about 1kg (2lb 2oz)
1 onion, sliced
1 carrot, roughly chopped
1 stick celery
1 large bay leaf
1 large sprig of thyme or rosemary

2 cloves
½ tsp black or white peppercorns
150g (5oz) split yellow or green peas, soaked
   for 2 hours in cold water and drained
good knob of butter
chopped parsley, to sprinkle

1   Place the joint in a large pan and cover with cold water. Add the vegetables, herbs, cloves and peppercorns. Bring slowly to the boil then turn the heat to a simmer. Skim off any scum that rises to the top.

2   Tip the peas into a large (25cm, 10in) square of clean cotton muslin or cheesecloth. Draw up into a loose pouch and tie tightly with string, allowing plenty of room for expansion. Drop into the simmering liquid and cook for 1 hour, or until the peas' bag swells and the meat is tender.

3   Pull out the bag and cut open. Mix the peas with some butter. Leave the bacon joint to cool for 30 minutes in the cooking liquor then remove, peel off the rind and slice the meat thickly. Sprinkle with parsley and serve with the pease pudding.

## 139 Roast leg of pork with apple sauce

**SERVES** 6    **PREPARATION TIME** 10 minutes    **COOKING TIME** 1 hour 30 minutes plus resting

1 joint pork leg, top end, about 1.25kg
  (2lb 12oz)
a little hot stock
sea salt and freshly ground black pepper

**APPLE SAUCE**
2 large cooking apples, each about 300g
  (10oz), peeled, cored and quartered
2 cloves
a little sugar, to taste
good knob of butter

1 Preheat the oven to 200°C (400°F, Gas Mark 6). Make sure the rind on the joint is well scored; if not use the tip of a razor-sharp knife or craft knife to score the skin in close lines. Sprinkle the rind evenly with salt. Cook for 20 minutes then reduce the temperature to 180°C (350°F, Gas Mark 4) and cook for a further 1¼ hours until the skin is crisp. Do not baste during cooking if you want crisp crackling. Remove and let stand 15 minutes.

2 Meanwhile make the sauce. Chop the apples into chunks. Place in a small pan with a splash of water and the cloves. Cover and cook gently for 10–15 minutes until the flesh is hot and fluffy. Remove and beat in a little sugar, to taste, the butter and a pinch of salt. Discard the cloves and keep the sauce warm.

3 When the pork is cooked, cut off the crackling, scrape off the fat on the back and snap into bite-sized pieces. Carve the joint in thick slices and serve with the apple sauce and the pan juices, seasoned and thinned down with a little hot stock.


## 140 Bacon fraize

**PREPARATION TIME** 5 minutes    **COOKING TIME** 12 minutes

250g (9oz) lean streaky bacon, chopped,
  or a pack of lardons

vegetable oil, for frying
1 recipe quantity Pancake batter (see page 17)

1 Heat a large non-stick frying pan and fry the chopped bacon in the oil until crisp and browned. Drain on kitchen paper. Pour the fat into a small jug and top up with some more oil.

2 Reheat the pan and return a quarter of the bacon. Pour in a quarter of the batter and stir gently to mix then cook until the mixture firms and small holes appear. Flip over and cook the other side for a few seconds, then slide the pancake out of the pan and keep rolled or folded on a warmed plate.

3 Repeat with the remaining oil, bacon and batter for 3 more pancakes. Serve hot.


## 141 Oxford sausages

**MAKES** 4–6    **PREPARATION TIME** 12 minutes plus chilling    **COOKING TIME** 15 minutes

2 slices of white bread, crusts removed
250g (9oz) lean minced pork
250g (9oz) lean minced veal
100g (3½oz) minced pork fat or
  shredded suet
1 tbsp finely chopped sage or 1 tsp dried

2 good pinches of dried thyme
  or marjoram
1 tsp fine sea salt
¼ nutmeg, ground
½ tsp ground white pepper
vegetable oil, for frying

1 Briefly soak the bread in cold water then squeeze dry and crumble into a large bowl. Mix in the meats, pork fat, herbs, salt and spices until well blended then shape into 4 or 6 sausages.

2 Chill for at least 2 hours, then shallow-fry in medium-hot oil for 5–7 minutes on each side until browned and firm. Drain on kitchen paper and serve.

## 142 Pork chops with spiced syrupy raisins

**PREPARATION TIME** 5 minutes    **COOKING TIME** 20 minutes plus resting

| | |
|---|---|
| 4 rindless thick-cut pork chops | 2 tbsp soft brown sugar |
| vegetable oil, for brushing | 5 cloves |
| 250 ml (9fl oz, 1 cup) red wine | 1 stick cinnamon |
| 1 tbsp red wine or cider vinegar | 2 strips of orange zest |
| 200g (7oz, 1¼ cups) raisins | sea salt and freshly ground black pepper |

1   Preheat the grill and trim the chops of excess fat. Brush with oil, season and cook for
    5–7 minutes on each side under a medium heat. Set aside for 10 minutes to rest.
2   Meanwhile, boil together the remaining ingredients until syrupy, about 12 minutes.
    Cool for 5 minutes, remove the whole spices and zest strips and serve with the chops.

## 143 Ham hock with lentils

**PREPARATION TIME** 10 minutes    **COOKING TIME** 1 hour 15 minutes

| | |
|---|---|
| 1 cured ham hock, about 800g (1lb 12oz) | 150g (5oz, ¾ cup) dried green lentils or yellow |
| 1 onion, sliced | split peas, pre-soaked and rinsed |
| 1 carrot, chopped | 2 tbsp chopped parsley |
| 1 stick celery | freshly ground black pepper |
| 1 large bay leaf | |
| 3 cloves or 1 small stick cinnamon | |

1   Put the hock into a large pan and cover with at least 1.5 litres (2½ pints, 6 cups)
    cold water. Bring to the boil then simmer for 30 minutes, skimming off any scum.
2   Add the vegetables, bay leaf, cloves and lentils, then grind in pepper to taste (no salt
    necessary). Return to the boil then reduce the heat to a gentle simmer and cook for
    35 minutes, checking the water level occasionally and topping up as necessary.
    The mixture should be slightly soupy and the lentils soft. Discard the bay leaf and
    whole spices.
3   Remove the hock and peel off the rind. Pull the meat off the bone and rip or fork it
    into shreds. Return to the pan, mix in the parsley and serve in shallow soup bowls.

## 144 Pork vindaloo

**PREPARATION TIME** 20 minutes    **COOKING TIME** 1 hour plus resting

| | |
|---|---|
| 1 tbsp ground coriander | 1 onion, sliced |
| 1 tbsp ground cumin | 2 fat cloves garlic, chopped |
| 2 tsp chilli powder, medium or hot | 1 tbsp flour |
| 1 tsp ground turmeric | 2 tbsp wine or cider vinegar |
| ½ tsp freshly ground black pepper | 1 large tomato, skinned and chopped |
| 600g (1lb 5oz) shoulder pork, cut in | 1 large bay leaf |
|   small cubes | sea salt |
| vegetable oil, for frying | chopped coriander, to sprinkle |

1   Mix together all the ground spices with 1 tsp salt then toss in the meat and coat well.
    Heat a thin layer of oil in a large non-stick frying pan and when hot, stir fry the meat,
    in two batches until nicely browned.
2   Transfer the meat to a plate, add a little more oil to the pan and stir-fry the onion
    and garlic for 5 minutes. Stir in the flour and cook for 1 minute, then stir in 600ml
    (1 pint, 2½ cups) boiling water.
3   Bring to the boil, stirring, return the meat and any leftover spice then mix in the
    vinegar, tomato and bay leaf. Cover and simmer gently for up to 1 hour, stirring
    occasionally and topping up with more boiling water as necessary. Check whether
    salt is required. Let stand for 15 minutes before serving sprinkled with coriander. For
    a more developed flavour, make a day ahead and reheat.

## 145   Buckingham bacon badger

**PREPARATION TIME** 20 minutes    **COOKING TIME** 40 minutes plus resting

1 large potato, about 300g (10oz)
1 onion, chopped
400g (14oz) bacon or gammon, chopped
vegetable oil, for frying
2–3 sage leaves, shredded
sea salt and freshly ground black pepper

**PASTRY**
200g (7oz, 1¹⁄₃ cups) self-raising flour
100g (3¹⁄₂oz, ³⁄₄ cup) shredded suet
¹⁄₂ tsp sea salt
ice-cold water, to mix
1 egg yolk mixed with 1 tsp cold water

1   Fry the potato, onion and bacon in a little oil in batches for about 10 minutes. Add seasoning to taste and the sage. Cool.

2   Preheat the oven to 190°C (375°F, Gas Mark 5). To make the pastry, mix the flour, suet and salt with just enough ice-cold water to give a firm dough. Roll out on a lightly floured board to a neat rectangle about 5mm (¹⁄₄ in) thick.

3   Spread the filling evenly over the pastry to within 1cm (¹⁄₂in) of the edges. Roll up and place join side down on a metal baking sheet lined with a sheet of non-stick baking parchment. Press the ends under neatly.

4   Brush egg yolk evenly over the pastry then bake for about 30 minutes until golden brown and crisp. Cool for 10–15 minutes before cutting in slices to serve. Good with a homemade or ready-made tomato sauce.

## 146   Mince-stuffed onions

**PREPARATION TIME** 10 minutes    **COOKING TIME** 1 hour plus cooling

4 large onions, each about 300g (10oz)
250g (9oz) lean minced pork, beef or lamb
1 fat clove garlic, crushed
1 small carrot, coarsely grated
vegetable oil, for frying
6 tbsp gravy or stock

1 tbsp tomato purée
1 tbsp chopped parsley
2 tbsp grated Cheddar-type cheese
2 tbsp dried breadcrumbs
1 sprig of thyme, leaves stripped
sea salt and freshly ground black pepper

1   Peel the onions, leaving the root ends trimmed but still attached. Boil in salted water for about 30 minutes until soft but still whole. Drain and cool until you can handle them.

2   Slice off the top quarter from each onion and push up the centres from the root ends leaving about 2 outer layers. (It doesn't matter if they split a little.)

3   Finely chop or process the cooked onion flesh. Brown the mince with the garlic and carrot in a hot frying pan with a little oil until crumbly. Mix in the chopped onion, a little gravy and the tomato purée. Season and cook, uncovered, until reduced and thickened. Stir in the parsley. Cool for 10 minutes.

4   Preheat the oven to 190°C (375°F, Gas Mark 5). Spoon the mixture into the hollowed onions, pressing down to firm. Transfer to a shallow ovenproof dish, sprinkle with the cheese, crumbs and thyme. Bake the onions for about 20 minutes until browned and crisp on top. Good with mashed potatoes.

# 147 Toad in the hole

**PREPARATION TIME** 10 minutes  **COOKING TIME** 35 minutes

8 chipolata pork sausages
good knob of lard or 1 tbsp vegetable oil

**BATTER**

125g (4oz, ¾ cup plus 1 tbsp) plain flour
½ tsp sea salt
2 eggs
300ml (10fl oz, 1¼ cups) milk

1  Preheat the oven to 190°C (375°C, Gas Mark 5). Beat the batter ingredients together until smooth. (No need to rest.)
2  Heat the lard in one large roasting pan or two smaller shallow ovenproof dishes for 5 minutes until smoking.
3  Carefully tip in the sausages higgledy piggledy and bake for 10 minutes, then pour over the batter and return to the oven for a further 20 minutes until the batter is risen and crisp. Serve as soon as possible with cabbage and gravy.

## 148 Braised pigeon

**PREPARATION TIME** 25 minutes  **COOKING TIME** up to 2 hours

4 wood pigeons
2 onions, thinly sliced
2 sticks celery, thinly sliced
1 carrot, chopped
1 bay leaf
2 sprigs of thyme
vegetable oil, for frying
6 rashers dry-cure streaky bacon

1 glass (175ml, 6fl oz, $\frac{2}{3}$ cup) red wine
1 tbsp softened butter mixed with 1 tbsp flour
3 cloves
2 star anise
1 small white cabbage, quartered and cored
a little freshly grated nutmeg
sea salt and freshly ground white pepper

1   Use kitchen scissors to cut the bony backs from the pigeons, leaving the breast and legs attached. Put the backs into a large pan with 1 onion, half the celery, the carrot, bay leaf and thyme. Add 1 litre ($1\frac{3}{4}$ pints, 4 cups) cold water. Bring to the boil then simmer, uncovered, until reduced by half. Strain and reserve.

2   Heat the oil in a large frying pan and brown the pigeons all over. Transfer to an ovenproof casserole. Preheat the oven to 170°C (350°F, Gas Mark 3).

3   Fry the bacon in the pan for 2–3 minutes and place on the pigeons, then add a little more oil and sauté the remaining onion and celery for 5–10 minutes until softened.

4   Sir in the wine and boil until reduced by half, then add the stock. Bring to the boil, beat in the butter and flour paste, add the whole spices then pour into the casserole. Season, cover and bake for about 1 hour.

5   Meanwhile, cut the cabbage quarters in half and blanch in boiling water for 2 minutes. Drain and stir into the pigeon casserole, cover and cook for a further 20 minutes or so. Uncover and grate over some nutmeg then serve hot with creamy mashed potato and celeriac mixed together.

## 149 Jugged hare

**SERVES** 4–6  **PREPARATION TIME** 30 minutes plus marinating  **COOKING TIME** 2 hours 20 minutes

1 young hare, about 2kg (4lb 8oz), skinned
   and jointed, blood reserved if liked
4 tbsp vegetable oil
4 rashers streaky bacon, chopped
150g (5oz) small onions or shallots
2 tbsp flour
2 sprigs of thyme
2 bay leaves
250ml (9fl oz, 1 cup) game or chicken stock
150g (5oz) small button mushrooms
1 tbsp lemon juice

sea salt and freshly ground black pepper
chopped parsley, to sprinkle

**MARINADE**
500ml (18fl oz, 2 cups) red wine
1 onion, chopped
1 stick celery, chopped
1 large carrot, chopped
2 cloves garlic, crushed
1 small stick cinnamon, crushed

1   Put the hare in a large bowl. Mix together the marinade ingredients and pour over the pieces. Leave for 1–2 days in the fridge, turning once or twice. Drain the meat, pat dry and strain the marinade into a jug. Discard all the vegetables.

2   Preheat the oven to 150°C (300°F, Gas Mark 2). Brown the hare pieces in a little hot oil then transfer to a casserole dish. Add a little more oil and brown the bacon and onions and add to the pot.

3   Sprinkle the flour into the pan, stirring, then gradually mix in the marinade, thyme and bay leaves. Bring to the boil and cook for 3 minutes then stir in the stock, season and return to the boil. Pour into the casserole, cover and cook for $1\frac{1}{2}$ hours. Uncover, add the mushrooms and cook for a further 30 minutes until tender.

4   If using the blood, mix in the lemon juice first to stop it coagulating. Stir the hot stock into the blood and cook gently in a pan over a low heat until it thickens. Pour over the hare and serve sprinkled with the parsley.

## 150 Roast partridge

**PREPARATION TIME** 10 minutes **COOKING TIME** 20 minutes plus resting

4 young partridge, livers reserved if supplied
50g (2oz) butter, softened
8 rashers streaky bacon
4 fat cloves garlic, roughly crushed
2 large sprigs of thyme, halved

250ml (9fl oz, 1 cup) Chicken or game stock
(see page 16)
150ml (5fl oz, 2/3 cup) white wine
4 slices of good bread, crusts removed
sea salt and freshly ground black pepper

1 Preheat the oven to 220°C (425°F, Gas Mark 7). Remove the livers if they are inside the birds and roughly chop. Set aside.
2 Smear the breasts with half the butter and cover with the bacon. Tuck a garlic clove and thyme sprig inside each cavity.
3 Place the birds in a roasting pan with the stock and wine. Roast for 10 minutes then remove the bacon, baste with the pan juices and roast for a further 10 minutes. Remove and stand for 10 minutes.
4 Sauté the livers in the remaining butter for 3–5 minutes, season then crush with a fork. Toast the bread, spread with the liver and cut in triangles. Serve with the birds, roasted bacon and strained pan juices.

## 151 Rabbit pie

**SERVES** 6–8 **PREPARATION TIME** 20 minutes **COOKING TIME** 2 hours plus resting

1 skinned and jointed rabbit, about
2kg (4lb 8oz)
3 tbsp flour
1 sprig of thyme and 1 sprig of rosemary,
leaves stripped and chopped
vegetable oil or lard, for frying
2 sticks celery, sliced
2 carrots, sliced
125g (4oz) lean streaky bacon, chopped

4 premium pork chipolatas
250ml (9fl oz, 1 cup) dry cider
250ml (9fl oz, 1 cup) Chicken or veal stock
(see page 16)
2–3 tbsp coarse grain mustard
500g (1lb 2oz) Shortcrust pastry (see page
18) or ready-made
1 egg yolk plus 1 tsp cold water
sea salt and freshly ground black pepper

1 Trim the joints of any thin bony parts. Mix together the flour, herbs, 1 tsp salt and some ground black pepper. Toss in the rabbit joints to coat, then shake off and reserve the excess flour.
2 Brown the rabbit in a large frying pan in batches in hot oil and transfer to a large saucepan while you cook the rest. Sauté the vegetables in the frying pan adding extra oil or lard, until softened, about 10 minutes. Transfer to the saucepan.
3 Stir-fry the bacon for 5 minutes. Twist and cut each sausage into 4, add to the frying pan to brown then add the bacon and the sausages to the saucepan.
4 Sprinkle the remaining seasoned flour into the frying pan, stir and cook for 1 minute then gradually mix in the cider and stock.
5 Bring to the boil, stirring, then simmer for 5 minutes. Mix in the mustard and pour into the rabbit pan. Cover and simmer for 45–55 minutes until tender. Remove from the heat and leave to cool to room temperature.
6 Spoon the cooled mixture into a large pie dish and spread evenly. Roll out the pastry to fit the top of the pie dish, allowing about 2cm (3/4in) overhang. Re-roll the trimmings and cut into long strips. Wet the edge of the pie dish and press these trimmings all around. Brush with egg glaze.
7 Lift over the pastry top, press onto the trimmings to seal well then trim to fit. Crimp the edges to neaten. Make a steam hole in the centre. Preheat the oven to 200°C (400°F, Gas Mark 6) while the pie rests.
8 Brush egg glaze over the pie top and bake on a metal baking sheet for 20 minutes, turning once or twice, then reduce the temperature to 170°C (325°F, Gas Mark 3) and cook for a further 20 minutes. Stand for 10 minutes before serving.

Double crust game pie

**PREPARATION TIME** 40 minutes   **COOKING TIME** 2 hours plus cooling

1kg (2lb 4oz) mixed lean game meat
(pheasant or pigeon breast, venison,
rabbit), cut into small chunks
2–3 tbsp vegetable oil
1 onion, chopped
6 rashers fatty smoked streaky
bacon, chopped
1 tsp dried mixed herbs or crumbled
dried sage

1 tsp juniper berries, crushed
2 tbsp flour
300ml (10fl oz, 1¼ cups) Game or chicken
stock (see page 16)
150ml (5fl oz, ⅔ cup) red wine
2 bay leaves
350g (12oz) Shortcrust pastry (see page 18),
1 egg yolk, beaten with 1 tsp cold water
sea salt and freshly ground black pepper

1   Sauté the meat briefly in 2 tbsp oil until lightly browned, season and set aside. Add
more oil to the pan and fry the onion, bacon, herbs and juniper for about 10 minutes.

2   Sprinkle and mix in the flour, cook for 2 minutes then stir in the stock, wine and bay
leaves and bring to the boil. Return the meat, cover and reduce the heat to a very
gentle simmer.

3   Cook for 1 hour then remove and cool to room temperature. Roll out half the pastry
and line a 20cm (8in) round or oval shallow pie dish, leaving the sides overhanging.
Spoon in the game stew. Roll out the remaining pastry and press on top. Seal then
trim and crimp. Make a steam hole in the centre. Glaze with the egg.

4   Chill for 20 minutes while you preheat the oven to 190°C (375°F, Gas Mark 5). Place
the pie dish on a metal baking sheet and bake for about 30 minutes until golden and
crisp. If you wish, decorate with sprigs of rosemary and thyme.

## 153 Roast pheasant and all the trimmings

**PREPARATION TIME** 10 minutes   **COOKING TIME** 40 minutes plus resting

1 brace of pheasants, oven ready
good knob of softened butter
2 large sprigs of thyme, halved
4 rashers smoked streaky bacon
2 fat cloves garlic
1 onion, halved
1 small glass (about 150ml, 5fl oz, ⅔ cup)
   ruby port
250ml (9fl oz, 1 cup) Game or chicken stock
   (see page 16)
sea salt and freshly ground black pepper

**TO SERVE**
Bread sauce (see page 17)
pack of potato sticks (game chips)
large bunch of watercress
Redcurrant or rowanberry jelly (see page 202)

1   Preheat the oven to 200°C (400°F, Gas Mark 6). Smear the pheasant breasts with butter, season and lay two halved thyme sprigs on each breast. Cover with the bacon rashers in a cross. Put a garlic clove and half an onion into each cavity and roast the birds for 30 minutes, basting every 10 minutes with extra butter or the pan juices.

2   Remove the bacon and thyme and return to roast for another 10 minutes, then let stand for 10 minutes. Tip the juices back into the roasting pan and put on the hob with the garlic, onion and port. Heat until bubbling, then stir in the stock and seasoning. Simmer until reduced by a third, then strain into a serving jug.

3   Cut each pheasant in half lengthways and serve with hot bread sauce, gravy, game chips, watercress sprigs and redcurrant jelly.

## 154 London pigeon pie

**SERVES** 6   **PREPARATION TIME** 25 minutes   **COOKING TIME** 1 hour 20 minutes

4 wood pigeons
2 onions, sliced
1 carrot, sliced
1 stick celery
1 bay leaf
2 blades mace or ½ tsp ground mace
½ tsp black peppercorns
3 tbsp ruby port
1 tbsp soft butter mixed with 1 tbsp flour
250g (9oz) premium-quality sausagemeat
   or 4 thick sausages, skinned

2 tbsp vegetable oil
4 rashers back bacon, roughly chopped
1 sprig of thyme
150g (5oz) button mushrooms, halved
1 recipe quantity Rough puff pastry
   (see page 18)
1 egg yolk plus 1 tsp cold water
sea salt and freshly ground black pepper

1   Slice off the 8 breasts from the pigeons with a small sharp knife and set aside. Place the carcasses (legs intact) in a large pan. Add 1 onion, the carrot, celery, bay leaf, mace, peppercorns and port and cover with 1 litre (1¾ pints, 4 cups) cold water. Bring to the boil then simmer, uncovered, until reduced by two-thirds.

2   Strain and reserve the stock. Discard the bones and vegetables. Return to the pan and, over a medium heat, whisk in the butter mixed with flour until thickened. Set to one side.

3   Preheat the oven to 190°C (375°F, Gas Mark 5). Shape the sausagemeat into 8 balls. Heat the oil in a large frying pan and fry the pigeon breasts lightly. Place into a medium pie dish. Brown the sausagemeat balls and bacon and add these to the dish.

4   Sauté the remaining onion in the pan for 5 minutes with the thyme sprig and remaining bay leaf, adding extra oil if necessary. Pour in the thickened stock, season then stir in the mushrooms. Cover with foil and bake for 45 minutes, then remove and allow to cool to room temperature.

5   Roll out the pastry to roughly fit the top of the dish. Cut some strips of pastry and press around the rim of the dish. Brush with some of the egg yolk glaze and fit over the remaining rolled-out pastry. Seal, trim and crimp the edges. Rest for 10 minutes, then bake for 35 minutes until golden brown and crisp.

## 155 Roast haunch of venison with juniper sauce

**SERVES** 6   **PREPARATION TIME** 15 minutes   **COOKING TIME** 1 hour 15 minutes

2kg (4lb 8oz) haunch of venison
butter, softened, to smear
2 sprigs of rosemary, leaves stripped
   and chopped
sea salt and freshly ground black pepper

**JUNIPER SAUCE**
1 large shallot or small onion, chopped
vegetable oil, for frying

1 tsp juniper berries, crushed
1 glass (175ml, 6fl oz, ⅔ cup) red or
   white wine
250ml (9fl oz, 1 cup) Game or beef stock
   (see page 16)
2 tbsp Redcurrant or rowanberry jelly
   (see page 202)
1 tbsp butter mixed with 1 tbsp flour
2 tbsp crème fraîche or double cream

1   Preheat the oven to 200°C (400°F, Gas Mark 6). Season the venison, smear some butter on the top and sides and sprinkle with the rosemary and seasoning.
2   Roast for 15 minutes then reduce the temperature to 180°C (350°F, Gas Mark 4) and roast for a further 45 minutes, basting once or twice with oil. Loosely cover the top if it begins to get too brown. Remove and let stand for 15 minutes while you make the sauce.
3   Sauté the shallots in a little oil with the juniper for 5 minutes then add the wine and cook for a further 5 minutes. Pour in the stock and redcurrant jelly. Season and simmer for 5 minutes.
4   Gradually work in the butter and flour mix, stirring until it thickens the sauce. Add the crème fraîche, season and strain into a jug. Carve the meat thinly and pour any carving juices into the sauce before serving.

## 156 Pan-fried venison fillets with red wine and chocolate

**PREPARATION TIME** 10 minutes   **COOKING TIME** 30 minutes

2–3 shallots, cut in wedges
2 rashers streaky bacon, chopped
1 sprig of thyme
1 tsp five-spice powder
vegetable oil, for frying
150g (5oz) chestnut or brown button
   mushrooms, sliced
2 tbsp raspberry vinegar

1 glass (175ml, 6fl oz, ⅔ cup) red wine
250ml (9fl oz, 1 cup) Game or beef stock
   (see page 16)
1 tbsp tomato purée
25g (1oz) dark chocolate
4 venison fillets, each about 150g (5oz)
sea salt and freshly ground black pepper

1   Sauté the shallots, bacon, thyme and five-spice powder in a pan with a little oil for about 5 minutes. Add a little more oil and fry the mushrooms for 3–5 minutes.
2   Deglaze the pan with the vinegar for 2 minutes then pour in the wine. Bring to the boil, then simmer until reduced by a third. Add the stock and tomato purée, return to the boil and cook until reduced by a half. Remove from the heat, discard the thyme sprig and stir in the chocolate. Keep warm.
3   Heat a thin film of oil in a heavy-based frying pan and season the fillets. Pan-fry for about 3–5 minutes on each side depending on how you like steaks – rare or medium-rare. The meat should be slightly springy when pressed with the back of a fork. Remove and allow to stand for 3 minutes, then serve with the sauce. Nice with green beans and a celeriac and potato mash.

## 157 Venison sausages with red onion marmalade

**PREPARATION TIME** 15 minutes plus soaking    **COOKING TIME** 35 minutes

2 large red onions, thinly sliced
2 fat cloves garlic, sliced
vegetable oil, for frying
½ stick cinnamon
1 star anise or ½ tsp five-spice powder
2 tbsp balsamic or sherry vinegar

2 tbsp raisins, soaked in hot water
1 tsp horseradish
sea salt and freshly ground black pepper
8 thick venison sausages
sprigs of thyme, to garnish (optional)

1   Cook the onions and garlic in just enough oil to cover over a low heat for a good
    20–30 minutes until reduced down and soft but not browned.
2   Add the spices and cook for 1 minute, then stir in the vinegar and cook until
    reduced, followed by the raisins and horseradish. Season and set aside.
3   Grill or pan-fry the sausages for a total of 15 minutes until just firm and still a little
    juicy. Stand for 5 minutes before serving with the onion marmalade and some creamy
    mashed potatoes. Garnish with sprigs of thyme, if you like.

## 158 Spiced venison casserole

**PREPARATION TIME** 20 minutes   **COOKING TIME** 1 hour 45 minutes

2 tsp coriander berries
2 cloves
¼ small stick cinnamon
4 juniper berries
½ tsp dried thyme
½ tsp freshly ground black pepper
750g (1lb 10oz) braising venison, cut in
   2cm (¾in) cubes
vegetable oil, for frying
1 large onion, chopped
1 carrot, chopped
1 stick celery, sliced

2 turnips, cut in cubes
2 fat cloves garlic
2 tbsp flour
2 tbsp tomato purée
700ml (1¼ pints, 2¾ cups) Beef or chicken
   stock (see page 16)
2 strips of orange zest and juice of 1 orange
2 bay leaves
sea salt and freshly ground black pepper
2–3 tbsp chopped coriander, to sprinkle
150ml (5fl oz, ⅔ cup) soured cream
   or half-fat crème fraîche, to drizzle

1   Grind the whole spices with a pestle and mortar or pulse in a small food processor. Mix with the thyme, pepper and 1 tsp salt. Toss the meat cubes in the mixture. Preheat the oven to 150°C (300°F, Gas Mark 2).
2   Heat a thin film of oil in a large frying pan and stir-fry the meat in batches until browned and lightly sealed. Transfer to a large casserole with a slotted spoon.
3   Add a little more oil to the pan and fry the vegetables and garlic for 5–10 minutes, stirring once or twice. Add any leftover spices, then mix in the flour and cook for 1 minute.
4   Combine the tomato purée and stock, pour into the pan and bring to the boil with the orange zest, juice and bay leaves.
5   Pour over the meat, stir to blend, cover and cook for about 1 hour–1 hour 15 minutes until the meat is just tender but not dry. Serve drizzled with the soured cream and scattered with coriander.


## 159 Roast boar with plum sauce

**SERVES** 6   **PREPARATION TIME** 10 minutes   **COOKING TIME** 1 hour 30 minutes plus resting

1 leg of boar, rind removed, about
   1.25kg (2lb 12oz)
1 tsp five-spice powder
1 tsp sea salt
¼ tsp freshly ground black pepper

**PLUM SAUCE**
4 large ripe red or black plums, stoned
   and chopped

150ml (5fl oz, ⅔ cup) red wine
4 tbsp port
2 cloves
½ small stick cinnamon
grated zest of 1 orange and juice of 2 oranges
juice of 1 lemon
1 tbsp brown sugar
2 tbsp Redcurrant or rowanberry jelly
   (see page 202)

1   Preheat the oven to 180°C (350°F, Gas Mark 4). Slash the fat on the leg several times with the tip of a sharp knife. Mix together the five-spice powder, salt and pepper, sprinkle evenly over the scored fat and rub in slightly.
2   Cook for about 45 minutes, turning once and basting with fat or juices, then continue for another 45 minutes or until the centre is just cooked. Remove and allow to rest for 20 minutes, covered in foil, before carving.
3   Meanwhile, make the sauce. Simmer all the ingredients for about 15 minutes until pulpy and syrupy. Cool for 30 minutes before serving.
4   Carve the meat into slices, drizzle over the juices from the roasting pan mixed with those from the carving board or dish. Serve with the sauce.

## 160 Roast grouse

**PREPARATION TIME** 10 minutes **COOKING TIME** 20 minutes

2 brace of grouse (4 birds)
50g (2oz) butter
8 rashers streaky bacon
2 slices of white bread, crusts removed

1 tbsp vegetable oil
150ml (5fl oz, ⅔ cup) red wine
150ml (5fl oz, ⅔ cup) port
sea salt and freshly ground black pepper

1   Preheat the oven to 230°C (450°F, Gas Mark 8). Do not wash the grouse – you need the blood inside for flavour. Smear each bird with half the butter, season and cover the breasts with the bacon.
2   Roast the birds for just 10 minutes then turn off the heat, remove the bacon and leave the birds in the oven for a further 10 minutes.
3   Meanwhile, fry the bread in the remaining butter and oil until golden and crisp, drain on kitchen paper and cut each slice in half diagonally. Place a bird on each triangle of toast and keep warm.
4   Add the wine and port to the pan juices and bubble up for 2–3 minutes. Season and strain and serve with the grouse.

## 161 Guinea fowl with tomato and tarragon dressing

**PREPARATION TIME** 15 minutes **COOKING TIME** 35–40 minutes plus resting and marinating

2 guinea fowl, each about 1kg (2lb 4oz)
3 tbsp vegetable oil, plus extra for brushing
1 tomato, skinned, seeded and
  finely chopped
2 sprigs of tarragon, leaves stripped
  and chopped
1 shallot, finely chopped

1 tbsp Worcestershire sauce
1 tbsp tomato ketchup
1 tsp coarse grain mustard
juice of ½ lemon
sea salt and freshly ground black pepper
Little Gem lettuce leaves, to serve

1   Preheat the oven to 190°C (375°F, Gas Mark 5). Untruss the birds but tie the feet loosely together. Season and brush with oil. Cover the breasts loosely with butter papers or foil.
2   Roast for about 35–40 minutes, basting twice with the juices. Remove and let stand for 10 minutes.
3   Meanwhile, mix together the tomato, tarragon, shallot, Worcestershire sauce, ketchup, mustard, lemon juice, 3 tbsp oil and seasoning.
4   Carve the birds into 4 whole breasts and 4 legs and thighs. Place them in a shallow dish. Tip any roasting juices into the dressing and spoon over the guinea fowl. Marinate for 15–20 minutes then serve on a platter lined with torn Little Gem leaves.

## 162 Roast chicken, bread sauce and bacon

**PREPARATION TIME** 10 minutes  **COOKING TIME** 1 hour plus resting

1 recipe quantity Bread sauce (see page 17)
1 roasting chicken, about 1.6kg (3lb 8oz)
50g (2oz) butter, softened
4–6 rashers streaky bacon
3 sprigs of thyme

2–3 cloves garlic
150ml (5fl oz, ²/₃ cup) Chicken stock
  (see page 16)
roasted vegetables (see pages 120 and 126)
sea salt and freshly ground black pepper

1   Preheat the oven to 200°C (400°F, Gas Mark 6). Prepare the Bread sauce up to step 2 (see page 17) then let it stand while you roast the bird.

2   Untruss the bird and pull out the pad of fat from the body cavity. Smear the bird with the butter. Grind over pepper to taste then lay the bacon diagonally over the breasts. Put the thyme and garlic into the cavity and roast for 15 minutes.

3   Baste with the melted butter and roast for a further 15 minutes. Reduce the temperature to 180°C (350°F, Gas Mark 4), remove and reserve the bacon, baste again and continue cooking for 30 minutes or until juices run clear when the thigh is pierced where it joins the body. Remove and allow to stand, covered loosely with foil, for 15 minutes. At this point, complete the preparation of the Bread sauce.

4   Drain the juices from the chicken into the roasting pan, place the bird on a platter, and keep warm with the bacon alongside.

5   Add the stock to the pan and bubble up for 2–3 minutes then strain into a small jug. Carve the chicken and serve with Bread sauce and the roasted vegetables.

## 163 Griddled spatchcock poussins

**PREPARATION TIME** 15 minutes   **COOKING TIME** 30 minutes plus resting

4 poussins, each about 500g (1lb 2oz)
50g (2oz) butter, melted, or vegetable oil
1 tsp ground paprika

1 tsp sea salt
1 tsp dried oregano
1 large lemon, quartered, to serve

1   Use poultry shears or strong kitchen scissors to cut the backs off the birds and flatten them out on a board, breast side up. Stick metal or thick wooden skewers through the legs diagonally in a cross to hold the birds flat. Brush with the butter.
2   Heat a griddle pan or barbecue to a steady medium-hot heat. Mix together the paprika, salt and oregano and sprinkle over the birds.
3   Griddle the poussins flesh side down for 10 minutes, turn and cook the other side for 10 minutes, then turn again for a final 5–10 minutes, ensuring the skin doesn't burn too much. Stand for 10 minutes then serve with the lemon quarters for squeezing over the birds.

## 164 Chicken and mushroom puff pie

**PREPARATION TIME** 15 minutes plus resting   **COOKING TIME** 40 minutes

250–300g cold cooked chicken, cut in
  thick chunks
250g (9oz) button or wild mushrooms, or
  a mixture, thickly sliced
50g (2oz) butter
1 sprig of thyme, leaves stripped
2–3 tbsp dry sherry

a little chopped parsley
200ml (7fl oz, ¾ cup) half-fat crème fraîche
any leftover chicken gravy
1 x 225g (8oz) sheet ready-rolled puff pastry
1 egg yolk, beaten with 1 tsp cold water
sea salt and freshly ground black pepper

1   Put the chicken into a pie dish, about 1 litre (1¾ pints, 4 cups) volume. Stir-fry the mushrooms in the butter until just wilted with the thyme and seasoning. Add the sherry and cook for a further 1–2 minutes. Stir in the parsley, then the crème fraîche and spoon over the chicken.
2   Tip the mushrooms over the chicken and fork together, adding any leftover chicken gravy. Allow to cool.
3   Cut out enough pastry to cover the pie dish top leaving a good overhang. Cut the leftover pastry into strips.
4   Brush the dish edges with egg yolk glaze, line with pastry strips and brush again with glaze. Then fit the pastry top and press down well on the edges. Rest for 15 minutes then trim the edges using kitchen scissors, pinch to crimp and seal. Make a large cross on top as a steam hole. Any remaining pastry can be used to make leaves. Glaze evenly with the egg and rest again.
5   Preheat the oven to 200°C (400°F, Gas Mark 6). Place the pie dish on a shallow metal tray and bake for 20 minutes, then turn and reduce the temperature to 180°C (350°F, Gas Mark 4) and bake for a further 20 minutes until crisp and golden.

**Note** To ensure a crisp pastry crust, make sure the filling fills the pie dish so that the pastry is slightly mounded. An old-fashioned cook's tip is to fit a pie funnel in the centre of the filling before covering with the pastry top. Often these funnels are shaped as blackbirds (after the nursery rhyme 'Four and Twenty Blackbirds Baked in a Pie') or chefs with tall hats. You can also use a large upturned china egg cup.

## 165 Hindle wakes (chicken poached with prunes)

**PREPARATION TIME** 25 minutes  **COOKING TIME** about 2 hours

1 chicken, about 1.6–1.8kg
  (3lb 8oz–4lb)
1 chicken stock cube
150ml (5fl oz, ⅔ cup) cider or malt vinegar
1 onion, chopped
1 carrot, chopped
1 stick celery, chopped
1 large sprig of marjoram, thyme,
  parsley and rosemary
1 large bay leaf
1 tsp black or white peppercorns

125g (4oz) stoned prunes, soaked in hot water
  for 10 minutes, drained and chopped
25g (1oz) butter
3 tbsp flour
grated zest and juice of 1 lemon
1 tbsp soft brown sugar
2 egg yolks
sea salt and freshly ground black pepper
3 tbsp chopped parsley, to sprinkle

1  Untruss the chicken and place in a large pan. Cover with water (about 1.5 litres, 2½ pints, 6 cups). Crumble in the stock cube and add the vinegar, onion, carrot, celery, herbs, bay leaf and peppercorns. Bring to the boil, then reduce the heat, cover and simmer gently for 1 hour–1 hour 15 minutes until the chicken is tender.

2  Transfer the bird to a platter and allow to cool. Boil the stock down by half to around 500ml (18fl oz, 2 cups) then strain into a jug.

3  When the chicken is cool enough to handle, strip off the meat and shred into large chunks and set aside.

4  Wipe out the pan, melt the butter and mix in the flour. Cook gently for 2 minutes then gradually whisk in the hot chicken stock. Bring to the boil until thickened and add the lemon zest, sugar and prunes. Simmer for a further 2 minutes.

5  Beat the egg yolks in a jug and gradually beat in a ladleful or two of the simmering sauce to amalgamate. Pour this back into the hot liquid, remove immediately from the heat and stir until thickened then add the lemon juice and seasoning to taste.

6  Mix in the chicken, reheat gently until very hot but not boiling and pour into a serving bowl. Sprinkle over the parsley and serve with new potatoes or rice.

## 166 Tudor chicken with parsley and verjus

**PREPARATION TIME** 10 minutes  **COOKING TIME** 1 hour plus resting

1 chicken, about 1.5kg (3lb 5oz)
handful of mixed herbs (thyme, parsley,
  rosemary, sage)
75g (3oz) butter, melted
3–4 tbsp verjus (fruit vinegar from grapes
  or apples)

2 tsp honey
sea salt and freshly ground black pepper
2–3 tbsp chopped parsley, to sprinkle

1  Season the bird all over and stuff the body cavity with herbs. Secure the openings with kitchen twine or thin skewers, then push onto a spit rotisserie and clamp in position. Brush with melted butter and grill, rotating slowly, on a medium heat for about 50 minutes with a drip tray underneath for the juices.

2  Baste every 10 minutes or so with the roasting juices and a little more melted butter until the skin turns a crisp deep golden colour. Watch the heat and adjust down if necessary.

3  When cooked (pierce the thickest part between the thigh and the body and if the juices run clear it is done), remove the bird from the oven but leave on the spit and rest for at least 15 minutes.

4  Carve as normal, reserving any juices. Tip all the cooking and carving juices into a small pan with any remaining butter. Bring to the boil with the verjus and bubble for 2–3 minutes, then stir in the honey.

5  Arrange the chicken on a platter and drizzle over the sauce, then sprinkle with the parsley and serve.

## 167 Chicken breasts with blue cheese pockets

**PREPARATION TIME** 12 minutes plus chilling   **COOKING TIME** 15 minutes plus resting

4 large boneless chicken breasts
180g (6oz) creamy blue cheese (Stilton,
    Beenleigh Blue, Cashel Blue, Dovedale)
grated zest of 1 lemon

1 sprig of thyme, leaves stripped
melted butter and vegetable oil
sea salt and freshly ground black pepper

1   Slit the breasts through the centre almost to the other side and open out. Mix together the cheese, lemon zest, thyme leaves and some pepper.
2   Divide between the chicken and fold back the flap, ensuring the cheese is fully enclosed. Chill for at least 1 hour if possible.
3   Heat a grill or griddle pan. Brush the chicken with a little butter and oil mixed, then cook for about 12–15 minutes, turning once, until the flesh feels just firm when pressed with the back of a fork. Do not overcook and keep checking the cheese stays inside.
4   Remove and stand for 5 minutes, then cut each breast in 3 diagonally and serve with watercress or rocket.

## 168 Poached chicken with lemon and tarragon sauce

**SERVES** 4–6   **PREPARATION TIME** 20 minutes   **COOKING TIME** 1 hour 30 minutes

250ml (9fl oz, 1 cup) dry white wine
1 onion, quartered
1 small bulb fennel, sliced, or 2 sticks celery
1 large carrot, cut in sticks
2 sprigs of thyme, rosemary and tarragon,
    tied as a bouquet garni
2 large bay leaves
½ tsp peppercorns
2 chicken stock cubes
1 fresh chicken, about 1.5kg
    (3lb 5oz)
sea salt and freshly ground black pepper

**LEMON AND TARRAGON SAUCE**
2 egg yolks
150ml (5fl oz, ⅔ cup) double cream
1 tbsp chopped tarragon (or rosemary
    or thyme)
juice of 1 lemon

1   Put the wine, vegetables, herbs, bay leaves, peppercorns and stock cubes in a large pan with 1.5 litres (2½ pints, 6 cups) cold water. Bring to the boil then simmer for 10 minutes.
2   Remove any fat from inside the chicken and lower the bird into the water. (Do not worry if the top of the breast is not completely submerged.)
3   Return the liquor to a simmer, cover and cook for 45 minutes–1 hour until the legs feel tender when pierced. Remove the pan from the heat, stand for 15 minutes then transfer the bird to a plate.
4   Strain 500ml (18fl oz, 2 cups) liquor into a pan and boil to reduce by half. (The remaining liquor may be frozen when cool and used subsequently.)
5   Divide the bird into neat portions, discarding the skin, wing tips and back. You may like to cut the breast halves in half again. Place on a platter, cover and keep warm.
6   To make the sauce, beat the egg yolks, cream and chopped tarragon in a jug. Ladle in a quarter of the reduced liquor and mix well, then pour it all back into the simmering stock and turn the heat right down.
7   Stir with a wooden spoon for 3–5 minutes until the sauce begins to thicken. Remove immediately, season then stir in the lemon juice. Pour a little sauce over the chicken and serve the rest in a jug.

## 169 Original coronation chicken

**PREPARATION TIME** 30 minutes **COOKING TIME** 1 hour 15 minutes plus cooling

1 chicken, about 1.5kg (3lb 5oz)
250ml (9fl oz, 1 cup) dry white wine
1 onion, ½ sliced, ½ chopped (used in
   the sauce)
1 carrot, chopped
1 stick celery, chopped
parsley stalks, sprigs of thyme and a bay leaf,
   tied as a bouquet garni
½ tsp black peppercorns

**SAUCE**
vegetable oil, for frying
1 tsp medium curry powder

1 tsp tomato purée
juice of ½ lemon
1 tbsp apricot jam or smooth mango chutney
200ml (7fl oz, ¾ cup) Mayonnaise (see page
   210), or bought
100ml (3½fl oz, ⅓ cup) single cream or
   half-fat crème fraîche
sea salt and freshly ground black or
   white pepper
chopped parsley and toasted flaked almonds,
   to sprinkle

1   Poach the chicken as in recipe on page 107 using half the wine, 1 litre (1¾ pints,
    4 cups) water, the sliced onion, carrot, celery, bouquet garni, peppercorns and
    1 tsp salt. Bring slowly to the boil, turn the heat right down and poach for
    45 minutes–1 hour or until the meat is very tender.
2   Meanwhile, make the sauce. Gently sauté the chopped onion in a little oil for
    5 minutes then add the remaining wine and cook for a further 5 minutes until soft.
    Mix in the curry powder and cook for 1 minute, then add the tomato purée and jam.
3   Remove from the heat and cool to room temperature, then gradually beat in the
    mayonnaise and cream. Season well.
4   Remove the chicken from the heat and cool in the cooking liquor for 20 minutes then
    remove and skin the meat. Shred it into large bite-sized chunks and cool. Mix with
    the sauce and chill until ready to serve. It may need to be lightened a little with a little
    more cream. Sprinkle with parsley and almonds and serve with a Summer rice salad
    (see page 134).

## 170 Chicken tikka masala

**PREPARATION TIME** 15 minutes plus marinating **COOKING TIME** 30 minutes

4 skinless, boneless chicken breasts

**MARINADE**
4 tbsp natural yogurt
1 tbsp freshly grated ginger
1 fat clove garlic, crushed
2 tsp garam masala spice mix
juice of 1 lemon
2 tbsp vegetable oil

**SAUCE**
1 large fresh green chilli, seeded and
   finely chopped
1 fat clove garlic, chopped
1 tbsp freshly grated ginger
2 tbsp vegetable oil
1 x 400g (14oz) can chopped tomatoes
2 tbsp tomato purée
2 whole cloves
4 cardamom pods
50g (2oz) butter
150ml (5fl oz, ⅔ cup) double cream
honey, to taste

1   Cut the chicken into small bite-sized pieces and place in a food bag. Mix together all
    the marinade ingredients, spoon into the food bag, rub well together then seal and
    chill for 4 hours.
2   Meanwhile, make the sauce. Gently sauté the chilli, garlic and ginger in the oil for
    5 minutes, then add the tomatoes, purée, cloves, cardamom and seasoning. Bring
    to the boil then simmer for 15 minutes. Remove and purée in a blender or food
    processor and rub through a sieve with the back of a ladle into a pan.
3   Preheat the oven to 190°C (375°F, Gas Mark 5). Lay the chicken pieces in a single
    layer in a roasting pan and bake for 10 minutes. Remove and stand for 5 minutes.
4   Reheat the sieved sauce and beat in the butter, then the cream. Add honey and
    seasoning to taste. Mix with the chicken and serve with rice or naan bread.

## 171 Chicken salmagundy

**PREPARATION TIME** 20 minutes  **COOKING TIME** 3 minutes

1 small poached or cooked chicken, skinned
grated zest of 1 lemon
4 hard-boiled eggs
100ml (3½fl oz, ⅓ cup) Vinaigrette
    dressing (see page 19)
a little chopped parsley
2 small Romaine or Cos lettuces,
    thickly shredded

1 x 50g (2oz) can anchovies, thinly
    sliced lengthways
150g (5oz) whole green beans, topped
    and tailed
12 salad onions sliced, white bulbs only
sea salt and freshly ground black or
    white pepper

1   Carve the breast meat of the chicken. Remove the leg meat and chop into small dice
    and mix with the lemon zest and seasoning.
2   Quarter two of the eggs and set aside. Remove the yolks from the other two, discard
    the whites and mash the yolks in a bowl with the vinaigrette dressing. Mix 2 tbsp
    dressing with the diced leg meat and chopped parsley.
3   Cover a meat platter with shredded lettuce and arrange the sliced breast meat
    around the sides, then spoon the chopped meat in the centre. Arrange the anchovy
    fillets over the chicken.
4   Blanch the beans in boiling water for 3 minutes, drain and cool under running water
    and pat dry. Scatter over the dish. Arrange the egg quarters and onions around.
    Drizzle over the remaining dressing and serve.

## 172 Chicken korma

**PREPARATION TIME** 15 minutes  **COOKING TIME** 25 minutes

1 onion, chopped
2 fat cloves garlic, chopped
1 tbsp freshly grated or puréed ginger
3 tbsp vegetable oil
1 tsp ground coriander
1 tsp ground cumin
½ tsp ground chilli, optional
seeds from 4 whole green cardamoms,
   crushed

1 x 400ml (14fl oz/1⅔ cup) can coconut milk
4 tbsp ground almonds
2 pinches of saffron strands, soaked in 2 tbsp
   boiling water
4 skinless, boneless chicken breasts, cut in
   small cubes
sea salt and freshly ground white pepper
coriander leaves, to garnish

1  Gently sauté the onion in a medium pan with the garlic and ginger in 2 tbsp of the
   oil for 5 minutes. Stir in the ground spices and crushed cardamom and sauté for a
   further 2 minutes.
2  Stir in the coconut milk, almonds, the saffron and soaking water and seasoning.
   Simmer for 5 minutes then drop in the chicken cubes. Return to a gentle simmer,
   cover and cook for 10 minutes. Serve with boiled basmati rice garnished with
   coriander.

## 173 Devon chicken casserole

**PREPARATION TIME** 15 minutes  **COOKING TIME** 1 hour 30 minutes plus resting

4 chicken legs, each about 250g
   (9oz), skinned
25g (1oz) butter
vegetable oil, for frying
100g (3½oz) back bacon, cut in thick strips
1 onion or large leek, sliced
1 bulb fennel, sliced wafer thin

1 sharp dessert apple (Charles Ross or Cox's)
2 large sprigs of tarragon, leaves
   stripped and chopped
250ml (9fl oz, 1 cup) dry cider
250ml (9fl oz, 1 cup) double cream
sea salt and freshly ground black pepper

1  Preheat the oven to 180°C (350°F, Gas Mark 4). Heat the butter with 1 tbsp of oil in
   a frying pan and brown the chicken legs, season, then transfer to a large casserole.
2  Add a little more oil to the pan and stir-fry the bacon and onion for 5 minutes, season
   and spoon over the chicken.
3  Add the fennel and apple to the pan juices and sauté for 5 minutes then stir in the
   tarragon and pour in the cider. Bring to the boil, simmer for 2 minutes, add the
   cream, and pour into the casserole.
4  Cover with foil then bake for up to 1 hour until the meat is tender when pierced.
   Remove, stand 10 minutes then serve. Good with rice or pasta or plain boiled
   potatoes.

# 174  Roast turkey and all the trimmings

**SERVES** 8  **PREPARATION TIME** up to 1 hour including making gravy, stuffing and bacon rolls
**COOKING TIME** 3 hours plus resting

4.5–5kg (10–11lb) turkey with giblets
100g (3½oz) butter, softened, or 125g (4oz)
  ripe Somerset Brie, cut into wedges
4–5 sprigs of thyme, leaves only
4 large sage leaves, chopped (optional),
  plus sprigs for garnish

1 large onion, quartered
1 lemon (can be left over from grating)
1 head garlic, halved (optional)
250g (9oz) lean streaky bacon
sea salt and freshly ground black pepper

1  Untruss the turkey, remove the giblets and pull out any thick wedges of fat from the
   cavity. Loosen the neck end and pat dry. Make the stuffing (see below) and press into
   the neck end of the bird and pull the skin back over it.
2  Mix the softened butter with the thyme and chopped sage, if using. Slip your hands
   inside the breast skin and make a pocket. Push the herb butter inside the skin and
   pull tight again, spreading the butter evenly. Place in a large roasting pan, sprinkle
   with seasoning and cover loosely with oiled or buttered foil.
3  Preheat the oven to 190°C (375°F, Gas Mark 5). Pop the onion, lemon and garlic
   inside the cavity and loosely tie the legs together. Roast for about 3 hours, turning the
   pan for even browning. If the skin is browning too quickly, reduce the temperature
   slightly. Remove the foil after 2 hours and baste with any pan juices. (To calculate
   other weights of bird allow 40 minutes/kg or 18 minutes/lb.)
4  Meanwhile, make the giblet gravy (see below).
5  For the bacon rolls, cut the rashers across in half, roll up and stick on wooden
   skewers. Grill or bake at the top of the oven for 15–20 minutes as the bird is nearing
   the end of cooking, turning once. Set aside.
6  Check the bird is cooked by piercing between the thigh and body: the juices should
   run clear. If they are pink, cook for a further 10–15 minutes. Once cooked, let the
   bird stand covered in a tent of foil to keep the heat in for up to 20 minutes. Carefully
   transfer to a warm serving platter and keep the roasting juices in the pan.
7  To serve, detach the drumsticks and loosen the thighs from the body. Carve the
   breast in long slices and the thigh meat in smaller ones. Accompany the meat with
   bacon rolls, stuffing, gravy, Roast potatoes (see page 126), Bread sauce (see page
   17) and Cranberry and port relish (see page 206).

### CHESTNUT SAUSAGE STUFFING

1 onion, grated or finely chopped
250g (9oz) prime-quality pork sausagemeat
2 tbsp chopped parsley
2 sage leaves, chopped finely

250g (9oz) canned or mi-cuit
  chestnuts, chopped
125g (4oz, 2 cups) fresh white breadcrumbs
sea salt and freshly ground black pepper

1  Mix all the ingredients in a large mixing bowl using clean hands.

### GIBLET GRAVY

turkey giblets
1 small onion, roughly chopped
1 carrot, chopped
1 stick celery, chopped
bacon rinds (optional)

1 small glass (150ml, 5fl oz, ⅔ cup)
  dry cider or white wine
1 bay leaf
2 tbsp flour
sea salt and freshly ground black pepper

1  Put everything except the flour into a medium pan with 1 litre (1¾ pints, 4 cups)
   water and some ground pepper. Bring to the boil then simmer, uncovered, for
   20–25 minutes until reduced by half. Strain and reserve stock.
2  While the cooked turkey is resting prior to carving, pour off the excess fat from the
   roasting pan, retaining the meaty juices, and place the pan over a medium heat. Mix
   in the flour, scraping up the meaty deposits, cook for 1 minute, then gradually add
   the giblet stock. Bring to the boil and simmer for 2–3 minutes, season with salt, then
   strain into a gravy boat or jug.

## 175   Boxing Day turkey pie

SERVES 6   **PREPARATION TIME** 30 minutes plus resting   **COOKING TIME** 40 minutes

1 recipe quantity Béchamel or Quick white
   sauce (see page 17)
any leftover turkey gravy
1 tbsp grated lemon zest
3 tbsp chopped parsley
600g (1lb 5oz) cooked turkey, diced
   or shredded
selection of cold cooked chipolatas,
   bacon rolls and stuffing, chopped into
   bite-sized pieces

3–4 hard-boiled eggs, quartered (optional)
200g (7oz) mushrooms, sliced (optional)
1 x recipe quantity Shortcrust pastry (see
   page 18), or 350g (12oz) ready rolled
   shortcrust or puff pastry
1 egg yolk, beaten with 1 tsp cold water

1   Make up the sauce then mix in any leftover gravy, the lemon zest and parsley. Cool.
2   Scatter the cooked turkey into a medium–large (20–23cm, 8–9in) pie dish with any cooked meats or stuffing. If liked, add some hard-boiled egg quarters or mushrooms then spoon over the cooled sauce and fork gently to mix in.
3   Roll out the pastry a good 2.5cm (1in) wider than the top of the pie dish and cut out roughly the same shape. Push a pie funnel into the centre of the pie, if you have one. Cut the leftover pastry into strips.
4   Brush the dish edges with egg yolk glaze, line with pastry strips and brush again with glaze. Then fit the pastry top and press down well on the edges. Rest for 15 minutes then trim the edges using kitchen scissors, pinch to crimp and seal. Make a large cross on top as a steam hole. Glaze evenly with the egg and rest again.
5   Preheat the oven to 200°C (400°F, Gas Mark 6). Place the pie dish on a shallow metal tray and bake for 20 minutes, then turn and reduce the temperature to 180°C (350°F, Gas Mark 4) and bake for a further 20 minutes until crisp and golden. Allow to cool for 10 minutes before serving.

## 176   Turkey meatballs in broth

**PREPARATION TIME** 15 minutes   **COOKING TIME** 25 minutes

500g (1lb 2oz) lean minced turkey or chicken
1 small onion, grated and very finely chopped
3 tbsp chopped parsley
1 tsp chopped thyme leaves
700ml (1¼ pints, 2¾ cups) Chicken or turkey
   stock, ideally homemade (see page 16)

125g (4oz) mushrooms, sliced
1 small leek, thinly sliced
3 tbsp double cream (optional)
sea salt and freshly ground black or
   white pepper

1   Beat the mince well with the onion, parsley, thyme and 1 tsp salt plus some ground pepper. With wet hands, shape into 12–16 small neat balls.
2   Bring the stock to the boil in a large shallow pan and drop in the balls. Partially cover and simmer gently for about 12–15 minutes until the balls feel firm when pressed. Transfer with a slotted spoon to a large, warm, shallow bowl.
3   Add the mushrooms and leeks to the stock and boil for at least 5 minutes until the liquid is reduced by half, then add the cream, if using, and boil again for 3 minutes until further reduced. Check the seasoning and pour over the meatballs. Serve hot with rice or pasta or mashed potatoes.

## 177 Slow-roast Gressingham duck legs with orange-braised fennel

**PREPARATION TIME** 15 minutes  **COOKING TIME** 1 hour

4 large Gressingham duck legs
1 tsp five-spice powder
1 tsp fine sea salt
4 small sprigs of rosemary or thyme
4 fat cloves garlic, split in half
1 large bulb fennel

50g (2oz) butter
1 tsp sugar
150ml (5fl oz, $2/3$ cup) dry cider
juice of 1 large orange
sea salt and freshly ground black pepper

1   Preheat the oven to 150°C (350°F, Gas Mark 3). Prick the duck legs all over with a knife tip. Mix together the five-spice powder and salt and rub into the duck skin. Sit the legs on the herb sprigs and 2 pieces of garlic each.
2   Roast the legs for 45–50 minutes, pouring off the melted fat twice during cooking. The skin should be crisp and the flesh tender.
3   Meanwhile, halve the fennel, remove the core, then thinly slice the rest. Melt the butter in a pan and gently sauté the fennel with the butter and sugar for a good 10 minutes until it starts to caramelize. Pour in the cider and bubble down until evaporated, about 5 minutes, then mix in the orange juice and continue cooking for a further 10 minutes. The fennel should be very tender.
4   Divide the fennel and sauce between 4 warmed plates and top with a duck leg. The garlic cloves can be served for spreading over the duck, if liked.

## 178 Bacon-wrapped quails

**PREPARATION TIME** 15-30 minutes  **COOKING TIME** 40-45 minutes plus resting

8 oven-ready quail
600g (1lb 5oz) wild (chanterelles or ceps)
   or brown button mushrooms
2 tbsp vegetable oil
50g (2oz) butter

1 sprig of thyme, leaves stripped
4 tbsp dry sherry or vermouth
16 rashers lean streaky bacon
sea salt and freshly ground black pepper
sprigs of watercress, to garnish

1   Preheat the oven to 190°C (375°F, Gas Mark 5). Untruss the birds and wash inside and out, then pat dry on kitchen paper. If you have time, bone out the breast bones by inserting a very sharp small knife down either side of the centre bone; they can be removed quite easily. Season the flesh.
2   Wash the mushrooms quickly in cold water, drain well, pat dry on kitchen paper, then chop roughly. Stir-fry over a high heat in a large frying pan in the oil and half the butter with the thyme leaves and seasoning for about 5 minutes until just wilted.
3   Add the sherry or vermouth to the pan and cook for a further 3 minutes or so, or until absorbed. Cool slightly then divide the mushrooms between the 8 quail, pushing the mixture into the body cavity.
4   Wrap 2 rashers of bacon around each bird to form a cross and smear with the remaining butter. Transfer the birds to one or two roasting pans and roast for about 35 minutes, basting in between with any roasting juices. (You may need to swap the pans over to ensure even cooking.) Remove and stand for 10 minutes. Serve 2 birds per head with the juices trickled over, garnished with watercress.

## 179 Pan-fried duck breasts with buttery apple rings

**PREPARATION TIME** 10 minutes   **COOKING TIME** 20 minutes plus resting

4 boned duck breasts
1 sprig of rosemary, leaves stripped
   and chopped
2 large Russet or Cox's apples
50g (2oz) butter

1 tbsp vegetable oil
1 tbsp honey
a few pinches of ground cinnamon
sea salt and freshly ground black pepper

1   Score the duck breasts right through the skin to the flesh in criss-cross fashion.
    Sprinkle with salt. Heat a griddled pan until hot and fry the duck, fat side down, for
    about 5 minutes. This creates a lot of steam so take care. Drain off the fat as it melts.
2   Turn the breasts over, sprinkle with salt, pepper and rosemary and reduce the heat
    to medium. Cook for a further 5 minutes until the flesh feels slightly bouncy when
    pressed. Do not overcook. Remove and let stand for 5–10 minutes.
3   Meanwhile, make the apples. Core with an apple corer then cut in 1cm (½in) slices.
    (If you have no corer, slice first and cut out the cores with the tip of a knife.)
4   Heat the butter and oil in a large frying pan and sauté the slices for 6–8 minutes
    on each side until golden brown and softened. Drizzle with honey and sprinkle with
    cinnamon and some pepper.
5   Slice each breast diagonally 4 or 5 times and serve the apples alongside.

## 180 Michaelmas roast goose with sausagemeat stuffing and apple sauce

**SERVES** 6 **PREPARATION TIME** 25 minutes **COOKING TIME** about 3 hours plus resting

1 oven-ready goose, 4.5–5kg (10–11lb)
giblets, if available, for Gravy (see page 111)
grated zest of 2 lemons
2 tsp fine sea salt
1 tsp five-spice powder
freshly ground black pepper
small handful each of parsley sprigs,
   thyme and sage, plus extra to garnish
2 cooking apples, peeled and chopped
good knob of butter
2 whole cloves

**STUFFING**
the goose liver, chopped
1 onion, chopped
2 tbsp vegetable oil
250g (9oz) premium-quality sausagemeat
50g (2oz, 1 cup) fresh white breadcrumbs
4–6 sage leaves, chopped

1 Separate the liver from the giblets and set aside. Boil the rest of the giblets in about 600ml (1 pint, 2½ cups) water with a little onion, carrot and bay leaf for about 20 minutes to give approximately 400ml (14fl oz, 1⅔ cups) stock.

2 Pull out any visible pads of fat inside the cavity and discard. Slash through the skin on the breast and the legs with the tip of a sharp knife in criss-cross fashion through to the flesh. Mix together the zest of 1 lemon, salt, five-spice powder and some ground pepper. Rub all over the goose, ensuring the mixture gets into the cuts you made. Let the bird rest while you make the stuffing.

3 Fry the chopped liver, onion and a third of the chopped apple in a little oil for about 5 minutes until lightly cooked. Season well and mix in the remaining lemon zest. Cool, then work in the sausagemeat, breadcrumbs and sage.

4 Lift up the neck skin flap, press in the cooled stuffing, then re-shape the skin. Place the bird in a large roasting pan. Push the herb sprigs into the body cavity. Halve the zested lemons and push these in too.

5 Preheat the oven to 200°C (400°F, Gas Mark 6). Roast the bird for 30 minutes until the fat starts to run. Pour off the fat once or twice more during cooking into a heatproof bowl (it is delicious for roasting potatoes, see page 126). Take care, you may need help to lift the heavy bird to drain off the fat.

5 Reduce the temperature to 180°C (350°F, Gas Mark 4) and continue to cook the goose for a further 2 hours–2 hours 15 minutes until the juices run clear when the thigh meat is pierced. If they are pink, cook for a further 15–20 minutes. Remove, cover loosely with a large sheet of foil and stand for 15 minutes before carving while you make Giblet gravy with the stock (see page 111).

6 Meanwhile, cook the remaining chopped apple with the cloves in some butter until soft and slightly pulpy. Season and add a little extra butter and keep warm.

7 To serve, detach the drumsticks and loosen the thighs from the body. Carve the breast meat in long slices, and the leg meat in thick shorter slices. Scoop out spoonfuls of sausagemeat stuffing from the neck and serve with the goose, along with the Giblet gravy and apple sauce.

# CHAPTER 4

# VEGETABLES
# & SALADS

The simple fare of the British kitchen has given rise to the
impression that we boil our vegetables to a pulp and view
them as no more than nondescript side dishes. The pages
of many British cookbooks and magazines show this to be a
myth. Kitchen gardens, allotments and vegetable plots confirm
the British love of fresh veg, best cooked simply with a light
dressing of buttery juices, pepper and chopped herbs.

In these days of globally sourced food, air-freighted
to our supermarkets all year round, seasonal vegetables
are losing their distinction. But produce that takes days to
reach our stores inevitably loses its 'just picked' flavour (and
texture). Fortunately, seasonal local produce can be found in
local farmers' markets the length and breadth of the country.

Many vegetable and salad recipes are simple, quick to
prepare and especially suited to light cooking. We are also
borrowing techniques from the Mediterranean, Near and Far
East for roasting, griddling and stir-frying our favourite roots
and shoots to enhance their sweetness and flavour.

## 181 Vine-ripened tomatoes baked with herby buttery crumbs

**PREPARATION TIME** 10 minutes  **COOKING TIME** up to 1 hour plus cooling

4 large vine-ripened tomatoes
vegetable oil, to drizzle
2 fat cloves garlic, sliced
50g (2oz) butter
50g (2oz, 1 cup) fresh white breadcrumbs
  (use slightly stale country-style bread)

2 tbsp sunflower seeds
1 large sprig of thyme or marjoram,
  leaves stripped and chopped
sea salt and freshly ground black pepper

1 Preheat the oven to 150°C (300°F, Gas Mark 2). Halve the tomatoes around the 'waists' and lay cut side up, tightly fitting, in a shallow ovenproof dish. Season, drizzle with a little oil and top with the garlic slices.
2 Bake, uncovered, for about 25–30 minutes until they begin to soften. Meanwhile, melt the butter and mix in the crumbs, sunflower seeds, herbs and seasoning.
3 Scatter over the tomatoes. Bake for a further 15–20 minutes until the crumbs are golden and crisp. Cool for 10–15 minutes before serving.

## 182 Beetroot in hot cream sauce

**PREPARATION TIME** 10 minutes  **COOKING TIME** 20–30 minutes

4 raw beetroot, about 500g (1lb 2oz)
1 recipe quantity Béchamel or Quick white
  sauce (see page 17)

3 tbsp chopped mixed green herbs
  (parsley, dill, tarragon, chives)
sea salt and freshly ground black pepper

1 Trim the stalks and roots of the beets and boil, unpeeled, in salted water until just tender, about 20 minutes. Drain and cool, then peel off the hot skin using rubber gloves to avoid staining.
2 Cut the beets into bite-sized chunks and place in a shallow heatproof dish. Make up the sauce and mix in the herbs. Check the seasoning and pour over the beets. Bake for a further 10 minutes, if liked, in a hot oven (200°C, 400°F, Gas Mark 6) and serve immediately.

## 183 Carrot sticks with tarragon, sugar and lemon

**PREPARATION TIME** 10–12 minutes  **COOKING TIME** 30 minutes

400g (14oz) carrots, peeled
good knob of butter
1 tbsp caster sugar
juice of 1 lemon

1 tbsp tarragon leaves, roughly chopped
sea salt and freshly ground white or
  black pepper

1 Cut the carrots into even sticks, about 1cm (1/2in) thick. Place in a pan and pour in enough boiling water just to cover, add a little salt and boil, uncovered, for 5 minutes until most of the water has evaporated.
2 Mix in the butter, sugar, lemon juice and tarragon. Bubble until the liquid is reduced to a glossy glaze, check the seasoning and serve.

## 184 Crushed peas and crème fraîche

**PREPARATION TIME** 2 minutes   **COOKING TIME** 5 minutes

250g (9oz) podded fresh peas (or use frozen)
2 tbsp chopped spring onions or chives

200ml (7fl oz, ¾ cup) tub half-fat
    crème fraîche
sea salt and freshly ground black pepper

1   Boil the peas for 3–5 minutes until just tender. Drain and return to the pan.
    Crush using a potato masher or large fork to a chunky purée.
2   Mix in the onions or chives and crème fraîche. Season and serve hot.

## 185 Cauliflower cheese

**PREPARATION TIME** 10 minutes   **COOKING TIME** 15 minutes

1 cauliflower, or 2 baby cauliflowers,
    trimmed, outer leaves removed
2–4 eggs, hard-boiled and quartered
    (optional)
1 recipe quantity Quick white sauce
    (see page 17)
1 tsp made English mustard

150g (5oz) mature Cheddar or Double
    Gloucester cheese, grated, or blue
    cheese, crumbled
2 tbsp dried breadcrumbs
1 tomato, cut into wedges
sea salt and freshly ground black pepper

1   Boil the cauliflower in enough salted water to cover for 5–7 minutes until just tender
    but not soft. (Note: you can substitute half the milk in the sauce with some of this
    cooking water.) Drain well and tip into a shallow ovenproof dish. Preheat the grill.
2   Tuck in the hard-boiled eggs, if using. Mix the hot sauce with the mustard and
    two-thirds of the cheese and pour over. Mix together the remaining cheese and
    crumbs and scatter over. Arrange the tomato on the dish, then grill until the topping
    is golden and crisp. Serve hot.

## 186 Leeks in cream sauce

**PREPARATION TIME** 5 minutes   **COOKING TIME** 20–25 minutes

4 leeks, trimmed and sliced diagonally into
    2cm (¾in) chunks
200ml (7 fl oz, ¾ cup) single cream

2 tbsp dried, natural colour breadcrumbs
2 tbsp grated Cheddar-style cheese
sea salt and freshly ground black pepper

1   Preheat the oven to 190°C (375°F, Gas Mark 5). Boil the leeks in salted water for
    5 minutes then drain well. Tip into a shallow heatproof dish.
2   Pour over the cream then sprinkle with the crumbs and cheese. Bake for 15–20
    minutes until bubbling and golden brown on top. Cool for 5 minutes before serving.

### VARIATION

#### Stuffed Staffordshire oatcakes
Divide the mixture between 4 Staffordshire oatcakes (ready-made oat pancakes), roll
and place join side down in a shallow heatproof dish. Pour over extra cream, sprinkle
with grated cheese and bake as above.

## 187 Fried green tomatoes

PREPARATION TIME 7 minutes   COOKING TIME 10 minutes

4 large green tomatoes
seasoned flour mixed with ½ tsp dried
   mixed herbs, to coat
1 egg, beaten

50g (2oz, ½ cup) dried, natural colour
   breadcrumbs or semolina
vegetable oil, for frying

1   Top and tail the tomatoes then slice each into 4. Dip first in flour, shaking off the
    excess, then into the beaten egg and finally into the dried breadcrumbs, again
    shaking off the excess. Set aside on a tray lined with baking paper.
2   Heat about 5mm (¼in) oil in a large non–stick frying pan. Fry the tomato slices for
    2–3 minutes on each side over a medium heat until golden and crisp. Drain and
    serve. Good with crispy bacon or mushrooms or both.

## 188 Crisp Brussels sprouts

PREPARATION TIME 10–12 minutes   COOKING TIME 10 minutes plus cooling

500g (1lb 2oz) Brussels sprouts
2–3 handfuls of icecubes
50g (2oz) butter

squeeze of fresh lemon juice
sea salt and freshly ground black
   or white pepper

1   Trim the stalk ends of the sprouts but do not cut crosses in them. Cut any large
    sprouts in half to ensure they cook evenly. Prepare a large bowl of water with
    the handfuls of icecubes.
2   Plunge the sprouts into a pan of boiling salted water. Return to the boil and cook
    for no more than 3 minutes.
3   Drain and tip the sprouts into the iced water. After 3 minutes, drain again and
    shake well. (They can be covered and chilled for up to 12 hours at this point.)
4   When ready to serve, heat the butter in a large pan until it stops foaming and starts
    to turn a nutty brown colour. Immediately toss in the sprouts and reheat at a low
    temperature, shaking the pan a few times, for about 3–5 minutes until piping hot.
5   Remove from the heat, stir in the lemon juice and seasoning, toss in the pan to coat,
    and serve immediately.

## 189 Honey-roasted roots

PREPARATION TIME 5 minutes   COOKING TIME 30 minutes plus resting

250g (9oz) small parsnips, ends trimmed
250g (9oz) small carrots, ends trimmed
vegetable or olive oil, to coat
1 sprig of thyme, marjoram or rosemary,
   leaves stripped and chopped

good knob of butter
2 tbsp clear honey
sea salt and freshly ground black pepper

1   Preheat the oven to 190°C (375°F, Gas Mark 5). Halve the vegetables lengthways
    then toss in enough oil to coat lightly. Tip into a roasting pan, season and sprinkle
    with herbs.
2   Roast for 20 minutes, then add the butter and honey and stir to coat. Return to
    the oven and roast a further 10 minutes. Let stand for 10 minutes then grind over
    extra freshly ground pepper.

# 190 Stuffed marrow rings with Cotherstone cheese

**SERVES** 4–6   **PREPARATION TIME** 15 minutes   **COOKING TIME** 1 hour 10 minutes plus cooling

1 marrow, about 1kg (2lb 4oz)
a little butter, to dot
1 onion, chopped or sliced
1 fat clove garlic, chopped
1 stick celery, chopped
vegetable oil, for frying

1 x 400g (14oz) can chopped tomatoes
1 large sprig of marjoram, leaves stripped,
   or 3 lovage leaves, chopped
125g (4oz) Cotherstone or Lancashire cheese
sea salt and freshly ground black pepper
raddichio or other salad leaves, to serve

1   Preheat the oven to 190°C (375°F, Gas Mark 5).
2   Top and tail the marrow then cut into rounds about 3cm (1¼in). Scoop out the seeds
    and place the rings in a single layer in a shallow ovenproof dish. Season, dot with a
    little butter, cover with foil, then bake for 35 minutes or until the skin is just tender
    and the flesh soft when pierced with a fork.
2   Meanwhile, sauté the onion, garlic and celery in a little oil for about 10 minutes
    until softened. Add the tomatoes with the herbs and seasoning and cook for a
    further 10 minutes until it forms a chunky purée.
3   Spoon the mixture into the centre of the marrow rings, crumble the cheese and
    sprinkle on top. Continue baking, uncovered, for a further 15 minutes then serve,
    with the salad leaves and the cooking juices from the pan.

## 191   Steamed English asparagus

**PREPARATION TIME** 5–10 minutes   **COOKING TIME** 5 minutes

400g (14oz) bunch of fresh asparagus spears
100g (3½oz) unsalted butter

squeeze of fresh lemon juice
sea salt and freshly ground black pepper

1   Fit a collapsible steaming basket into the base of a wide, shallow, lidded pan.
2   Snap off the hard woody end of each spear. If liked, peel the ends with a swivel vegetable peeler. Lay the spears in the steamer basket and pour in enough salted boiling water just to reach the base of the basket. Season, bring to the boil then cover and steam for 5 minutes.
3   Meanwhile, melt the butter until hot, mix in the lemon and keep warm.
4   Transfer the stems carefully (steam can burn) onto 4 warmed plates. Drizzle with the butter and grind over pepper to taste. Alternatively, increase the butter to 150g (5oz) and serve in 4 small ramekins as a dipping sauce.

## 192   Spicy red cabbage

**PREPARATION TIME** 15 minutes   **COOKING TIME** 45 minutes

1 red cabbage, quartered, cored and
   finely shredded
1 red onion, thinly sliced
1 Bramley apple, quartered, cored
   and chopped
3 cloves
1 stick cinnamon
1 star anise

2 tsp coriander berries, roughly crushed
50g (2oz) butter
2 tbsp soft brown sugar
2 tbsp cider vinegar
1 large bay leaf
1 sprig of thyme or rosemary, or both
250ml (9fl oz, 1 cup) red wine
sea salt and freshly ground black pepper

1   Mix together the cabbage, onion, apple and spices. Heat the butter and sugar in a large pan with about 100ml (3½fl oz, ⅓ cup) water and bring to the boil. Tip in the cabbage mixture, stir well, then add the remaining ingredients and seasoning.
2   Return to the boil, lower the heat to a simmer, cover and cook gently for about 30 minutes, stirring once or twice. Then uncover the pan and bubble up until the liquid reduces right down, and serve.

## 193   Woolton pie

**PREPARATION TIME** 30 minutes   **COOKING TIME** 30 minutes plus cooling

1kg (2lb 4oz) mixed root and winter
   vegetables (carrots, leeks, celery, parsnips,
   turnips, swede, etc), peeled and roughly
   chopped
2–3 spring onions, chopped
1 vegetable stock cube or 2 tsp bouillon
   powder

2 tbsp porridge oats
good knob of butter
2–3 tbsp chopped parsley
50g (2oz) mature Cheddar-type cheese
1 quantity Shortcrust pastry (see page 18)
2 tbsp creamy milk
sea salt and freshly ground black pepper

1   Put all the vegetables in a large pan with enough lightly salted water to cover and boil until just tender, about 15 minutes. Drain, reserving 500ml (18fl oz, 2 cups) of the cooking water. Tip the vegetables into a pie dish. Scatter over the onions.
2   Return the vegetable water to a pan and mix in the stock cube, oats and butter. Return to the boil, stirring until thickened, simmer for 5 minutes, then mix in the parsley and ground pepper. Remove and cool for 5 minutes, then mix in the cheese and pour over the vegetables. Cool to room temperature.
3   Preheat the oven to 200°C (400°F, Gas Mark 6). Roll out the pastry to fit the top of the pie dish. Cut long strips from any trimmings and press on the rim of the pie dish. Cover with the pastry, cut a cross in the centre, crimp the edges and glaze with the milk. Bake for 25–30 minutes until crisp and golden. Cool for 10 minutes then serve.

# 194 Roasted peppers and raisins

**PREPARATION TIME** 10 minutes    **COOKING TIME** 20 minutes

1 red, 1 yellow and 1 green pepper, quartered and seeded
75g (3oz, ½ cup) raisins

a little olive oil
a little cider vinegar
sea salt and freshly ground black pepper

1   Preheat the oven to 200°C (400°F, Gas Mark 6). Place the prepared peppers, skin side up, in a single layer in a shallow non-stick roasting pan.
2   Roast for about 15–20 minutes, turning once, until the skins begin to blister and char. Remove and cover the pan with a clean tea towel (the trapped steam will help to loosen the skins).
3   Meanwhile, cover the raisins with boiling water and steep for 10 minutes until they plump up. Drain well.
4   When the peppers are lukewarm, peel off and discard as much of the skin as possible and slice the flesh. Tip into a dish and mix in some oil and vinegar to taste plus seasoning. Mix in the raisins and leave to cool further. This is best served at room temperature.

## 195 Roasted squash and sage

PREPARATION TIME 12 minutes   COOKING TIME 30 minutes plus cooling

1 squash or small pumpkin
1 red onion, thinly sliced
3 tbsp vegetable oil
50g (2oz) butter
2 large sprigs of sage, leaves
stripped and shredded

50g (2oz, ½ cup) chopped walnuts or
hazelnuts, optional
sea salt and freshly ground black pepper

1 Halve the squash, scoop out the seeds, peel then cut into bite-sized chunks.
Preheat the oven to 190°C (375°F, Gas Mark 5).
2 Tip the squash chunks into a roasting pan and mix in the onion slices and oil.
Dot with butter, scatter with the sage and seasoning.
3 Roast for about 25 minutes, stirring once or twice, until just tender. Scatter over the
nuts and roast for a further 5 minutes. Cool for 10 minutes before serving.

## 196 Oven-baked barley and mushroom pilaff

PREPARATION TIME 10 minutes   COOKING TIME up to 1 hour

1 small onion, chopped
2 tbsp vegetable oil
50g (2oz) butter
150g (5oz) chestnut or wild mushrooms,
roughly chopped
125g (4oz, ⅔ cup) pearl barley
100g (3½oz, ½ cup) brown or green lentils,
pre-soaked

850ml (1½ pints, 3⅓ cups) Vegetable,
chicken or game stock (see page 16)
2 bay leaves
2–3 tbsp chopped parsley
sea salt and freshly ground black pepper

1 Preheat the oven to 190°C (375°F, Gas Mark 5). Sauté the onion in the oil in a
large pan for 5 minutes, stir in the butter until melted, then mix in the mushrooms
and cook for a further 3 minutes.
2 Stir in the barley, lentils, stock, bay leaves and seasoning. Bring to the boil, stir once
then tip into a large ovenproof casserole. Cover and bake in the oven 50 minutes.
Remove the bay leaves and mix in the parsley, then serve.

## 197 Barbecued sweetcorn

PREPARATION TIME nil   COOKING TIME 12–15 minutes

4 corn on the cobs, husks on
4 good knobs of butter
few drops of hot pepper sauce or
Worcestershire sauce
sea salt and freshly ground black pepper

1 Preheat a barbecue or griddle until hot. Cook the corns in their husks over the heat
for 12–15 minutes depending on size, turning occasionally, until the husks blacken.
2 Remove, cool for 5 minutes, then strip off the husks. Serve topped with knobs of
butter and seasoning. Shake over the sauces to taste.

## 198 Tudor butter bean tart

**PREPARATION TIME** 25 minutes **COOKING TIME** about 1 hour plus cooling

125g (4oz, 1 cup) wholemeal flour
125g (4oz, ¾ cup plus 1 tbsp) plain flour
50g (2oz) lard or shortening
75g (3oz) butter
sea salt and freshly ground black pepper

**FILLING**
1 large shallot, sliced
25g (1oz) butter
1 x 410g (14oz) can butter beans, drained
200ml (7fl oz, ¾ cup) double cream
2 egg yolks
½ tsp dried winter savory or thyme
2 tbsp chopped parsley

1   Make the pastry according to the method for Shortcrust pastry (see page 18). Roll out thinly and use to line a 20cm (8in) flan case or tart tin. Allow to rest while you preheat the oven to 190°C (375°F, Gas Mark 5).
2   Fill the case with non-stick baking parchment and baking beans and bake blind for 15 minutes. Remove the parchment and beans. Trim the pastry level with the top of the flan dish. Reduce the temperature to 170°C (325°F, Gas Mark 3).
3   Sauté the shallot in the butter for 5 minutes, then remove and whiz in a food processor with the butter beans, cream, yolks, herbs and seasoning. Pour into the flan case and return to the oven for 35–40 minutes until risen and firm. Cool for 10 minutes and serve in wedges.

## 199 Buttered broad beans with summer savory

**PREPARATION TIME** 10 minutes **COOKING TIME** 7 minutes

500–600g (1lb 2oz–1lb 5oz) fresh broad
  beans, unpodded weight, or 250g (9oz)
  frozen beans
50g (2oz) butter

2 sprigs of summer savory or wild thyme,
  leaves stripped
sea salt and freshly ground black pepper

1   Pod the beans then boil in lightly salted water for 5 minutes. Drain and rinse under cold running water, then peel off the grey skins, if liked.
2   Return the beans to the pan with the butter. Add the savory and seasoning, reheat for 1–2 minutes and serve. Delicious with home-cooked ham.

## 200 Sautéed potatoes

**PREPARATION TIME** 10 minutes **COOKING TIME** 10 minutes

800g (1lb 12oz) large potatoes, cooked
  and drained
3–4 tbsp vegetable oil
large knob of butter

1–2 tbsp finely chopped parsley
1–2 tbsp small capers
sea salt and freshly ground black pepper

1   Slice the cooked potatoes to an even thickness, about 1cm (½in). Heat the oil in a large frying pan and when hot add the potato slices in an even layer. Work in batches if necessary.
2   Cook for 2 minutes without turning, slide in the butter and cook for a further minute until golden and crisp, then flip over and cook the other side for 2 minutes. Remove, drain on kitchen paper, then toss in the parsley and capers. Season and serve hot.

## 201 Perfect roast potatoes

**PREPARATION TIME** 10 minutes **COOKING TIME** 50 minutes

50g (2oz) goose fat or beef dripping or 4 tbsp
    vegetable oil
800g–1kg (1lb 12oz– 2lb 4oz) roasting
    potatoes (about 6–8), peeled and cut into
    even-sized chunks

sprig of thyme or rosemary, leaves
    stripped and chopped
sea salt and freshly ground black pepper

1   Preheat the oven to 200°C (400°F, Gas Mark 6). Put the fat into a shallow roasting
    pan and place in the oven on the middle shelf. Boil the potatoes for 5 minutes in
    lightly salted water then drain.
2   Carefully remove the roasting pan. Stir the par-boiled potatoes into the hot fat,
    season well and scatter with chopped herbs. Return to the oven and cook for
    45–55 minutes, turning once or twice until nicely golden all over.
3   Drain on kitchen paper. Keep warm in a low oven, uncovered, so they stay crisp.

## 202 Chunky chips

**PREPARATION TIME** 10 minutes plus soaking    **COOKING TIME** 12 minutes

800g–1kg (1lb 12oz–2lb 4oz) large
    potatoes, peeled
about 1 litre (1¾ pint, 4 cups) vegetable
    oil or beef dripping

fine sea salt and freshly ground black pepper
    (optional)

1   Cut the potatoes into 1cm (½in) wide slices, discarding the trimmings, then cut
    each slice into 1cm (½in) wide sticks. Soak in a large bowl of cold water for 1 hour.
    Drain and pat dry between 2 clean tea towels.
2   Heat the oil in a heavy, deep-sided frying pan or medium pan to 160°C (325°F)
    if you have a thermometer (or until a cube of white bread turns pale gold in
    1 minute). Blanch the chips in two batches in a metal frying basket in the oil for
    about 5 minutes until just softened but uncoloured.
3   Drain on kitchen paper while you reheat the oil between batches back to the
    correct temperature.
4   Raise the temperature to 190°C (375°F), then re-fry the chips in 2–3 batches for
    2–3 minutes until golden and crisp. Drain again on kitchen paper and sprinkle with
    salt and pepper if liked. Keep warm, uncovered, for a few minutes before serving.

## 203 Scalloped potatoes

**PREPARATION TIME** 10 minutes    **COOKING TIME** 1 hour 20 minutes plus resting

375ml (13fl oz, 1½ cups) milk
2 tbsp flour
50g (2oz) butter, plus extra for greasing
500g (1lb 2oz) potatoes, thinly peeled
1 fat clove garlic, crushed

1 small onion, thinly sliced (optional)
½ tsp ground paprika
about 3 tbsp dried, natural colour
    breadcrumbs
sea salt and freshly ground black pepper

1   Put the milk, flour and half the butter into a non-stick pan and bring slowly to the
    boil, stirring constantly with a wooden spoon. Season and add the garlic. Simmer
    for 1 minute then remove from the heat.
2   Preheat the oven to 180°C (350°F, Gas Mark 4). Lightly grease a medium shallow
    ovenproof dish with butter then layer in the potato and onion, trickling in the sauce
    and sprinkling with paprika between each layer. Cover with foil and bake for about
    45 minutes, or until the potatoes start to soften.
3   Meanwhile, melt the remaining butter and mix with the breadcrumbs. Uncover the
    dish, sprinkle with the breadcrumbs and return to the oven for a further 30 minutes
    until cooked. Let stand for 10 minutes before serving.

## 204 Boxty potato pancake

**PREPARATION TIME** 12 minutes    **COOKING TIME** 15–20 minutes

800g (1lb 12oz) potatoes (3–4 large ones),
    peeled
3 tbsp flour
1 tsp baking powder

a little milk, to mix
good knob of dripping, lard or butter
sea salt

1   Coarsely grate the potato. Tip into a clean tea towel and wring out the excess liquid.
2   Mix the grated potato with the flour and baking powder. Add about ½ tsp salt and
    2–3 tbsp milk.
3   Heat some fat in a large non-stick frying pan. When hot, drop in dessertspoonfuls
    of the mixture, shaping to neat rounds with a palette knife and pressing down lightly.
    Cook until golden brown on one side, approximately 3–4 minutes, then flip over
    to cook the other side. Serve with bacon and eggs or with apple sauce for a main
    meal accompaniment.

## 205 Mash supreme

SERVES 4–6   **PREPARATION TIME** 10 minutes   **COOKING TIME** 15–20 minutes

800g–1kg (1lb 12oz–2lb 4oz) large floury
  potatoes (Desirée, King Edward), peeled
50g (2oz) butter

150ml (5fl oz, ²⁄₃ cup) whole milk
sea salt and freshly ground black pepper

1   Cut the potatoes into even-sized chunks, about 3cm (1¼in) square. Boil in plenty
    of salted water for 10–20 minutes until tender. Drain and return to the hot pan set
    on the lowest heat and dry off for 2–3 minutes.
2   Remove from the heat and start to mash with a masher, adding the butter.
3   Meanwhile, heat the milk until almost boiling. Pour onto the part-mashed potatoes
    and continue to mash and stir until smooth and creamy. Check the seasoning and
    scoop into a warmed dish. This mash is the basis for other side dishes.

### VARIATIONS

### Champ
Make the mash as in Step 1 above, then chop 3 spring onions and simmer in the
milk for 5 minutes, then beat into the mashed potatoes with seasoning.

### Colcannon
Make the mash as above, then finely shred ½ small crinkly cabbage and 1 trimmed
leek and blanch together in boiling water for 3 minutes. Drain well then mix into
the mashed potatoes with seasoning. You could also substitute the butter for bacon
fat for a true Irish flavour.

## 206 Northumberland pan haggarty

**PREPARATION TIME** 15 minutes plus soaking   **COOKING TIME** about 50 minutes plus resting

3 potatoes, each about 250g (9oz),
  peeled
1 large onion, halved and thinly sliced
2 tbsp vegetable oil

25g (1oz) beef dripping or butter, melted
about 100g (3½oz) Cheddar-type cheese,
  coarsely grated
sea salt and freshly ground black pepper

1   Thinly slice the potatoes, ideally on a mandolin or Japanese food slicer. Soak in
    a large bowl of cold water for 30 minutes, then drain and dry thoroughly between
    two clean tea towels.
2   Meanwhile, fry the onion slices gently in the oil in a frying pan for about 5 minutes
    until they start to soften. Remove the onions with a slotted spoon.
3   Layer the onions with the potatoes in a shallow ovenproof baking dish or shallow
    cast-iron pan, seasoning well and trickling in the melted fat.
4   Halfway through, sprinkle with half the cheese and continue the potato and onion
    layers. Finish with the rest of the cheese. Cover with a lid and cook on a low heat
    for 30–40 minutes, shaking the pan occasionally to loosen the base, but don't stir it.
5   Test to see if the potato is cooked with a thin knife. When soft, place under a
    preheated grill to brown the cheese topping. Let stand for a good 10 minutes before
    cutting into wedges to serve.

## 207 Bubble 'n' squeak

**MAKES** 8 cakes   **PREPARATION TIME** 30 minutes   **COOKING TIME** 10–15 minutes

1kg (2lb 4oz) floury potatoes, peeled
  and quartered
½ small green cabbage, shredded
40g (1½oz) butter

a little flour, to coat
bacon fat, lard or vegetable oil, for frying
sea salt and freshly ground black pepper
tomato ketchup, to serve

1   Boil the potatoes until tender, about 12–15 minutes, then drain and return to the
    hot pan on a low heat for 1–2 minutes to dry out. Mash well and set aside.
2   Boil the cabbage for 3–5 minutes until just tender but still a little crunchy. Drain,
    cool quickly under cold running water and drain again.
3   Mix with the potatoes, butter and seasoning to taste. Spread the mixture on a dinner
    plate and leave to cool.
4   Divide into 8 portions and shape into neat round cakes. Toss in the flour, shaking
    off the excess.
5   Shallow-fry in 5mm (¼in) hot fat in two batches for 2 minutes on each side, turning
    carefully. Drain and serve with ketchup.

## 208 Perfect jacket potatoes

**PREPARATION TIME** 5 minutes   **COOKING TIME** 50–60 minutes

4 baking potatoes, each about 250g (9oz), such as Desirée, King Edward, Marfona or Idaho

vegetable oil, to coat (optional)
knob of butter or cream cheese

1   Preheat the oven to 190°C (375°F, Gas Mark 5). Choose unblemished, even-sized potatoes so that they cook to a light fluffiness. Remove any 'eyes'. Wash and score the largest side in a cross with the tip of a sharp knife. (Alternatively, prick several times with a fork or skewer on a potato roasting rack.) If you want a tender skin, rub lightly with some vegetable oil, otherwise for a crisp skin leave as is.
2   Cook for 50–60 minutes or until soft when a skewer is inserted in the centre.
3   Remove and cool for 10 minutes and cut through the scored cross. Using both hands, push the base up to open out the cross and add a good knob of butter or cream cheese in the centre of each 'spud'.

## 209 Scottish tattie scones

**PREPARATION TIME** 15 minutes   **COOKING TIME** 15–20 minutes

1 floury potato, about 250g (9oz), peeled
25g (1oz) butter, plus extra
    for greasing
50g (2oz, ⅓ cup) plain flour, plus extra
    for rolling

¼ tsp baking powder
2 good pinches of salt

1   Cut the potato into even-sized chunks and boil until just tender, for about 12 minutes. Drain well, return to the pan on a low heat for a few seconds to dry out, then mash with the butter.
2   Sift the flour, baking powder and salt into a bowl and mix in the warm potato to a firm, but still soft dough. Shape into 2 balls.
3   Roll out each ball on a lightly floured board to a circle about 5mm (¼in) thick. Cut into quarters and prick well with a fork.
4   Heat a griddle and when you feel a good heat rising, brush quickly with a little butter. Cook the scones for 3 minutes on each side until golden brown and firm. Repeat with the remaining dough ball. Serve for breakfast with bacon and eggs, or with butter and jam.

## 210 Warm cauliflower salad

**PREPARATION TIME** 5 minutes   **COOKING TIME** 5 minutes

1 small cauliflower, broken into roughly
    equal florets
3 tbsp Vinaigrette (see page 19)
1 tsp fennel or caraway seeds

2 tbsp chopped parsley
2–4 eggs, hard-boiled and
    peeled (optional)
sea salt and freshly ground black pepper

1   Boil the cauliflower in lightly salted water for 5 minutes then drain, run under cold water for a few seconds to cool a little and shake dry. Tip into a shallow bowl.
2   Toss in the vinaigrette, season and mix with the seeds and parsley, then set aside until warm. To turn into a light main meal, halve the eggs and serve with the florets.

## 211 Kitchen garden salad

**PREPARATION TIME** 15 minutes    **COOKING TIME** nil

1 small bulb fennel
1 crisp lettuce
good handful of spinach leaves
small handful of young dandelion leaves
small handful of parsley sprigs
1 carrot, coarsely grated

small handful of chives, snipped or
  2 spring onions, shredded
½ recipe quantity Vinaigrette (see page 19)
sea salt and freshly ground black or
  white pepper

1   Halve the fennel lengthways, remove the core, then slice wafer thin on a mandolin
    or Japanese slicer. Submerge in a bowl of iced water for 20 minutes, then drain
    and spin or pat dry.
2   Separate out the lettuce leaves and tear into bite-sized pieces. Wash in ice-cold
    water with the remaining salad leaves and parsley and spin or pat dry.
3   Toss everything together with the carrot and chives. Cover and chill until required.
    Season to taste and toss with the dressing just before serving.

## 212 Cucumber and mint salad

**PREPARATION TIME** 10 minutes plus resting    **COOKING TIME** nil

½ cucumber
fine sea salt, for sprinkling
1 tbsp cider vinegar

freshly ground black pepper
2 tbsp shredded mint, to scatter

1   Use a swivel vegetable peeler to remove 3 strips of peel from the cucumber then
    slice it very finely into daisy shapes with a razor-sharp knife, or on a mandolin or
    Japanese slicer.
2   Layer the slices in a colander, sprinkling lightly in between with salt. Leave to drain for
    20 minutes over the sink then rinse with cold water and pat dry with kitchen paper.
3   Tip into a small shallow bowl and sprinkle with the vinegar and pepper. Leave for
    10 minutes, then scatter over the mint and serve. Good with cold salmon or chicken.

## 213 Tomato, spring onion and cress salad

**PREPARATION TIME** 5 minutes plus resting    **COOKING TIME** nil

4 large tomatoes, tops scored once
fine sea salt, to sprinkle
2 tbsp olive oil
1 bunch of watercress, washed

2 spring onions, finely shredded
freshly ground black pepper
1 tbsp roughly chopped marjoram, to scatter

1   Dunk the tomatoes into a pan of just-boiled water. Remove after 30 seconds and
    peel. Take out the stalk ends with the tip of a small, sharp knife and slice thinly
    with a serrated blade.
2   Layer in a colander, sprinkling lightly in between with salt and drain for 20 minutes
    over a bowl to catch the juices. Mix these juices with the oil.
3   Arrange the watercress on a platter and season with pepper. Place the tomatoes
    on top and pour over the oil and juices, sprinkling with the onions. Scatter with the
    marjoram and serve.

## 214 Broad bean, asparagus and cos lettuce salad

**PREPARATION TIME** 12 minutes   **COOKING TIME** 5–7 minutes

500g (1lb 2oz) unpodded fresh broad beans
250g (9oz) bunch of green asparagus spears
1 small Cos lettuce or 2 Little Gems
4–6 tbsp Vinaigrette (see page 19)

2 tbsp each chopped parsley, chives
  and mint
sea salt and freshly ground black or
  white pepper

1   Pod the beans and blanch in a pan of boiling water for 3 minutes. Drain and rinse under cold running water then peel off the grey skins. Season the beans and cool.
2   Trim the woody ends of asparagus and cut each spear in half. Blanch in boiling water for 2–3 minutes, drain and rinse in cold running water. Pat dry with kitchen paper.
3   Tear the Cox lettuce into bite-sized chunks or use whole Little Gem leaves. Toss with the herbs then the vinaigrette and beans. Tip onto a platter and scatter the asparagus tips on top. Grind over pepper and serve.

## 215 Best-ever potato salad with herbs

**PREPARATION TIME** 10 minutes plus cooling   **COOKING TIME** 15 minutes

500g (1lb 2oz) new potatoes, scrubbed
 and halved
3 tbsp Vinaigrette (see page 19)
2 tbsp Mayonnaise (see page 210)
2 tbsp single cream

2 spring onions, sliced thinly on the diagonal
1 large sprig of tarragon, leaves stripped
2 tbsp chopped parsley
sea salt and freshly ground black pepper

1   Boil the potatoes in their skins in lightly salted water for about 15 minutes until just tender. Drain and return to the pan. Season and toss in the vinaigrette. Leave to cool to room temperature.
2   Beat together the mayonnaise and single cream and stir into the potatoes along with the onions and herbs. Check the seasoning and transfer to a salad bowl to serve.

## 216 Grated carrot and lemon salad

**PREPARATION TIME** 10 minutes   **COOKING TIME** nil

300g (10oz) large carrots, peeled
juice of 1 lemon
1 tbsp olive oil
2 tbsp chopped parsley

1 tbsp chopped mint
3 tbsp sunflower seeds
sea salt and freshly ground black pepper

1   Coarsely grate the carrot into a bowl. Mix with the lemon juice, oil, herbs and seasoning. Chill for 1 hour, then toss in the sunflower seeds and serve.

## 217 Spinach and bacon with brown bread croûtons

**PREPARATION TIME** 10 minutes   **COOKING TIME** 10 minutes

200g (7oz) smoked streaky bacon
4 slices of brown (wheatmeal) bread,
 crusts removed
3 tbsp olive or vegetable oil

2 tbsp raspberry vinegar
250g (9oz) baby spinach leaves
freshly ground black pepper

1   Chop the bacon into 1cm (½in) strips. Cut the bread into 2cm (¾in) squares.
2   Heat a non-stick frying pan and dry-fry the bacon on a medium heat until the fat starts to run and the bacon crisps. Transfer the bacon to a plate.
3   Heat the oil in the pan, then add the bread squares in a single layer. Cook for about 2 minutes on each side until crisp and golden. Remove, return the bacon to the pan, and toss with the vinegar.
4   Tip the spinach into a bowl and toss in the bacon with some ground black pepper. Scatter over the croûtons and serve.

## 218 Roasted baby beets with orange and rocket

**SERVES** 4–6    **PREPARATION TIME** 15 minutes    **COOKING TIME** 45 minutes

500g (1lb 2oz) bunch of raw baby beetroots
2 tbsp vegetable or olive oil
juice of 1 small orange
2–3 pinches of ground cumin
1 small sprig of thyme, leaves stripped

2–3 tbsp chopped parsley
100g (3½oz) rocket leaves
1 tbsp Vinaigrette (see page 19)
sea salt and freshly ground black pepper

1   Preheat the oven to 190°C (375°F, Gas Mark 5). Trim the roots from the beets and
either scrub well in cold water or peel thinly with a swivel vegetable peeler (wear
rubber gloves to stop your fingers getting stained). Cut in half and mix with the oil
and seasoning.
2   Tip the prepared beetroot into a small, shallow roasting pan and roast for about
40–45 minutes, stirring once or twice, until just tender when pierced. Remove, toss
in the orange juice, cumin and thyme. Cool then mix with the parsley.
3   Toss the rocket with the vinaigrette and seasoning and scatter over a small platter.
Tip the beets and their juices on top and grind over black pepper.

## 219 Lentil and red onion salad

**PREPARATION TIME** 10 minutes plus soaking and cooling    **COOKING TIME** 2 minutes

1 small red onion, sliced thinly
1 x 400g (14oz) can green lentils, drained
3–4 tbsp Vinaigrette (see page 19)

1 carrot, peeled and coarsely grated
1 small bunch of watercress, leaves stripped
sea salt and freshly ground black pepper

1   Soak the onion slices in plenty of cold water for 1 hour, stirring once or twice, then
drain and pat dry. This helps soften them.
2   Rinse the lentils and shake dry. Heat gently in a pan with the vinaigrette until
hot, then tip into a bowl and mix in the onion, carrot and watercress. Check the
seasoning, cool for 10–15 minutes and serve.

## 220 Summer rice salad

**PREPARATION TIME** 10 minutes    **COOKING TIME** 12 minutes

150g (5oz, 1 cup) basmati or long-grain rice
   (not easy cook/parboiled)
⅓ recipe quantity Vinaigrette (see page 19)
½ small red pepper, seeded, halved
   widthways and very thinly sliced
¼ cucumber, halved, seeded and chopped

2 tbsp sliced black olives
2 tbsp mayonnaise
2 tbsp single cream or low-fat natural yogurt
2 tbsp chopped chives
2 tbsp chopped parsley
sea salt and freshly ground black pepper

1   Rinse the rice in a sieve under cold running water. Leave to drain. Boil at least
1.5 litres (2½ pints, 6 cups) water in a pan with 1 tsp salt. Stir in the rice, return
to a medium boil and cook for 10 minutes for basmati rice, 12 minutes for
long-grain or according to the packet instructions
2   Drain, rinse under cold water for a few seconds and leave for 5 minutes in the sieve.
Then tip into a large bowl and mix in the vinaigrette and some seasoning. Allow to
cool for 30 minutes, then mix in the pepper, cucumber and olives.
3   Blend together the mayonnaise and cream and fork through the rice along with the
chopped herbs. Serve lightly chilled.

## 221 Celery, apple and walnut salad

**PREPARATION TIME** 15 minutes   **COOKING TIME** nil

4 large sticks celery, trimmed and sliced
   thinly on the diagonal
1 large Cox's apple (or Laxton or Russett),
   quartered, cored and chopped
100g (4oz, 1 cup) fresh walnuts, roughly
   chopped
2 tbsp roughly chopped parsley

1 sprig of tarragon, leaves stripped
   and chopped
1 recipe quantity Old English salad dressing
   (see page 210) or 2 tbsp mayonnaise
   mixed with 2 tbsp single cream or
   natural yogurt
sea salt and freshly ground black pepper

1  Mix together the celery, apple, walnuts and herbs and stir in the dressing or
   mayonnaise and yogurt. Season to taste and serve as a side salad or light starter
   on a bed of thinly sliced apple.

# CHAPTER 5

# PUDDINGS & DESSERTS

Knickerbocker Glory, Whim Wham, Eton Mess … whatever the frivolous name there is no doubting the wealth of great British desserts or puddings. A homely fruit crumble, creamy bread and butter pudding or special trifle brought to the table cause whoops of delight. A special occasion is a great excuse to produce lots of desserts that few guests can resist!

Country cooks, not *haute cuisine* chefs, brought about British puds. It was the milkmaid churning creamy curds and butter, the farmer's wife using her glut of apples, plums and leftover beef suet that led to our sweet treasure trove. Spices have been used since seafaring medieval explorers and traders returned home with these exotic flavourings and, from the eighteenth century, sugar from the West Indies. Richly spiced fruit puddings once included meat (hence the name mincemeat) and white chicken thickened with pounded almonds made 'blancmange'. The tradition for exchange and adaptation of personal favourite recipes is reflected in many of the delightful personalized titles.

## 222 Irish apple and potato pie

**SERVES** 6–8  **PREPARATION TIME** 25 minutes plus cooling  **COOKING TIME** 40 minutes plus cooling

500g (1lb 2oz) floury potatoes, peeled
and cut into even-sized chunks
25g (1oz) butter, plus extra to dot
2 tsp caster sugar
1/2 tsp ground ginger or 1 teaspoon
ginger purée

about 4 tbsp flour, plus extra for rolling
800g (1lb 12oz) cooking apples
(e.g. Bramleys, Grenadier), cored, peeled
and thinly sliced
3 tbsp demerara sugar

1   Boil the potatoes in lightly salted water until tender. Drain well and return to the
pan. Mash with a quarter of the butter, the sugar and ginger. Cool for 10–15 minutes
until you can handle it, then work in enough flour to make a smooth dough. Divide
into 2 equal portions.
2   On a well-floured board, roll or pat out 1 portion to a 25cm (10in) round and lift onto
a china plate or metal pie plate. Pile the apples onto the pastry, sprinkling in between
with the sugar and dotting with the remaining butter.
3   Roll out the second portion to a slightly larger round. Dampen the pie edges with
water and lift the second round on top, pressing firmly to seal. Trim and crimp
and cut a cross in the centre.
4   Preheat the oven to 200°C (400°F, Gas Mark 6). Bake for 30–40 minutes or until
the pastry is golden and the apples soft when pierced. Allow to cool completely
and chill before serving.

## 223 Treacle and coconut tart

**SERVES** 6–8  **PREPARATION TIME** 25 minutes plus chilling  **COOKING TIME** 30 minutes

225g (8oz) warmed golden syrup
50g (2oz, 1 cup) fresh white breadcrumbs
40g (1 1/2 oz, 1/2 cup) desiccated coconut
1 egg, beaten
120ml (4fl oz, 1/2 cup) double cream
1 recipe quantity Sweet dessert or Shortcrust
pastry (see page 18), thawed if frozen

about 3 tbsp raspberry or apricot jam, slightly
warmed until runny
handful of fresh raspberries (optional)
a little sifted icing sugar, to dust

1   Beat the syrup in a bowl with the breadcrumbs, coconut, egg and cream. Ideally
chill for 24 hours for a lighter filling.
2   Roll out the pastry on a lightly floured board to a thickness of 5mm (1/4in), about
30cm (12in) diameter. Use to line a 23cm (9in) loose-bottomed flan tin, about
1.5cm (5/8in) deep. Press the pastry well into the sides and trim the top while leaving
it slightly overhanging over the rim. Leave to chill for 20 minutes while you preheat
the oven to 190°C (375°F, Gas Mark 5).
3   Spread the jam in the flan base using the back of a spoon. Scoop the filling on top; it
should come three-quarters of the way up the flan. If using, drop in the raspberries.
4   Bake for about 30 minutes until the filling is risen and golden brown. Allow the tart
to cool to room temperature before serving dusted with icing sugar.

**HINT** for measuring syrup and honey.
Stand the can of syrup or jar of honey in a pan of just boiled water for about
5 minutes to soften it a little. Place a mixing bowl on the scales and pour in the
runny syrup to the required weight.

## 224 Rhubarb crumble tart

**SERVES** 6–8   **PREPARATION TIME** 20 minutes plus chilling   **COOKING TIME** 1 hour 10 minutes

400–500g (14oz–1lb 2oz) fresh rhubarb,
  washed and cut into 4cm (1½in) lengths
100g (3½oz, ½ cup) caster sugar
25g (1oz) butter
1 tsp vanilla extract
1 recipe quantity Sweet dessert pastry
  (see page 18) or 1 x 20cm (8in) ready-to-
  bake dessert pastry case

**TOPPING**
75g (3oz, ½ cup) plain flour
50g (2oz) butter
40g (1½oz, ⅓ cup) demerara sugar
50g (2oz, ½ cup) chopped roasted hazelnuts

1   Pat the washed rhubarb lightly with kitchen paper so it is not too wet. It should still be a little damp. Heat a large non-stick frying pan until you can feel a good heat rising. Toss the damp rhubarb in the sugar, then immediately tip into the pan and spread to a single layer.

2   Cook on a high heat for 1 minute until the sugar begins to caramelize, then reduce the heat and cook for 5 minutes, stirring occasionally, so the fruit is evenly coated in a light caramel. Mix in the butter and vanilla and cook for a further 5 minutes. Remove the pan from the heat and cool.

3   Roll out the pastry to 3mm (¼in) thickness and line a fluted 20cm (8in) flan tin with sides at least 2.5cm (1in) deep. Do not trim the pastry edges yet. Prick the base with a fork. Line with non-stick baking paper and baking beans and set aside to chill for 20 minutes while you preheat the oven to 200°C (400°F, Gas Mark 6).

4   Place the flan case on a baking sheet and bake blind for 15 minutes. Reduce the temperature to 180°C (350°F, Gas Mark 4). Remove the paper and beans and return the case to the oven for 5 minutes.

5   Remove and trim the pastry case with a sharp knife.

6   For the topping, whiz the flour and butter in a food processor to fine crumbs then mix in three-quarters of the demerara sugar and all the nuts.

7   Spoon the rhubarb filling into the pastry case, cover with the topping, and sprinkle over the last of the demerara.

8   Return the tart to the oven and bake for a further 20 minutes until the topping is golden and crunchy. Cool and turn out of the flan tin. Delicious served warm or at room temperature with Real custard (see page 19), pouring cream or ice cream.

## 225 Bakewell tart

**SERVES** 6–8   **PREPARATION TIME** 25 minutes plus resting   **COOKING TIME** 55 minutes

1 recipe quantity Rough puff pastry
  (see page 18)
2–3 tbsp raspberry jam, warmed
125g (4oz) butter, softened
125g (4oz, ½ cup plus 2 tbsp) caster sugar
125g (4oz, 1½ cups) ground almonds or half
  cake crumbs and half ground almonds

1 large egg, beaten
1 tsp almond extract, if available
2 tbsp icing sugar, to dust OR 6 tbsp icing
  sugar plus a squeeze of fresh lemon juice

1   Roll out the pastry and use to line a 20cm (8in) round flan tin at least 2.5cm (1in) deep. Allow a little overhang. Line with baking paper and baking beans and chill for 20 minutes while you preheat the oven to 200°C (400°F, Gas Mark 6).

2   Bake the flan case on a heavy metal baking sheet for 20 minutes, removing the paper and beans after 15 minutes. Rest for 5 minutes, then trim the pastry top neatly with a very sharp knife. Spread the base with the jam. Reduce the temperature to 170°C (325°F, Gas Mark 3).

3   Beat together the butter, sugar, almonds, egg and extract and spread over the jam. Return to the oven for a further 25–30 minutes until risen and golden. Cool.

4   To serve, either dust lightly with icing sugar or, for a more special occasion, mix together the icing sugar and lemon juice, adding warm water in dribbles to make glacé icing. Spread over the top of the cooled filling and leave to set.

## 226 Bramley apple plate pie

**SERVES** 6–8  **PREPARATION TIME** 20 minutes plus resting  **COOKING TIME** 35 minutes

1½ recipe quantity Shortcrust pastry (see
    page 18) or 1 x 500g (1lb 2oz) pack ready-
    rolled shortcrust pastry, thawed if frozen
3 Bramley apples, about 750g (1lb 10oz),
    peeled, cored and thinly sliced

2–3 tbsp sugar, caster or granulated, plus
    extra to sprinkle
few cloves or pinches of cinnamon
1 egg white, beaten

1    Divide the pastry and knead into 2 balls. Roll out both balls to fit a 23cm (9in)
    pie dish or china plate. Press one of the rounds into the base, allowing the edges
    to overhang, and prick the base a few times.
2    Pile the apples into the pie dish, mounding in the centre and scatter with sugar to
    taste. Add the cloves or cinnamon.
3    Brush the rim with egg white, lift over the second round of pastry and press together.
4    Hold the pie up in one hand and with the other trim the overhanging dough using a
    sharp knife angled slightly outwards. Pinch the edges together with the thumb and
    finger of one hand and the index finger of the other, making a scalloped edge.
5    Cut a cross in the centre. Glaze with egg white and sprinkle with extra sugar to give
    the crust a sparkle. Rest for 15 minutes while you preheat the oven to 190°C
    (375°F, Gas Mark 5).
6    Place the pie on a metal baking sheet, then bake for 30–35 minutes, turning the
    plate once or twice, until golden brown.

### VARIATION

#### Warden pie
Wardens were an old variety of old cooking pear (mentioned in Shakespeare's
*The Winter's Tale*) from Warden Abbey in Bedfordshire. To make the pie, follow the
Bramley Apple Pie recipe above, substituting firm Conference pears for the apples
and crushed saffron strands for the cloves. Quinces are also suitable for the filling,
but slice them thinly as, raw, they are quite hard.

## 227 Custard tart

**SERVES** 6–8  **PREPARATION TIME** 20 minutes plus resting  **COOKING TIME** 1 hour

125g (4oz, ¾ cup plus 1 tbsp) plain flour,
    plus extra to dust
good pinch of salt
2 tsp grated lemon zest
75g (3oz) butter

125g (4oz, ½ cup plus 2 tbsp) caster sugar
6 egg yolks
250ml (9fl oz, 1 cup) whipping cream
1 whole nutmeg

1    For the pastry, rub together the flour, salt, lemon zest and butter until the mixture
    resembles breadcrumbs. Stir in a third of the sugar. Beat 1 egg yolk with 1 tbsp ice-
    cold water and mix into the crumbs with a table knife, then knead to form a ball of
    dough adding extra water if necessary. Wrap in cling film and chill for 2 hours.
2    Roll out the pastry on a lightly floured surface and use to line a 20cm (8in) flan tin,
    about 2.5cm (1in) deep, allowing some overhang. Trim away the excess pastry but
    press the dough back up the sides to allow for shrinkage.
3    Rest for 15 minutes while you preheat the oven to 190°C (375°F, Gas Mark 5). Line
    the case with baking paper and baking beans, then bake blind for about 15–20
    minutes or until the pastry is starting to turn golden brown. Remove the paper and
    beans, return to the oven for 5 minutes. Reduce the temperature to 130°C
    (275°F, Gas Mark 1).
4    For the filling, whisk together the remaining yolks and sugar. Lightly heat the cream
    until tepid then beat into the yolk mixture. Strain through a sieve into the pastry
    case and return to the centre of the oven, still on the baking sheet. Bake for 30–35
    minutes or until the custard appears just lightly set. Remove from the oven and grate
    over about a third of a whole nutmeg. Cool to room temperature, then use a very
    sharp knife to trim away the top of the pastry overhang. Remove from the tin to serve.

## 228 Lemon meringue pie

**SERVES** 6–8    **PREPARATION TIME** 20 minutes plus chilling    **COOKING TIME** 1 hour

⅓ recipe quantity Sweet dessert pastry (see page 18) or 175g (6oz) ready-made shortcrust or sweet pastry
45g (1½oz, ⅓ cup) cornflour

250g (9oz, 1¼ cups) caster sugar
grated zest and juice of 2 lemons
2 large eggs, separated

1  Roll out the pastry thinly and use to line a 20cm (8in) loose-bottomed flan tin, leaving the edges overhanging. Prick the base and line with baking paper and baking beans. Chill for 20 minutes while you preheat the oven to 200°C (400°F, Gas Mark 6).

2  Bake the case blind for 15 minutes, then remove the paper and beans and return to the oven for a further 5 minutes. Remove and cool. Using a very sharp knife, trim the pastry edges to the top of the flan case, taking care not to crack the pastry. Lower the temperature to 150°C (300°F, Gas Mark 2).

3  Blend the cornflour with 150g (5oz, 1 cup) of the sugar, the lemon zest and 250ml (9fl oz, 1 cup) water in a medium pan. Bring slowly to the boil, stirring constantly until smooth and thickened. Simmer for 1 minute then remove and mix in the lemon juice. Cool for 2 minutes, then mix in the yolks and pour into the pastry case.

4  Whisk the egg whites in a large, very clean mixing bowl until they form firm, soft peaks. Gradually whisk in the remaining sugar to give a glossy meringue. Spoon over the filling, roughing into peaks, and bake for 30 minutes until golden and crisp.

5  Remove and cool completely to room temperature, then cut in wedges to serve.

## 229 Pear or quince and almond tart

**SERVES** 6–8 **PREPARATION TIME** 25 minutes plus resting **COOKING TIME** 55 minutes

1 recipe quantity Sweet dessert pastry (see page 18)
2–3 tbsp apricot jam, warmed
125g (4oz) butter, softened
125g (4oz, ½ cup plus 2 tbsp) golden
  caster sugar
125g (4oz, 1½ cups) ground almonds or half
  cake crumbs and half ground almonds

1 large egg, beaten
1 tsp almond extract
2 Conference pears or 1 large quince,
  quartered, peeled and sliced
1 tbsp caster sugar
strip of lemon zest

1   Roll out the pastry and use to line a 20cm (8in) round flan tin at least 2.5cm (1in) deep, allowing the edges to overhang. Line with baking paper and baking beans and chill for 20 minutes while you preheat the oven to 200°C (400°F, Gas Mark 6).
2   Bake the flan case on a metal baking sheet for 20 minutes, removing the paper and beans after 15 minutes. Rest for 5 minutes, then trim the pastry top neatly with a very sharp knife. Spread the base with the jam. Reduce the temperature to 170°C (325°F, Gas Mark 3).
3   Beat together the butter, sugar, almonds, egg and extract and spread over the jam. Poach the fruit with the sugar, zest and a splash of water for about 10 minutes to soften, then arrange over the creamed filling. Bake for a further 25–30 minutes until risen and golden. Cool before serving

## 230 Strawberry flan

**SERVES** 6–8 **PREPARATION TIME** 20 minutes plus resting **COOKING TIME** 20 minutes

1 recipe quantity Sweet dessert pastry
  (see page 18)
150ml (5fl oz, ⅔ cup) double cream

4–6 tbsp Lemon curd (see page 205)
400g (14oz) fresh strawberries, hulled
sifted icing sugar, to dust

1   Roll out the pastry on a lightly floured board to 3mm (¼in) and line a 20cm (8in) loose-bottomed flan tin at least 3cm (1¼in) deep. Leave the edges untrimmed. Prick the base. Line with baking paper and baking beans. Chill for 20 minutes.
2   Preheat the oven to 190°C (375°F, Gas Mark 5). Bake the pastry blind for 15 minutes, and then remove the paper and beans. Trim the edges with a sharp knife, return the case for 5 minutes or until cooked. Allow to cool.
3   When ready to serve, whip the cream until thick then gradually mix in the lemon curd. Spread over the base of the tart case.
4   Slice the strawberries and scatter over the top. Dust with icing sugar and serve.

## 231 Oldbury gooseberry cakes

**MAKES** about 12 **PREPARATION TIME** 25 minutes **COOKING TIME** 25 minutes

400g (14oz, 3 cups) plain flour
100g (3½oz) butter
100g (3½oz) lard or shortening

250g (9oz) fresh dessert gooseberries,
  topped and tailed
150g (5oz, ¾ cup) caster or demerara sugar

1   Tip the flour into a large bowl. Melt the butter and lard with 4 tbsp water and bring to the boil. When melted pour into the flour and mix to a dough with a wooden spoon. Knead lightly when cool enough to handle.
2   Divide into two-thirds and one third. Roll out the bigger portion thinly and cut out 12 x 8cm (3¼in) rounds. Press these into a 12-hole bun tin, pressing them up the sides. Roll out the remaining pastry and cut out 6cm (2½in) rounds for the tops.
3   Divide the gooseberries between the tarts, sprinkle in the sugar, wet the edges with some water and press on the tops. Cut a cross in the centre of each.
4   Preheat the oven to 200°C (400°F, Gas Mark 6) and bake for 20–25 minutes, turning if necessary to cook evenly. Cool for 5 minutes then remove to a wire rack to cool fully. Serve at room temperature.

## 232 Plum and almond tart

**SERVES** 6–8  **PREPARATION TIME** 20 minutes plus resting  **COOKING TIME** 55 minutes

1 recipe quantity Sweet dessert pastry
  (see page 18)
125g (4oz) butter, softened
125g (4oz, ½ cup plus 2 tbsp) caster sugar
125g (4oz, 1½ cups) ground almonds
3 tbsp plain flour

1 large egg, beaten
2 tbsp brandy or rum
6 tbsp plum jam or apricot jam glaze
  (see page 19)
6 large ripe plums, ideally Victorias
  or greengages

1 Roll out the pastry to 3mm (¼in) thick and use to line a 23cm (9in) loose-bottomed
  flan tin. Allow some overhang. Prick the base and line with baking paper and
  baking beans. Chill for 20 minutes while you preheat the oven to 190°C (375°F,
  Gas Mark 5).
2 Meanwhile, beat together the butter and sugar until creamy, then add the almonds,
  flour, egg and brandy.
3 Bake the pastry case for 20 minutes, removing the paper and beans after 15
  minutes. Return the case for 5 minutes or until cooked. Cool for 5 minutes then use
  a very sharp knife to trim the top neatly. Turn the oven to 170°C (325°F, Gas Mark 3).
4 Spread half the jam on the base and spoon in the creamed mixture. Halve the plums
  around the centre and twist apart. Press the cut side into the filling and return to the
  oven for 30–35 minutes until risen and golden.
5 Cool slightly and brush the top with the remaining jam. Serve at room temperature.

## 233 Mince pies

**MAKES** 12  **PREPARATION TIME** 5 minutes  **COOKING TIME** 12–15 minutes

350g (12oz) Sweet dessert pastry (see page 18)
Mincemeat (see below)

1 egg yolk, beaten with 1 tsp cold water
sifted icing sugar, to dust

1 Roll out the pastry thinly and cut out 12 x 8cm (3¼in) rounds. Fit into a 12-hole
  bun tin. Spoon in a heaped tsp of mincemeat and flatten slightly.
2 Re–roll the pastry trimmings and cut out 12 x 6cm (2½in) rounds and press
  lightly on top. Snip the tops once with scissors or cut small crosses, glaze with
  the egg and bake at 190°C (375°F, Gas Mark 5) for 12–15 minutes until cooked
  and golden. Cool for 3 minutes before lifting out onto a wire rack. Dust with icing
  sugar and serve warm.

### Mincemeat

**MAKES** 1¼kg (2lb 12oz)  **PREPARATION TIME** 25 minutes  **COOKING TIME** nil

250g (9oz, 1½ cups) each raisins, sultanas
  and currants
150g (5oz, 1 cup) dried cranberries or mixed
  wild berries
250g (9oz, 1½ cups) soft brown sugar
1 cooking apple or quince, quartered, cored
  and coarsely grated

125g (4oz, 1 cup) shredded suet (optional)
1 tbsp mixed spice
½ nutmeg, finely grated
grated zest and juice of 1 lemon
grated zest and juice of 1 small orange
3 tbsp dark rum or brandy
120 ml (4fl oz, ½ cup) ruby port

1 Simply mix everything together in a large non-metallic bowl. Cover and leave for
  3–4 weeks, stirring once a week and then pot in sterilized jam jars and store in a
  cool dark cupboard.

# 234 Jam roly poly

**SERVES** 4–6   **PREPARATION TIME** 20 minutes   **COOKING TIME** 1 hour 30 minutes

150g (5oz, 1 cup) self-raising flour
75g (2½oz, ½ cup) shredded suet
4–6 tbsp jam or golden syrup

1 Mix the flour and suet with about 6 tbsp cold water to a firm, but not dry dough.
Roll out on a lightly floured board to a neat rectangle, about 5mm (¼in) thick.
The narrowest end should be the diameter of the steaming basket.

2 Spread the jam right up to the edges then roll up from the narrow end. Place join
side down on a large sheet of baking paper and roll up, allowing room for expansion,
folding the paper over to enclose. Overwrap in foil, scrunching the ends together for a
watertight seal.

3 Steam in a metal basket, join side up, in a pan of simmering water for about 1 hour
30 minutes, checking the water level 2–3 times. Let stand for 5 minutes before
unwrapping carefully and serve in slices with Real custard (see page 19) or more
jam, thinned with a little boiling water.

## VARIATION

### Mincemeat roly poly
Make the suet crust as above using stout or ale instead of water and spread with
home-made Mincemeat (see page 143) or use 1 x 425g (15oz) jar mincemeat and
1 coarsely grated apple. Sprinkle with some cinnamon, roll up and cook as above.

**Note** You can also bake a roly poly wrapped in foil and placed in a roasting tin at
180°C (350°F, Gas Mark 4) for about 30 minutes until firm and golden.

## 235 Richmond maids of honour

**MAKES** about 18 tartlets   **PREPARATION TIME** 25 minutes plus resting   **COOKING TIME** 20 minutes

1 recipe quantity Rough puff pastry
 (see page 18) or 375g (13oz) pack
 ready-rolled puff pastry

**FILLING**
75g (3oz) butter, softened
100g (3½oz) curd cheese
1 egg plus 1 egg yolk

50g (2oz, ½ cup plus 1 tbsp) ground almonds
2 tbsp caster sugar
1 tbsp rum or brandy
50g (2oz, ⅓ cup) currants
40g (1½oz, ¼ cup) chopped mixed peel
sifted icing sugar, to dust

1   Roll the pastry out thinly, to about 3mm (¼in) thick. Cut out 18 x 8cm (3¼in)
   rounds. Press these into bun tins (or you may have to do these in batches).
   Leave them to stand while you preheat the oven to 200°C (400°F, Gas Mark 6)
   and make the filling.

2   Beat together the butter, cheese, egg and yolk, almonds, sugar and rum until the
   mixture is smooth and creamy. Stir in the currants and peel and divide the mixture
   between the pastry cases.

3   Bake for 15–20 minutes until golden and firm. Cool for 5 minutes in the tins before
   turning out onto a wire rack. Dust with a little icing sugar to serve.

## 236 Lemon canary pudding

**SERVES** 4–6   **PREPARATION TIME** 15 minutes   **COOKING TIME** 1 hour 30 minutes

125g (4oz) butter, softened, or soft margarine,
 plus extra for greasing
125g (4oz, ½ cup plus 2 tbsp) caster sugar,
 ideally golden unrefined
grated zest and juice of 1 lemon

2 eggs
125g (4oz, ¾ cup) self-raising flour
a little milk, if necessary
1–2 tbsp syrup or clear honey (optional)

1   Thoroughly grease a 1 litre (1¾ pint, 4 cup) pudding basin. Place a small round
   disc of baking paper in the base to ensure the pudding will turn out easily.

2   Beat together the butter, sugar, lemon zest and juice, eggs and flour until smooth
   and creamy. Add a spoonful or two of milk if necessary for a soft dropping
   consistency. Spoon syrup or honey into the basin if you want a glossy top then
   spoon the mixture on top.

3   Tear off a sheet each of baking paper and foil the same size and fold together in
   a pleat in the centre to allow for expansion during cooking.

4   Mould over the basin top and secure with string or a large elastic band. Place
   in a steamer basket inside a large pan with enough water to come half-way up
   the basin. Cover, bring to a good boil for 5 minutes, then reduce the heat to a
   simmer for 1 hour 30 minutes, checking the water level every 20–30 minutes and
   topping up with boiling water.

5   Remove carefully, let stand for 5 minutes before turning out onto a plate.
   Serve with Real custard (see page 19).

## 237 Spotted dick with lemon syrup sauce

**SERVES** 4–6  **PREPARATION TIME** 20 minutes  **COOKING TIME** 2 hours

75g (3oz, ½ cup) self-raising flour
75g (3oz, 1¼ cups) fresh white breadcrumbs
75g (3oz, ½ cup) shredded suet
50g (2oz, ¼ cup) caster sugar
grated zest of 1 lemon
100g (3½oz, ⅔ cup) currants or raisins

about 6 tbsp milk

**SAUCE**
4 tbsp golden syrup
juice of ½ lemon

1  Mix together all the dry ingredients in a large bowl then bind to a moist dough with milk. Knead lightly and shape to a roll about 7.5cm (3in) diameter on a sheet of baking paper. Roll up loosely to allow for expansion then overwrap in foil, scrunching the joins to seal.

2  Place in a steamer basket over boiling water, cover and boil for 5 minutes, then reduce the heat and cook for 2 hours, checking the water level and topping up with boiling water about 3 times.

3  Let stand for 5 minutes before carefully unwrapping. Slice to serve.

4  For the sauce, simply heat the syrup and lemon juice with 2–3 tbsp water, then pour over the slices of pudding.

## 238 Sussex pond pudding

**SERVES** 6  **PREPARATION TIME** 25 minutes plus boiling the lemon  **COOKING TIME** 2 hours

1 large thin-skinned lemon
250g (9oz, 1⅔ cups) self-raising flour
125g (4½oz, 1 cup) shredded suet
175ml (6fl oz, ¾ cup) milk

3 tbsp golden syrup
125g (4oz) butter
125g (4oz, ⅔ cup) demerara sugar
½ tsp ground ginger or cinnamon

1  Place the lemon in a pan with enough water to cover and simmer for 40 minutes until soft. Drain and cool.

2  Mix together the flour and suet to a dough with the milk. Lightly grease a 1 litre (1¾ pint, 4 cup) pudding basin. Roll out the dough to form a round large enough to line the inside of the basin. Cut out a quarter of the dough, reshape into a ball and set aside.

3  Spoon the syrup into the base of the basin. Mould the three-quarters cut round into a cone shape and press inside the basin to fit neatly. Chop the lemon roughly and place inside the basin. Chop up the butter and mix the sugar with the ginger. Tip both on top of the lemon.

4  Roll out the reserved ball of dough to fit the top of the basin, lightly dampen the edges and press to seal. Tear off a sheet each of baking paper and foil the same size and fold together with a pleat in the centre to allow for expansion during cooking. Mould over the pudding and tie round the rim with kitchen string or secure with a large elastic band.

5  Steam on a steamer basket in a large pan with enough water to come halfway up the sides for 2 hours, checking the water level occasionally and topping up with boiling water as required.

**VARIATION**

Substitute 150g (5oz, 1 cup) raisins or mixed dried fruit for the boiled lemon and mix with the chopped butter, sugar and spice.

## 239 Christmas pudding

**PREPARATION TIME** 25 minutes plus 4 hours soaking   **COOKING TIME** 3 hours for large pudding or 2 hours for small

175g (6oz, 1¼ cups) raisins
175g (6oz, 1¼ cups) sultanas
75g (3oz, ½ cup) dried cranberries
10 stoned prunes, chopped
1 sharp dessert apple, quartered, cored
  then coarsely grated
3 tbsp dark rum or brandy
75g (3oz, ½ cup) dark soft brown sugar
100g (3½oz, 2 cups) fresh white
  breadcrumbs

100g (3½oz, ¾ cup) shredded suet
3 tbsp flour
1 tsp each ground cinnamon, ginger and
  all-spice
½ whole nutmeg, finely grated
2 large eggs
1 tbsp marmalade
2 tbsp black treacle or molasses, warmed
6 tbsp milk or brown ale

1. Put the dried fruits, grated apple and rum into a pan. Heat until sizzling, stirring, then remove and let stand for about 4 hours (or overnight).
2. The following day, tip into a large mixing bowl and add the sugar, breadcrumbs and suet. Sift together the flour and spices and mix in. Beat the eggs with the marmalade, treacle and milk and stir in. Get all the family to stir and make a wish.
3. Grease 1 x 1.25 litre (2 pint, 5 cup) or 2 x 750ml (15fl oz, 3 cup) pudding basins and line the base with a small round of baking paper. Spoon in the mix and flatten on top. Tear off a sheet each of baking paper and foil the same size and fold together in a pleat in the centre to allow for expansion during cooking. Shape over the basin and tie with kitchen string or secure with a large rubber band.
4. Steam or boil for a good 3 hours for the larger pudding, or 2 hours for the smaller ones in a large covered pan with enough water to come half way up the sides. Check the water level 2–3 times and top up with more boiling water as necessary. Cool the pudding out of the pan and store, covered, until Christmas Day.
5. Reboil as before for 1 hour. Serve with Brandy or Rum butter (see page 206) and either cream or Real custard (see page 19).

## 240 Banoffee pie

**SERVES** 6   **PREPARATION TIME** 20 minutes plus boiling   **COOKING TIME** 2 hours

1 x 397g (14oz) can condensed milk or
  1 x 450g (1lb) jar Dulce de Leche
250g (9oz) digestive biscuits
125g (4oz) butter

2 large ripe bananas
250ml (9fl oz, 1 cup) double cream
a little grated chocolate, or 1 chocolate
  flake, crushed

1. If using condensed milk, place the unopened can in a large pan of boiling water and boil steadily for 2 hours, checking and topping up the water as necessary, to ensure the can is covered at all times. Cool before opening.
2. Crush the biscuits in a food processor to fine crumbs. Melt the butter and mix with the crumbs. Press into the base of a 22–23cm (8½–9in) flan tin and up the sides then chill until firm.
3. Slice the bananas over the base then spread with the caramelized milk. Whip the cream to soft peaks and dollop on top. Sprinkle with the grated or crushed chocolate and serve lightly chilled.

**Note** It is a good idea to boil 3 cans of condensed milk at the same time. The milk turns into a rich caramel and keeps for many months, unopened, for other pies.

## 241 Sticky toffee and date pudding

**SERVES** 6–8  **PREPARATION TIME** 30 minutes plus soaking  **COOKING TIME** 2 hours plus resting

**TOPPING**
100g (3½oz, ¾ cup) unrefined light
    muscovado sugar
50g (2oz) butter, softened
50g (2oz, ½ cup) walnut halves, roughly
    chopped, optional

**PUDDING**
150g (5½oz, 1 cup) chopped dates
1 Bramley apple, cored and peeled

zest and juice of 1 lemon
125g (4oz) butter, softened
100g (3½oz, ½ cup) caster sugar
3 eggs
100g (3½oz, 1 cup) self-raising flour
¼ tsp fine sea salt
½ tsp baking powder
75g (3oz, 1½ cups) fresh white
    breadcrumbs

1   First, cover the dates in boiling water and soak for 15 minutes. Drain well and
    squeeze out the excess liquid. Set aside.
2   Lightly grease a 1 litre (1¾ pint, 4 cup) heatproof pudding basin and put a small
    round disc of greaseproof paper in the base. To make the topping, cream 50g (2oz)
    of the muscovado sugar and the butter until nicely blended, then spread it around
    the base and a third of the way up the sides of the basin. Scatter over the chopped
    nuts, if using. Coarsely grate the apple and mix with the lemon juice.
3   To make the pudding, cream together the remaining muscovado sugar with the
    butter, caster sugar, eggs, flour, salt, baking powder and lemon zest. Add the
    grated apple, dates and breadcrumbs and incorporate lightly.
4   Spoon into the pudding basin. Tear off a sheet each of baking paper and foil of the
    same size and fold together with a pleat in the centre. Mould over the basin and
    tie with kitchen string or secure with a large rubber band.
5   Steam over a pan of boiling water for 2 hours, checking the water level every
    30 minutes, topping up with boiling water as necessary.
6   Stand the pudding for 10 minutes, before running a table knife around the sides
    and shaking it out onto a warm plate. Serve with Toffee Sauce, below.

### Easy toffee sauce

250ml (9fl oz, 1 cup) double cream
175g (6oz, 1¼ cups) light muscovado sugar

4 tbsp liquid glucose
75g (3oz) unsalted butter

1   Put half the cream in a heavy-based pan with the rest of the ingredients and bring
    slowly to the boil, stirring frequently. When the sugar has dissolved and no longer
    feels gritty, increase the heat and boil to a light toffee colour, about 10 minutes,
    stirring once or twice so it doesn't burn on the base.
2   Immediately remove from the heat and cool, stirring occasionally to prevent a thick
    skin forming. When cool, beat in the remaining cream and serve.

## 242 Plum crumble

**PREPARATION TIME** 20 minutes **COOKING TIME** 30 minutes

500g (1lb 2oz) ripe plums, halved and stoned
grated zest and juice of 1 orange
5 tbsp soft brown or demerara sugar
½ tsp ground cinnamon or ginger

100g (3½oz, 1 cup) plain flour
50g (2oz) butter
25g (1oz, ¼ cup) chopped walnuts
or hazelnuts

1   Place the fruit in a pan with the orange juice, 3 tbsp sugar and spice. Simmer for
10–15 minutes until the fruit is soft but not mushy. Cool, and check for any wayward
stones. Strain off the juice back into the pan. Tip the fruit into a medium pie dish.
Boil the juice down by half and pour back over the plums.

2   Preheat the oven to 180°C (350°F, Gas Mark 4). Rub together the flour and butter to
fine crumbs. Mix in the remaining sugar, the nuts and orange zest. Sprinkle over the
plums and bake for about 20 minutes until lightly brown. Cool for 10 minutes before
serving with Real custard (see page 19) or pouring cream.

## 243 Gypsy tart

SERVES 6   PREPARATION TIME 25 minutes plus resting   COOKING TIME 35–40 minutes

1 recipe quantity Sweet dessert pastry
  (see page 18)
175g (6oz, 1¼ cups) light muscovado sugar

1 x 170ml (6fl oz) can evaporated milk
'hundreds and thousands' sugar dragees
  (optional)

1   Lightly knead the pastry, then roll out to fit a loose-bottomed 20cm (8in) tart tin. Trim the edges level with the top of the tin, then press up the pastry a little around the sides. Prick the base a few times and chill while you make the filling and preheat the oven to 200°C (400°F, Gas Mark 6).
2   Fill the tin with baking paper and baking beans and bake blind on a metal baking sheet for 20 minutes. Remove the paper and beans after 15 minutes. Reduce the oven to 180°C (350°F, Gas Mark 4).
3   Meanwhile, use an electric whisk to beat together the sugar and evaporated milk for a good 10 minutes until it forms a thick, toffee-coloured foam. Pour into the pastry case and return to the oven for 15–20 minutes until lightly set. Remove, sprinkle with the dragees, if using, and cool.

## 244 Chocolate and raspberry roulade

SERVES 6   PREPARATION TIME 30 minutes   COOKING TIME 12 minutes

200g (7oz) dark chocolate, at least 60%
  cocoa solids
4 tbsp strong coffee or espresso
4 large eggs
125g (4oz, ½ cup plus 2 tbsp) caster sugar,
  plus extra for the filling

250ml (9fl oz, 1 cup) double cream
250g (9oz) fresh raspberries
1 tbsp sifted icing sugar, to dust

1   Preheat the oven to 200°C (400°F, Gas Mark 6). Lightly grease a Swiss roll tin approximately 23 x 33cm (9 x 13in) and line completely with a large sheet of baking paper, snipped at the corners to fit.
2   Break up the chocolate into a heatproof bowl and add the coffee. Melt over a pan of gently simmering water or place in the microwave on medium for about 2 minutes, stirring once or twice. Remove and cool.
3   Put the eggs into a large heatproof bowl and whisk over a large pan of simmering water for about 7 minutes until they form a thick pale-golden foam that holds its shape when you trail some foam over itself. Remove from the heat and allow to cool for 5 minutes, then whisk again.
4   Fold in the melted chocolate and scoop into the prepared tin, spreading to level. Bake for about 12 minutes until the top forms a thin crust and feels lightly firm when gently pressed.
5   Remove, cool and turn out onto another sheet of baking paper, then peel off the paper and trim the crusty edges. Wrap up in the paper into a loose roll and leave until completely cool.
6   Whip the cream until holding soft peaks and beat in the sugar. Lightly crush the raspberries, reserving a few to serve. Fold the crushed fruits lightly into the cream for a rippled effect.
7   Unwrap the roulade, and don't worry if it cracks a little but leave it on the paper.
8   Spread over the raspberry cream and re-roll. It doesn't matter if it is not too neat. Tip onto an oval serving plate and chill until ready to serve. Sift liberally with the icing sugar and scatter the reserved berries on top. Cut in thick oozy slices.

## 245 Bread and butter pudding

**SERVES** 6   **PREPARATION TIME** 20 minutes plus soaking   **COOKING TIME** 35 minutes plus cooling

150g (5oz, 1 cup) raisins, or mixed dried fruit
  or dried cranberries
1 small artisan baker's style white loaf,
  thinly sliced
50g (2oz) butter, softened
4 tbsp demerara sugar

**CUSTARD**
2 eggs plus 2 egg yolks
250ml (9fl oz, 1 cup) double cream
400ml (14fl oz, 1¾ cup) milk
3–4 tbsp caster sugar
few drops almond or vanilla extract

1   Put the dried fruits in a small bowl and cover with hot water. Soak for 10 minutes until they plump up, then drain.
2   Cut the crusts thinly from the bread, spread the slices thinly with butter and cut diagonally in half. Stack in slightly angled layers in a large lightly buttered ovenproof dish, scattering the soaked fruits in between.
3   Beat together the eggs, yolks, cream, milk, sugar (to taste) and extract. Slowly pour the custard over the bread, pressing the slices into the liquid so they are well soaked. Set aside for a good hour to allow the custard to be absorbed.
4   Sprinkle lightly with demerara sugar and preheat the oven to 180°C (350°F, Gas Mark 4). Place the dish in a roasting pan and pour in boiling water to come half way up the sides of the dish.
5   Bake for about 35 minutes until the top is light golden brown and crisp. Cool for 10–15 minutes before serving. Serve with pouring cream or Irish Baileys icecream (or both) for the ultimate lily gilding.

## 246 Cherry and peach cobbler

**PREPARATION TIME** 20 minutes   **COOKING TIME** 25 minutes plus cooling

2 ripe peaches, halved and stoned
250g (9oz) fresh cherries, stoned
60g (2½oz) caster sugar
200g (7oz, 1½ cups) plain flour

50g (2oz) butter or margarine
about 100ml (3½fl oz, ⅓ cup) milk,
  plus extra to glaze

1   Preheat the oven to 190°C (375°F, Gas Mark 5). Slice the peaches into a heatproof pie dish and scatter in the stoned cherries and half the sugar.
2   Rub together the flour and butter to fine crumbs. Stir in the remaining sugar, then add enough milk to form a soft dough. Knead lightly and roll out a round about 1cm (½in) thick. Use a scone cutter to cut out as many 5cm (2in) rounds as possible, kneading and re-rolling as necessary.
3   Place these over the fruits in neat lines, brush with more milk to glaze and bake for 20–25 minutes or until risen and golden. Cool for 10 minutes before serving.

## 247 Hot jam or marmalade omelette

**SERVES** 2   **PREPARATION TIME** 2 minutes   **COOKING TIME** 10 minutes

3 eggs
1 tbsp caster sugar
good knob of butter plus a little vegetable oil

2 tbsp jam or thin-cut marmalade
sifted icing sugar, to dust

1   Beat the eggs with 2 tbsp cold water and the sugar.
2   Heat the butter and a little oil in a large non-stick frying pan over a medium heat. Pour in the eggs and cook the egg, drawing it in from the sides and tilting the pan so that the uncooked egg slips underneath.
3   When most of the egg is set, lightly spread in the jam or marmalade with the back of a spoon and roll the omelette away from you, holding the pan over a large plate. Slide the omelette out of the pan and cut it in two. Serve on warm dessert plates dusted with a little icing sugar.

## 248 Alice's baked rice pudding

**PREPARATION TIME** 5 minutes  **COOKING TIME** 1 hour

100g (4oz, ⅔ cup) pudding rice
1 litre (1¾ pints, 4 cups) full cream
   or Jersey milk
2 tbsp soft brown or granulated sugar

1 bay leaf (optional)
good knob of butter or 1 heaped tbsp
   shredded suet
freshly grated nutmeg

1  Preheat the oven to 160°C (325°F, Gas Mark 3). Put the rice, milk and sugar into
a pan, bring to the boil, stirring, then pour into a medium pudding dish.

2  Add the bay leaf, if using, stir in the butter or suet and sprinkle with nutmeg.
Place the dish in a shallow roasting tin and bake for 1 hour, stirring twice. Stand for
30 minutes before serving.

### VARIATIONS

For a fragrant rice, use Thai jasmine. For a creamy rice, try Arborio risotto rice.
Add a variety of whole spices (cinnamon stick, lemon grass stem, a few whole
cloves or 1 star anise) to vary the flavours.

## 249 Athol brose

**PREPARATION TIME** 10 minutes plus resting   **COOKING TIME** nil

50g (2oz, ½ cup) oatmeal or porridge oats
1 tbsp clear honey, ideally Scottish
   heather honey
4 tbsp whisky

250ml (9fl oz, 1 cup) double cream
fresh raspberries (optional)
Shortbread/petticoat tails (see page 191),
   to serve

1   Mix the oatmeal with 120ml (4fl oz, ½ cup) cold water and let stand for 1 hour. Strain
    the liquid into a jug, pressing down well in the sieve. Discard the oats.
2   Mix the honey and whisky into the liquid. Whip the cream until forming firm, but not
    stiff, soft peaks and gradually whisk in the strained oaty liquid.
3   Divide the raspberries, if using, between 4 tumblers and spoon over the cream. Chill
    and serve with shortbread.

## 250 Cranachan

**PREPARATION TIME** 15 minutes   **COOKING TIME** 5 minutes

100g (3½oz, 1 cup) porridge oats
75g (3oz, ½ cup) soft brown sugar
250ml (9fl oz, 1 cup) double cream
3 tbsp whisky

150–200g (5–7oz) fresh raspberries,
   or frozen and thawed
4–8 tsp clear honey, ideally Scottish
   heather honey

1   Preheat a grill to medium. Lay a sheet of foil on the grill pan and scatter over the oats
    and sugar, roughly mixed together. Heat for about 5 minutes until they brown, stirring
    once or twice. Watch carefully so that they don't burn. Remove and cool.
2   Whisk the cream until it forms firm but soft peaks and mix in the whisky. Gently
    fold in most of the sugary oatmeal and raspberries. Divide between 4 tumblers
    and scatter over the remaining oatmeal and berries. Chill until ready to serve and
    trickle with the honey.

## 251 Raisin and rosewater flummery

**SERVES** 6   **PREPARATION TIME** 20 minutes plus soaking   **COOKING TIME** 30 minutes

75g (3oz, ½ cup) pinhead oatmeal
800ml (1⅓ pints, 3⅓ cups) milk
3 strips of lemon zest
75g (3oz, ½ cup) raisins
a little demerara sugar or honey

about 1 tbsp triple-strength rosewater
150ml (5fl oz, ⅔ cup) double cream
3 tsp (1 sachet) gelatine crystals softened in
   2 tbsp water

1   Cover the raisins in boiling water and soak for 1 hour, then drain and cool. Stir in
    the lemon zest, sugar or honey to taste.
2   Meanwhile, simmer the oatmeal in the milk for about 30 minutes until thick and
    creamy, stirring often so that it doesn't stick and burn.
3   When the oatmeal resembles a light porridge remove and cool, stirring frequently
    until cold, then mix in the raisins and rosewater to taste.
4   Dissolve the soaked gelatine in the microwave for 30 seconds or in a small pan
    of simmering water. Mix a little oatmeal into the dissolved gelatine then stir it back
    into the oatmeal. Chill until lightly set.
5   Whisk the cream until it forms soft, floppy peaks and fold into the setting mixture.
    Spoon into tumblers and serve lightly chilled. You could top it with some toasted
    porridge oats, if liked (see recipe 250 above).

## 252 Vanilla and lemon junket

**PREPARATION TIME** 5 minutes   **COOKING TIME** 3 minutes

500ml (18fl oz, 2 cups) rich whole milk,
e.g. Jersey or Channel Islands milk
about 1 tbsp caster sugar, plus extra to
sprinkle, if liked

2 drops of vanilla extract
2 strips of lemon zest
1 tsp liquid rennet

1   Heat the milk very gently until it is blood temperature (37°C, 98°F) – it will feel neither warm nor cold. Stir in sugar to taste, the extract and lemon zest.
2   Pour into a pretty glass bowl placed where it will be undisturbed. Mix in the rennet and leave until ready to serve. Within an hour the milk will have set lightly. Sprinkle lightly with extra sugar and serve.


## 253 Apple charlotte

**PREPARATION TIME** 25 minutes   **COOKING TIME** 45 minutes

2 Bramley apples, each about 250g (9oz),
peeled, cored and chopped
50g (2oz, 1/4 cup) caster sugar plus 1 tbsp
extra to coat

2 tbsp light orange or grapefruit marmalade
125g (4oz) butter
8–9 slices of white sliced bread,
crusts removed

1   Simmer the apples gently with a splash of water and the sugar for about 15 minutes until soft and pulpy. Remove, mix in the marmalade and cool.
2   Soften a fifth of the butter in a microwave for a few seconds then mix with 1 heaped tbsp of sugar. Spread the mixture around the base and sides of a small 1 litre (1³/₄ pint, 4 cup) soufflé dish or other small dish with straight sides.
3   Melt the remaining butter and pour into the dish. Cut 2 slices of bread in rounds to fit the base and top of the dish and cut the remainder into half slices like thick fingers. Dip the bread quickly in the butter to coat and press 1 round on the base and surround the fingers around the sides.
4   Spoon the apple in the centre and finally dip the last round bread in the butter. Place on top of the apple, pressing down lightly. Preheat the oven to 190°C (375°F, Gas Mark 5).
5   Stand the pudding in a small roasting tin and bake for 25–30 minutes until crisp and golden. Let stand for 5 minutes then run a table knife around the outside and upturn on a plate to serve.


## 254 Queen of puddings

**SERVES** 4–6   **PREPARATION TIME** 20 minutes plus standing   **COOKING TIME** 50–55 minutes plus cooling

knob of soft butter
150g (5oz, 2½ cups) fresh white breadcrumbs
500ml (18fl oz, 2 cups) creamy milk
75g (3oz, 1/3 cup) caster sugar

½ tsp vanilla extract or grated zest
of 1 lemon
3 large eggs, separated
2 tbsp raspberry, blackcurrant or plum jam

1   Preheat the oven to 180°C (350°F, Gas Mark 4). Grease a medium pie dish with the butter. Tip the breadcrumbs into a large bowl.
2   Scald the milk until almost boiling, then stir in half the sugar, the extract or zest. Mix into the breadcrumbs. Beat the yolks and stir into the mixture, then spoon it into the pie dish. Place the pie dish in a roasting pan and pour in enough boiling water to reach halfway up the sides of the dish. Bake for 30 minutes until the mixture sets.
3   Remove the pie dish from the pan and cool for 10 minutes then spread with the jam.
4   Whisk the egg whites to firm peaks and gradually whisk in the remaining sugar. Pile the meringue on top of the jam layer and return to the oven for a further 15–20 minutes until the meringue browns and is crisp on the outside. Cool for 20 minutes before serving with pouring cream.

# 255 Summer pudding

**PREPARATION TIME** 30 minutes plus chilling  **COOKING TIME** 5 minutes

1kg (2lb 4oz) mixture of fresh soft summer fruits (strawberries, raspberries, stoned and chopped cherries, blackcurrants, redcurrants, gooseberries, etc)
100–150g (3½–5oz, ½–¾ cup) caster sugar

2 passion fruits (optional) or 2 tbsp crème de cassis (optional)
1 small sliced white loaf, crusts removed (you need about 10 slices)

1   Prepare the fruits. Hull the strawberries and halve or slice if large. Put into a large pan with a choice of the other fruits and the lesser amount of sugar. Bring slowly to the boil so that the juices begin to run, then simmer gently for 3–5 minutes. Taste for sweetness, adding extra sugar if required.

2   If using passion fruits, scoop the pulp into the pan (rub them through a sieve to remove pips if you wish, although the mixture is already quite pippy). Or mix in the cassis. Cool the fruits and strain off excess juice into a jug.

3   Line the base of a 1 litre (1¾ pint, 4 cup) pudding basin with a small disc of baking paper. Cut out a round of bread to fit the base and press in. Cut out another larger round for the top of the basin (or 2 half moons) and set aside. Square up the remaining bread slices, and cut each one in half, slightly on a diagonal, to form trapeziums. Then fit inside the basin alternating the wide and narrow ends so that they fit neatly together with no gaps.

4   Spoon in the fruits, pressing down lightly. Dip the top round quickly in the reserved juices and press on top. Cover with a round of baking paper then a small plate that fits exactly inside, if possible. Place in the fridge with a large can on top to weigh down the pudding. Chill for 24 hours.

5   Turn out and brush or spoon the reserved juice over any unstained pieces of bread. Serve with lightly whipped cream, half-fat crème fraîche or natural yogurt.

## 256 Lemon posset

**PREPARATION TIME** 15 minutes   **COOKING TIME** nil

250ml (9fl oz, 1 cup) double cream
75–100g (3–3½oz, ⅓–½ cup) caster sugar
grated zest and juice of 1 large
    unwaxed lemon

4 tbsp medium dry sherry
4 Brandy snaps (see page 193)

1   Whisk the cream with the smaller amount of sugar and the lemon zest until it forms
    floppy peaks. Add the juice and whisk slowly until the cream thickens more.
2   Fold in the sherry and taste to see whether it needs extra sugar. Spoon into 4 small
    wine glasses and chill until ready to serve. Stick a brandy snap into each glass just
    before serving.


## 257 Poor knights of Windsor

**PREPARATION TIME** 2 minutes   **COOKING TIME** 15–20 minutes

4 thick slices of white bread, crusts removed
2 large eggs
3 tbsp creamy milk or single cream
2 tbsp medium dry sherry or sweet wine

good knob of butter plus 1 tbsp vegetable oil
2 tbsp caster sugar mixed with 1 tsp ground
    cinnamon, to dust
plum or raspberry jam, to serve

1   Cut each slice of bread into three. Beat together the eggs, milk and sherry.
2   Heat the butter and oil in a large frying pan and, as it heats, quickly dip the bread
    into the eggy mixture on both sides then put straight into the pan. Cook for 2 minutes
    or so on each side until golden brown. Remove, reheat the pan with more butter
    and oil and dip and fry the remaining bread slices.
3   Dust the slices with the cinnamon sugar and spoon jam on top.


## 258 Wet Nelly (Liverpool bread pudding)

**MAKES** 20 squares   **PREPARATION TIME** 15 minutes   **COOKING TIME** 35 minutes

300g (10½oz) slightly stale white loaf
100g (3½oz, ⅔ cup) raisins
100g (3½oz, ⅔ cup) sultanas
75g (3oz, ½ cup) shredded suet
75g (3oz, ½ cup) soft brown sugar

1 tsp mixed spice or cinnamon
2 large eggs
200ml (7fl oz, ¾ cup) milk
2 tbsp warmed black treacle or molasses

1   Break up the bread (including crusts) and blitz in a food processor to make coarse
    breadcrumbs. Tip into a bowl and mix in the dried fruits, suet, sugar and spice.
2   Beat together the eggs, milk and treacle and pour over the dry ingredients, mixing
    well. Let stand while you preheat the oven to 180°C (350°F, Gas Mark 4) and grease
    and line the base of a small roasting pan with baking paper.
3   Scoop in the mixture, spread to level and bake for 30–35 minutes or until the centre
    feels firm and springy. Remove, cool for 10 minutes, then turn out onto a wire rack to
    cool completely. Cut into about 20 squares.

## 259 Gooseberry fool

**PREPARATION TIME** 20 minutes    **COOKING TIME** 10 minutes

500g (1lb 2oz) fresh ripe gooseberries,
   topped and tailed
about 50g (2oz, ¼ cup) caster sugar
1 sprig of mint, plus a few small sprigs
   or leaves

½ recipe quantity cold Real custard
   (see page 19)
150ml (5fl oz, ⅔ cup) double cream

1   Rinse the gooseberries, drain and tip into a pan with the sugar. Stew gently for about 10 minutes until pulpy and cooked. Cool, and drain off some of the juice if it is very liquid. Mash the fruit, but don't purée. Steep a sprig of mint in the fruit as it cools, then remove and chill.
2   Prepare and cool the custard. When cold stir roughly into the fruit. Whip the cream until it forms firm but soft peaks and fold in the gooseberry custard. Spoon into glass dishes and decorate with mint leaves, if liked.

**VARIATIONS**

### Blackcurrant fool
Stew 250g (9oz) fresh blackcurrants in a little water with sugar and mint until soft and pulpy and follow the recipe above.

### Rhubarb fool
Chop, rinse and stew 400g (14oz) rhubarb and follow the recipe above. Omit the mint but add a strip or two of orange zest.

## 260 Boodles orange fool

**PREPARATION TIME** 15 minutes plus chilling    **COOKING TIME** nil

4 trifle sponges or 8 boudoir or Italian
   sponge fingers
3 oranges, grated zest of 2 and juice of 3

grated zest and juice of 1 lemon
50g (2oz, ¼ cup) caster sugar
250ml (9fl oz, 1 cup) double cream

1   Break up the sponges and divide between 4 wine glasses. Stir together the orange zest, juice and sugar until the sugar is dissolved.
2   Whip the cream until it just starts to thicken and gradually whisk in the sweet juice until the mixture becomes thickened.
3   Spoon over the sponges and chill for a good 3–4 hours. Serve as is, or topped with a few fresh orange segments.

## 261 Apple brown betty

**PREPARATION TIME** 30 minutes    **COOKING TIME** 30 minutes

150g (5oz) dates, stoned and chopped
75g (3oz) butter, softened
2 tbsp caster sugar, plus extra for the top

8 slices of white sliced bread, crusts removed
2 large dessert apples (Cox's or Granny
   Smith), peeled, cored and thinly sliced

1   Cover the dates in boiling water and soak for 30 minutes, then drain well.
2   Cream a third of the butter with the sugar and spread on the base and up the sides of a medium pie dish.
3   Spread the remaining butter on the bread. Now layer the apple with the dates and buttered bread, ending with a layer of bread, buttered side up. Sprinkle the top with a little extra sugar.
4   Preheat the oven to 190°C (375°F, Gas Mark 5). Stand the pie dish in a roasting pan and bake for 25–30 minutes until the top is golden brown and crisp. Let stand for 10 minutes then serve from the dish with Real custard (see page 19) or pouring cream.

# 262 Old English strawberry trifle

**SERVES** 6  **PREPARATION TIME** 30 minutes  **COOKING TIME** for custard (see page 19)

1 homemade Swiss roll (see page 177), or
  8 trifle sponges
strawberry jam, to spread (optional)
5 tbsp medium dry sherry or raspberry and
  orange juice
400g (14oz) fresh strawberries, hulled

small handful of ratafia or amaretti biscuits
1 recipe quantity thickened Real custard
  (see page 19)
250ml (9fl oz, 1 cup) double cream
3–4 tbsp chopped unsalted pistachios or
  almond flakes

1   Slice the Swiss roll, if using, and arrange around the sides of a pretty glass bowl
    with one round on the base, or use individual bowls if you have them. If using trifle
    sponges, split in half, spread with jam and arrange in the bowl, jam side up.
2   Sprinkle over the sherry or juice. Set aside 6 even-sized perfect strawberries and slice
    the rest. Scatter over the cake or sponges. Save 6 ratafia biscuits and roughly crush
    the rest over the berries. Chill while you make the custard and cool, then spoon it
    over the ratafias and return to the fridge to chill again.
3   Whisk the cream to form soft peaks, but don't over-whip. The texture should be soft
    enough to dollop on top of the custard in little swirls. Sprinkle with the nuts and
    decorate with the reserved strawberries and ratafias.

**Note** If you like a jelly layer, heat 300ml (10fl oz, 1 1/4 cups) hot raspberry juice.
Soak 2 tsp gelatine crystals in 2 tbsp cold water, then stir into the hot liquid until
dissolved. Cool until setting and spoon over the sliced strawberries and chill until
set. Proceed with the rest of the recipe.

**VARIATION**

## Christmas sherry trifle
Follow the recipe for Strawberry Trifle above, substituting fresh seasonal fruits for
the strawberries (e.g. sliced apricots or plums) or use a 400g (14oz) can of fruits in
natural juices (e.g. peaches, apricots or pears) and some frozen raspberries.

## 263 Whim wham

**PREPARATION TIME** 10 minutes   **COOKING TIME** nil

8 boudoir or Italian sponge fingers
a little sweet white wine or German hock
6–8 tsp redcurrant jelly or seedless
   raspberry jam

250ml (9fl oz, 1 cup) double cream
toasted almond flakes, to sprinkle
candied angelica, cut into diamonds.
   to decorate

1  Break up the biscuits into 4 wine glasses. Trickle with enough wine to just moisten, about 2 tbsp each, then drizzle in the jelly or runny jam.

2  Whisk the cream until it forms soft floppy peaks and dollop on top. Sprinkle with flaked nuts and decorate with angelica spikes.

## 264 Aunt Polly (baked trifle)

**SERVES** 6–8   **PREPARATION TIME** 15 minutes   **COOKING TIME** 50 minutes

4 trifle sponges or about 150g (5oz) sponge
   or Victoria sandwich cake
1 x 400g (14oz) can apricots in natural
   juice, drained
1 vanilla pod or 1 tsp vanilla extract
500ml (18fl oz, 2 cups) single cream
   or creamy milk

2 large eggs
50g (2oz, ¼ cup) caster sugar
3 tbsp raspberry or apricot jam, warmed
250ml (9fl oz, 1 cup) whipping cream
toasted almond flakes, to decorate

1  Lightly butter or oil a medium heatproof glass baking dish and cover the base with the trifle sponges or cake, roughly sliced. Scatter over the drained apricots. Preheat the oven to 170°C (325°F, Gas Mark 3). Slit open the vanilla pod, if using, and scrape the sticky seeds with the tip of a sharp knife into the cream or milk with the pod. Heat slowly until on the point of boiling.

2  Meanwhile, beat the eggs and sugar in a heatproof bowl. Remove the vanilla pod and slowly whisk the hot cream onto the eggs. Strain this over the cake and apricots, pressing the cake down, and place the dish in a deep-sided roasting pan and pour enough boiling water around the sides to come halfway up the dish.

3  Bake for 40–45 minutes until the custard-soaked sponge sets lightly. Remove the dish from the oven and pan. Allow to cool.

4  Spread the top with jam and chill thoroughly. When ready to serve, whisk the cream until it forms soft peaks and dollop on top of the custard cake and decorate with the toasted almond flakes.

## 265 Cambridge burnt cream

**SERVES** 6   **PREPARATION TIME** 10 minutes   **COOKING TIME** 15 minutes

1 vanilla pod
500ml (18fl oz, 2 cups) whipping cream (or
   half single and half double cream)

125g (4oz, ½ cup plus 2 tbsp) caster sugar
4 egg yolks

1  Split the vanilla pod lengthways and scrape out the sticky seeds with the tip of a sharp knife. Heat the cream in a non-stick pan, add the seeds and pod, then heat gently until almost boiling. Remove the pan from the heat and discard the pod. Preheat the oven to 170°C (325°F, Gas Mark 3).

2  Whisk together a quarter of the sugar and the egg yolks until thick and creamy, then whisk in the hot cream. Strain into 6 ramekins or small ovenproof glass dishes and place in a shallow roasting pan.

3  Bake for 8–10 minutes until a skin forms on top. Remove, cool and chill overnight.

4  When ready to serve, heat a grill until glowing hot. Sprinkle the remaining sugar evenly on top of the ramekins and grill until the sugar dissolves and begins to caramelize. Alternatively, brown with a cook's blowtorch.

## 266  Hot fruity fritters

**PREPARATION TIME** 10 minutes  **COOKING TIME** 10 minutes

1 x  400g (14oz) can pineapple rings, drained,
    or 2 dessert apples, cored and thickly
    sliced, or 2 large just-ripe bananas,
    halved and split

**BATTER**
100g (3½oz, 1 cup) plain flour
1 tbsp caster sugar
2 eggs
2 tbsp creamy milk
vegetable oil, for frying
caster or sifted icing sugar, to dust

1  Prepare the fruits, patting dry if necessary.
2  Beat together the flour, sugar, eggs and milk in a bowl using a whisk to form
   a thick smooth batter.
3  Heat a deep frying pan a third full of oil to 170°C (325°F). Dip the prepared fruits,
   working in batches, first in the batter, coating evenly; then lower carefully into the
   hot oil, ideally with a frying basket.
4  Fry for 2–3 minutes until crisp and golden. Drain on kitchen paper. Repeat with
   remaining fruit, reheating the oil as necessary. Serve lightly dusted with sugar.

## 267  Hot rum bananas with cinnamon cream

**PREPARATION TIME** 5 minutes  **COOKING TIME** 10 minutes

4 large ripe bananas
about 25g (1oz) butter
2–3 tbsp demerara or soft brown sugar
2–3 tbsp white or dark rum
juice of 1 lime

150ml (5fl oz, ⅔ cup) double or
    whipping cream
a little caster sugar
2 good pinches of cinnamon or
    freshly grated nutmeg

1  Halve and split the bananas. Heat the butter in a large frying pan until melted
   and mix in the sugar.
2  Fry the bananas in the mixture for about 5 minutes, turning once or twice in the
   juices, then add the rum and bubble down for 1–2 minutes. (Or light with a match
   and flambé.) Mix in the lime juice and set aside to cool.
3  Whip the cream to form floppy peaks, adding sugar to taste and the spice. Serve
   with the warm bananas.

## 268  Baked apples with marmalade

**PREPARATION TIME** 15 minutes  **COOKING TIME** 40 minutes

4 large cooking apples (e.g. Bramleys), each
    about 250g (9oz)
4 tbsp light orange or grapefruit marmalade

2 tbsp demerara sugar
4 tbsp raisins
good knob of butter

1  Preheat the oven to 180°C (350°F, Gas Mark 4). Core the apples with an apple corer
   making the hole a good 2.5cm (1in) wide. Score around the circumference of each
   apple, cutting through the skin. Place in a baking dish.
2  Mix together the marmalade (snip the peel strips if they are too long), sugar, raisins
   and butter, then spoon into the cored holes. Bake for about 35–40 minutes until the
   apples become very tender when pierced. Do not stir or disturb, but turn the dish
   if they overbrown. Remove and let cool, then serve warm or chill. Good with Real
   custard (see page 19) or pouring cream.

# 269 Susie's simple milk chocolate mousse

**PREPARATION TIME** 5 minutes    **COOKING TIME** 2 minutes plus setting

150g (5½oz) good-quality milk chocolate,
  at least 30% cocoa solids
350ml (12fl oz, 1⅓ cups) double cream

freshly grated nutmeg or 2 tbsp brandy,
  rum or Cointreau
2 egg whites

1   Break up the chocolate into a heatproof bowl and pour in half the cream. Melt in the microwave on low, stirring until dissolved, or place over a pan of gently simmering water. Remove and cool to room temperature.

2   Whip the remaining cream until it forms floppy peaks and gently fold into the melted chocolate with the nutmeg or spirits. Whisk the egg whites until they form soft but firm peaks and fold in, using a large metal spoon. Scoop into four small teacups, wine glasses or a small bowl. Chill until set. For an extra treat, decorate with a few slivers of your favourite chocolate.

## 270 Port and claret jelly

**SERVES** 6   **PREPARATION TIME** 15 minutes   **COOKING TIME** 2 minutes

35cl (½ bottle) light red wine
200ml (7fl oz, ¾ cup) cranberry or
    raspberry juice
5 tbsp ruby port
2–3 tbsp caster sugar, or to taste
3 strips of orange or lemon zest

juice of 1 small orange or 1 lemon
1 sachet (3½ tsp) gelatine crystals
handful of fresh raspberries, or halved
    strawberries or canned cherries,
    stoned (optional)

1   Heat together the wine, juice, port, sugar to taste, zest strips and juice until on the
    point of boiling. Remove from the heat.
2   Meanwhile, soak the gelatine in a cup with 2 tbsp cold water and when solid,
    stir briskly into the hot liquid until dissolved. Pour into a small jelly mould, cool
    then chill until set.
3   If you wish to add fruits to the jelly, sprinkle these first into the base of a suitable
    mould, then just cover with cooled jelly mix. Chill until set and slowly pour on the
    remaining jelly and return to the fridge until firm. To serve, dip briefly in a bowl of
    hot water, pull the sides away with your fingers, then upend onto a wet plate,
    shaking sharply to demould.

## 271 Poached peaches with redcurrants

**PREPARATION TIME** 15 minutes   **COOKING TIME** 5 minutes

4 just-ripe peaches, ideally white ones
250g (9oz) fresh redcurrants (or half
    raspberries and half redcurrants)

50g (2oz, ¼ cup) caster sugar
1 split vanilla pod (optional)
3 tbsp white wine

1   Dip the peaches for about 20 seconds into a pan of boiling water, then remove to
    a large bowl of very cold water. Drain and score in half, then twist to separate the
    halves and remove the stones. Peel and halve each half. Place in a pretty glass bowl.
2   Strip the redcurrants from the stalks and place in a pan with the sugar, vanilla pod,
    if using, and about 120ml (4fl oz, ½ cup) water. Bring to the boil, then simmer for
    2 minutes. Mix in the wine and pour over the peaches, mixing well. Cool and chill.

## 272 Knickerbocker glory

**PREPARATION TIME** 25 minutes plus setting the jelly   **COOKING TIME** 2 minutes

1 packet (135g, 4½oz) red, orange, yellow
    or green jelly
150g (5oz) fresh over-ripe raspberries
1 x 500ml (18fl oz) tub luxury icecream
    (e.g. vanilla or strawberry)
2 ripe peaches, sliced, or 1 small can
    (200g, 7oz) mandarin oranges, drained

8 large fresh strawberries, sliced
handful of ratafia biscuits or amaretti or
    4 fan icecream wafers, roughly crushed
a little whipped cream
some chopped nuts

1   Make up the jelly according to the packet instructions and chill in a shallow bowl until
    set, then chop into small chunks. Purée the raspberries and rub through a sieve to
    remove the pips.
2   Take 4 knickerbocker glasses or tall tumblers and make layers of jelly, scoops of
    icecream, sliced fruits and crushed biscuits, trickling raspberry purée in between.
    Finish with a scoop of icecream and a dollop of whipped cream and chopped nuts.
    The taller and more colourful the better!

## 273 Lemon and ginger cheesecake

**MAKES** 1 x 20cm (8in flan)    **PREPARATION TIME** 25 minutes plus setting    **COOKING TIME** 3 minutes

200g (7oz) digestive biscuits
100g (3½oz) butter
1 tbsp golden syrup
zest and juice of 1 unwaxed lemon, washed
1 sachet (3½ tsp) gelatine crystals

200g (7oz, ¾ cup) cream cheese, softened
2 tbsp chopped stem or crystallized ginger
50g (2oz, ¼ cup) caster sugar
350g (12oz, 1¾ cups) half-fat crème fraîche
  or full-fat yogurt

1   Crush the biscuits in a food processor to fine crumbs. Melt the butter and syrup
    and mix into the crumbs. Line the base of a loose-bottomed 20cm (8in) flan tin
    with baking paper.
2   Tip in the crumbs and spread over the base and up the sides of the tin, patting firmly
    with the back of a spoon. Chill for about 1 hour.
3   Pour the lemon juice into a cup and sprinkle in the gelatine. Leave until it goes solid
    then dissolve either by placing the cup in a small pan of simmering water or in the
    microwave on low for 1–2 minutes. When it is clear, let cool for 5 minutes.
4   Beat together the cream cheese, ginger and sugar until smooth and creamy then
    mix in the crème fraîche or yogurt. Lastly, mix in the gelatine.
5   Scoop the mixture into the flan tin and chill for 2–3 hours until set. This is good
    topped with a choice of soft fruits, or sliced oranges or plums and chopped ginger.

## 274　Eton mess

**PREPARATION TIME** 5–10 minutes　**COOKING TIME** nil

250ml (9fl oz, 1 cup) double cream or
　1 x 500ml (18fl oz) tub luxury icecream,
　softened
3–4 ready-made meringue nests
250g (9oz) fresh strawberries, hulled and
　sliced or halved

125g (4oz) fresh slightly over-ripe raspberries
toasted almond flakes or roughly chopped
　unsalted pistachios (optional)

1　Whip the cream, if using, until it forms soft peaks. Alternatively, mash the icecream
　　to a slush. Crush in the meringues and stir gently to combine.
2　Fork through the strawberries and raspberries and divide between 4 glass dishes.
　　Sprinkle with the nuts, if liked.

## 275　Molly's light lemon soufflé

**PREPARATION TIME** 20 minutes　**COOKING TIME** 2 minutes

2 tsp gelatine crystals
3 large eggs, separated
150g (5oz, ¾ cup) caster sugar

grated zest of 1 lemon
100ml (3½fl oz, ⅓ cup) fresh lemon juice

1　Soak the gelatine in 2 tbsp cold water in a cup and when solid dissolve by standing
　　the cup in a small pan of gently simmering water or in the microwave on low for
　　1–2 minutes. Remove and cool.
2　Whisk the egg yolks and sugar in a large bowl over a pan of simmering water until the
　　mixture leaves a trail when you lift up the whisk, about 7 minutes. Remove from the
　　heat, add the lemon zest and juice and whisk for a further 3–5 minutes until cool.
3　Mix in a little lemon mixture with the gelatine, then tip back into the whole mixture
　　and stir in thoroughly.
4　Whisk the egg whites until they form soft but firm peaks and fold in. Scoop the
　　mixture into a small soufflé dish or pretty glass bowl. Chill until lightly set.

## 276　Anne's pinky pud

**SERVES** 4–6　**PREPARATION TIME** 10 minutes plus setting　**COOKING TIME** 2 minutes

1 packet (135g, 4½oz) raspberry or
　strawberry jelly
1 x 375ml (13fl oz) can evaporated
　milk, chilled

about 250g (9oz) fresh raspberries or
　strawberries, sliced

1　Dissolve and make up the jelly according to the packet instructions but use only
　　450ml (16fl oz, 1¾ cups) water to dissolve. Cool until on the point of setting. Tip
　　the fruits into a glass bowl.
2　Using electric beaters whisk the milk in a large bowl for a good 5–7 minutes until
　　you have a thick foam. Whisk in the cooled, almost set, jelly then scoop the mixture
　　on top of the fruit and chill until set. Perfect for children in the summer when soft
　　fruits are at their best.

## 277 Blackcurrant leaf or lemon geranium leaf water ice

**PREPARATION TIME** 5 minutes plus steeping and freezing   **COOKING TIME** 3 minutes

125g (4oz, ½ cup plus 2 tbsp) caster sugar
fresh young blackcurrant or lemon geranium
  leaves, enough to fill 3 cups, washed

grated zest and juice of 2 lemons

1   Dissolve the sugar in 500ml (18fl oz, 2 cups) boiling water, then simmer for 3 minutes and stir in the fragrant leaves, lemon zest and juice. Press well to bruise the leaves, then set aside to steep until cold.
2   Strain off the liquid, pressing down on the leaves to extract all the flavour, then churn in an icecream machine until slushy. Scoop into a plastic freezer container and freeze. Alternatively, pour into a shallow freezer container and open freeze, beating about 3 times as it freezes to break up the ice crystals. Serve in small dainty scoops as a palette cleanser.

## 278 Brown bread icecream

**SERVES** 4–6   **PREPARATION TIME** 20 minutes plus churning and freezing   **COOKING TIME** 15 minutes plus making the custard

100g (3½ oz, 2 cups) fresh wholemeal or
  brown breadcrumbs
3 tbsp caster sugar

1 recipe quantity Real custard (see page 19)
2 tbsp rum (optional)

1   Preheat the oven to 180°C (350°F, Gas Mark 4). Spread the breadcrumbs in a shallow roasting tin and sprinkle over the sugar. Heat until the crumbs are crisp and brown, stirring once or twice, about 10–15 minutes. Remove and cool completely.
2   Make up and cool the custard, then churn in an icecream maker with the rum until thick and slushy. Mix in the crumbs until just combined and scoop into a plastic container. Freeze for no longer than 1 hour and serve in scoops. Lovely with raspberries or crushed and lightly stewed red or blackcurrants.

## 279 Lavender honey icecream

**SERVES** 4–6   **PREPARATION TIME** 5 minutes plus cooling and freezing   **COOKING TIME** 15 minutes plus standing

250ml (9fl oz, 1 cup) double or
  whipping cream
1 tbsp dried lavender flowers
2½–3 tbsp caster sugar

1 large egg plus 2 egg yolks
1–2 tbsp clear honey

1   Heat the cream with the lavender in a non-stick pan and set aside for 30 minutes, then strain off the lavender and return the cream to reheat in the pan again.
2   Meanwhile, beat the sugar with the egg and yolks in a heatproof bowl. When the cream starts to bubble, whisk it gradually onto the yolks and sugar.
3   Strain back into the pan and cook on the lowest heat possible, stirring until the mixture starts to thicken, about 5 minutes.
4   Immediately pour back into the bowl and stir in the honey to taste. Cover with cling film and cool, then chill and churn in an icecream machine until thick and semi-frozen. Scoop into a shallow freezerproof container and freeze until just solid. Serve in scoops.

## 280 Raspberry ripple icecream

**PREPARATION TIME** 3 minutes    **COOKING TIME** nil

1 x 500ml (18fl oz) tub luxury vanilla
   icecream, softened
250g (9oz) fresh ripe raspberries

4 ginger nut or 3 digestive biscuits,
   roughly crushed
a little Drambuie liqueur, to serve (optional)

1   Scoop out the icecream into a bowl. Crush the raspberries with a fork until they
    become slightly juicy.
2   To get the pink rippled effect, fork the berries through the softened icecream along
    with the biscuits. Pour a tot of Drambuie, if liked, over each portion just before serving.

## 281 Pimms water ice

**PREPARATION TIME** 10 minutes plus steeping and freezing  **COOKING TIME** 5 minutes

200g (7oz, 1 cup) caster sugar
zest strips and juice of 1 large unwaxed lemon
¼ cucumber, roughly chopped
1 large sprig of mint or lemon balm

150ml (7fl oz, ⅔ cup) Pimms
sliced lemons, cucumber, sprigs of mint or
   lemon balm or borage flowers, to serve

1 Dissolve the sugar with 500ml (18fl oz, 2 cups) boiling water in a pan and simmer
for 5 minutes. Add the lemon strips, juice, cucumber and mint or lemon balm sprig.
Cool, then stir in the Pimms.
2 Strain into a shallow bowl, pressing down with the back of a ladle to extract the
flavour. Freeze in a shallow container, beating frequently with a fork until gritty and
almost frozen. Serve in scoops in small tumblers and decorate with sliced lemons,
cucumber, herb sprigs or borage flowers.

## 282 Lemon curd icecream

**SERVES** 4–6  **PREPARATION TIME** 10 minutes plus freezing  **COOKING TIME** nil

250ml (9fl oz, 1 cup) double cream
50g (2oz, ½ cup) icing sugar

200g (7oz, 5 tbsp) Lemon curd, ideally
   homemade (see page 205)
2 egg whites

1 Whisk the cream with the icing sugar until thick but still soft. Mix in the lemon curd.
2 Whisk the egg whites until stiff and fold into the mixture.
3 Scoop into a shallow freezer container, and freeze for about 3 hours. Serve in scoops
or slices. Nice with sliced strawberries or raspberries and blueberries.

## 283 Earl Grey tea icecream

**SERVES** 6  **PREPARATION TIME** 10 minutes plus cooling and freezing  **COOKING TIME** 7 minutes

20g (¾oz, 3 tbsp, 8 bags) Earl Grey tea
3 large eggs
100g (3½oz, ½ cup) caster sugar

squeeze of fresh lemon juice
250ml (9fl oz, 1 cup) double cream

1 Pour 500ml (18fl oz, 2 cups) boiling water onto the tea and leave to mash for
10 minutes. Strain the tea into a bowl and cool completely, then chill.
2 Whisk the eggs and sugar with the lemon juice in a large heatproof bowl over a
pan of gently simmering water until thick and creamy, about 7 minutes. Remove
and cool, whisking occasionally, until room temperature, then whisk in the cold tea.
3 Whip the cream to form soft floppy peaks and fold into the mixture. Freeze in a
shallow freezer container, whisking 2–3 times as it freezes. Serve in scoops before
it becomes too hard.

## 284 Coffee ice cream

**SERVES** 4–6  **PREPARATION TIME** 10 minutes plus cooling and freezing  **COOKING TIME** see custard (page 19)

1 recipe quantity Real custard (made with
   double cream, see page 19)
125ml (4fl oz, ½ cup) espresso-strength
   coffee

1–2 shots of rum or Tia Maria (optional)

1 Make up the custard and while it is cooling mix in the coffee and rum, if using. Chill
and then churn in an icecream machine until thick.
2 Scoop into a shallow freezer container and freeze until required. Thaw for 15 minutes
or so until soft enough to scoop.

# CHAPTER 6

# TEATIME TREATS

Afternoon tea, a quintessentially British affair made fashionable by the Duchess of Bedford two centuries ago, bridges the gap between lunch and dinner. If it faded from fashion at the end of the last century, it is now enjoying a revival in British high-class hotels, with tourists flocking to enjoy this great social occasion.

True afternoon tea means thinly sliced, dainty bread and butter sandwiches followed by a selection of cake slices – iced sponge fancies, rich fruit cake or light, creamy puffs piled high on a tiered china or silver stand. In times past there was a certain formality, for children could sit down to tea with adults but were permitted some cake only once they had eaten their buttered bread, spread with a little jam if they were lucky!

Unlike continental gâteaux, our cakes are homely and wholesome, rather than multi-layered and adorned. British cakes are easy to make and bake in the most humble kitchen and often last all week, and indeed improve on keeping. Taking tea is a tradition that thrives in many parts of the former British Empire, particularly those settled by Scottish and Irish farming immigrants.

## 285 Teatime sandwiches

**MAKES** 4 rounds  **PREPARATION TIME** 10 minutes  **COOKING TIME** nil

8 slices of fresh, baker's-quality bread
softened butter or other fat spread

sea salt and freshly ground black pepper

1   Spread each bread slice with the softened butter. Make up with the fillings of your
choice (see right). Season lightly and stack the 4 rounds on top of one another then
cut off the crusts using a serrated knife. Cut into triangles, quarters or 3 rectangular
fingers and serve immediately.

**FILLINGS  (enough to make 4 rounds)**

## Country house cucumber

½ large cucumber, peeled if liked                      sea salt and freshly ground white pepper
a few drops of white wine vinegar (optional)

1   Slice the cucumber as thinly as possible – a mandolin or Japanese food slicer helps.
    Layer in a colander, lightly sprinkling in between with salt. Leave to drain over the
    sink for 30 minutes, then rinse and pat dry on kitchen paper.
2   Season with pepper and sprinkle with a little vinegar, if liked.

## Egg and cress

3 large eggs, hard-boiled                      sea salt and freshly ground black or
   and peeled                                     white pepper
1 tbsp mayonnaise or salad cream
1 tub mustard and cress, snipped from
   tub, or 3 tbsp alfalfa sprouts

1   Chop the eggs finely (or use an egg slicer). Mix with the mayonnaise to bind, season
    and stir in the cress lightly to blend. Traditionally served in fingers.

## Tomato

4 vine-ripened tomatoes                      sea salt and freshly ground black pepper
a few snipped fresh chives (optional)

1   Dip the whole tomatoes briefly into boiling water, then peel off the skins. Remove
    the cores with the tip of a sharp knife and slice as thinly as possible onto a plate.
    Sprinkle lightly with salt and leave for 20 minutes, then drain off the juice and pat
    dry on kitchen paper.
2   Make up the sandwiches, sprinkling with chives and pepper.

## Smoked salmon and horseradish

2 tsp horseradish relish                      200g (7oz) thinly sliced smoked salmon
125ml (4fl oz, ½ cup) crème fraîche or        a little fresh lemon juice
   half-fat cream cheese                       freshly ground black pepper

1   Beat together the horseradish and crème fraîche. Spread on half the bread slices.
2   Top with the salmon, squeeze over a little lemon juice and sprinkle with pepper.
    Make up the sandwiches and serve.

## Coronation chicken

150g (5oz) cooked chicken breast,             1 tbsp mayonnaise
   chopped finely                             ½ tsp curry paste or powder
1 spring onion, finely chopped, or 2 tbsp     2 tsp chutney (mango, plum, tomato, etc.)
   snipped fresh chives                       sea salt and freshly ground black pepper

1   Simply combine everything together. Make up the sandwiches and serve.

## 286   Cheese and onion toasty

**MAKES** 1   **PREPARATION TIME** 3 minutes   **COOKING TIME** 5 minutes

2 thin slices of good country bread, ideally
   brown or crusty white
a little softened butter
50g (2oz) best-quality mature farmhouse
   Cheddar, Cheshire or Lancashire cheese,
   sliced or grated

½ mild onion, thinly sliced
freshly ground black pepper

1   Grill or griddle 1 side of both bread slices. Spread the untoasted sides lightly with
butter, and top 1 slice with cheese and onion, season with pepper and top with the
second slice. Alternatively, make up the sandwich before toasting, then griddle or grill.

### VARIATION

### Cheese and chutney toasty

Omit the onion and use 1–2 spoonfuls tomato or mango chutney, bought pickle or
Cranberry and port relish or Red onion marmalade (see pages 206 and 209).

## 287   Easy white bread

**MAKES** 1 medium loaf   **PREPARATION TIME** 20 minutes plus proving   **COOKING TIME** 25 minutes

500g (1lb 2oz, 3⅓ cups) strong white
   bread flour
1 tsp fine sea salt

large knob of butter or margarine
1 sachet fast-action or easy-blend yeast
a little vegetable oil, to grease

1   Tip the flour into a large bowl and mix in the salt. Rub in the butter until finely
blended, then stir in the yeast, mixing well.
2   Mix in 250ml (9fl oz, 1 cup) tepid water with a table knife, adding extra trickles if
the mixture seems a little dry. When it starts to clump together, mix to a ball then
tip out onto the worktop.
3   Shape the dough into a roll and knead it by holding down one end and pushing
the other backwards and forwards with the heel of your hand as if you were
scrubbing it. (This helps to work the gluten in the flour to give a good texture.)
Knead for 3–5 minutes, turning the ball as you work, until the dough no longer feels
sticky and is very smooth. Pop back into the bowl, cover with cling film and leave in a
warm spot until doubled in size. This could take 1–2 hours.
4   When risen and spongy, punch down the dough, tip it out and knead again for
1–2 minutes. Grease a 1kg (2lb) loaf tin lightly with oil. Shape the dough into a
roll the length of the tin, drop it in, cover loosely with cling film and leave to prove.
Meanwhile, preheat the oven to 200°C (400°F, Gas Mark 6).
5   When the dough almost reaches the top of the tin, bake for 25 minutes or until risen
and crusty on top. Check to see it is cooked by loosening from the tin with a knife,
tipping out and tapping the base. It should sound hollow – if not, return the loaf to
the oven for a further 5 minutes. Cool.

### VARIATION

### Cottage loaf

After the first rising, pull off one-third of the dough and shape into a ball. Shape
the remainder into a bigger ball. Place the smaller ball on top and press the two
together, wetting lightly at the join. Place on a greased baking tray and, using the
handle of a wooden spoon dipped in flour, press a hole right through the middle.
Leave to prove for 25–30 minutes until doubled in size, brush lightly with a little
milk and bake as above.

**Note** For a more traditional texture, you can use fresh yeast instead of a sachet
of easy yeast. Allow 15g (½oz) fresh yeast and crumble it into a little warm water,
stirring to blend. Leave for about 15–20 minutes to froth. Then mix into the flour
with the tepid water and proceed with the recipe as above.

## 288  Irish soda bread

**MAKES** 1 loaf   **PREPARATION TIME** 15 minutes   **COOKING TIME** 35 minutes

250g (9oz, 1²/₃ cups) plain flour plus extra
   to sprinkle
250g (9oz, 1²/₃ cups) strong white bread flour
1 tsp cream of tartar
1 tsp bicarbonate of soda

1½ tsp fine sea salt
450ml (16fl oz, 1³/₄ cups) buttermilk, or use
   half and half live natural yogurt and
   skimmed milk, mixed together

1   Preheat the oven to 190°C (375°F, Gas Mark 5). Grease a shallow 15cm (6in)
    cake tin and line with baking paper. (If you have no tin, then shape the dough into
    a smooth round on a baking tray.)
2   Sift together the flours, cream of tartar, bicarbonate of soda and salt in a large bowl.
3   Mix in the buttermilk to form a smooth, soft dough. Drop into the tin, score the top in
    a cross and dust lightly with extra flour.
4   Bake for 30–35 minutes. Check to see it is cooked by loosening from the tin with a
    knife, tipping out and tapping the base. It should sound hollow – if not, return the
    loaf to the oven for a further 5 minutes. Cool for 5 minutes in the tin then turn out
    on a wire rack to cool completely.

## 289 Wheaten loaf

**MAKES** 1 large loaf  **PREPARATION TIME** 10 minutes  **COOKING TIME** 40 minutes

250g (9oz, 1²/₃ cups) plain flour
250g (9oz, 1²/₃ cups) wholemeal flour
50g (2oz, 1 cup) wheat bran (optional)
1 tsp bicarbonate of soda
1 tsp salt

good knob of butter or margarine (optional)
350–400ml (12–14fl oz, 1¹/₃–1³/₄ cups)
   buttermilk, or half and half live natural
   yogurt and skimmed milk, mixed together

1  Preheat the oven to 200°C (400°F, Gas Mark 6). Grease and line a large non-stick
   1kg (2lb) loaf tin.
2  Thoroughly mix together the flours, bran, if using (it gives a good nutty texture),
   bicarbonate of soda and salt in a large bowl. Rub in the butter or margarine, if using.
3  Quickly stir in the buttermilk and mix to a dough, but don't overmix. Scoop into the
   tin, bang it 2–3 times on the worktop to level and bake for 35–40 minutes, turning if
   the top browns. Check it is cooked by turning out the bread and tapping on the base.
   It should sound hollow. Cool for 10 minutes in the tin then turn out to cool completely.

## 290 Doris Grant country wholemeal loaf

**MAKES** 1 large loaf  **PREPARATION TIME** 15 minutes  **COOKING TIME** 35 minutes

500g (1lb 2oz, 3¹/₃ cups) wholemeal organic
   stoneground flour
1 tsp sea salt

1 tsp organic soft brown sugar or honey
1 sachet easy-blend yeast

1  Preheat the oven to 200°C (400°F, Gas Mark 6). Grease a 1kg (2lb) non-stick loaf tin
   and line the base with baking paper. Spoon out 1 tbsp of the flour and reserve.
2  Thoroughly mix together the flour, salt, sugar and yeast in a large bowl. Then make
   up 450ml (15fl oz, 1³/₄ cups) tepid water by mixing three-quarters cool water with
   one-quarter hand-hot water. (The temperature is important for a quick rise.)
3  Using a large wooden spoon, quickly beat in about ⁷/₈ of the water to a soft dough.
   Add the rest if the mixture seems a little dry. It should be quite moist and thick,
   depending on the flour.
4  Scoop into the tin, bang it 2–3 times on the worktop to level, sprinkle over the
   reserved flour, cover loosely with cling film and leave in a warm spot for about 30
   minutes until it rises by about one-third – almost to the top of the tin.
5  Bake for 30–35 minutes, turning the tin if the top browns, until the base sounds
   hollow when you turn out the bread and tap it. Cool on a wire rack.

## 291 Sticky gingerbread

**SERVES** 8–10  **PREPARATION TIME** 15 minutes  **COOKING TIME** 40 minutes

300g (10oz, 2 cups) plain flour
2 tsp ground ginger
1 tsp mixed spice or ground cinnamon
1 tsp bicarbonate of soda
150g (5oz, ²/₃ cup) black treacle

150g (5oz, ²/₃ cup) golden syrup
100g (3¹/₂oz) butter
100g (3¹/₂oz, ³/₄ cup) soft dark brown sugar
2 eggs, beaten
30g (1oz) stem ginger or raisins (optional)

1  Preheat the oven to 180°C (350°F, Gas Mark 4). Lightly grease a 20cm (8in) square
   shallow tin and line with baking paper. Put the flour, spices and soda into a large
   bowl and mix well together.
2  Warm the treacle, syrup, butter and sugar until melted and beat into the dry
   ingredients along with the eggs to give a smooth thick batter. Stir in the stem ginger,
   finely chopped, or raisins, if using. Scoop into the tin and bake for about 40 minutes
   until firm and springy on top.
3  Cool in the tin then turn out and peel off the paper. Wrap in cling film and store in an
   airtight tin for 3–5 days before cutting into slices. Nice served buttered.

## 292 Sally Lunn bread

**MAKES** 2 round loaves   **PREPARATION TIME** 20 minutes plus 3 risings   **COOKING TIME** 15 minutes

20g (¾oz) fresh yeast
50g (2oz, ¼ cup) caster sugar
300g (10oz, 2 cups) strong white bread flour

grated zest of 1 lemon
1 large egg, beaten
50g (2oz) butter, softened

1   Cream the yeast with 2 tsp of the sugar, 50g (2oz, ½ cup) flour and 150ml (5fl oz, ⅔ cup) tepid water in a small bowl. Cover with cling film and set aside in a warm spot to froth, about 15–20 minutes. Lightly grease 2 x 15cm (6in) sandwich tins.

2   Tip the remaining flour into a large bowl and mix in the remaining sugar and lemon zest. Make a well in the centre, spoon in the yeasty mix and almost all the egg (save a spoonful for glazing). Use a large wooden spoon to mix well, then knead in the softened butter with your hands until the dough leaves the side of the bowl, adding a little extra flour if necessary.

3   Cover with lightly oiled cling film and leave in a warm spot to rise, about 1 hour.

4   Knock back, knead lightly and divide into 2 neat rounds. Drop into the sandwich tins, glaze the tops with the last of the egg and cover loosely with oiled cling film. Preheat the oven to 220°C (425°F, Gas Mark 7). When the dough has risen by half, bake the loaves on the same shelf for about 15 minutes until risen and golden brown. Serve warm.

## 293 Madeira cake

**MAKES** 1 x 20cm (8in) cake   **PREPARATION TIME** 20 minutes   **COOKING TIME** 1 hour 15 minutes

125g (4oz) butter, softened
125g (4oz, ½ cup plus 2 tbsp) caster sugar
3 eggs, beaten
grated zest of 1 lemon

200g (7oz, 1⅓ cups) self-raising flour
3–4 thin slices of candied citron or lemon peel (optional)

1   Preheat the oven to 180°C (350°F, Gas Mark 4). Lightly grease a deep 20cm (8in) cake tin and line the base with baking paper.

2   Put the butter, sugar, eggs, zest and flour into a food processor or bowl of an electric mixer. Beat well for a good 3 minutes, scraping down the sides twice.

3   Scoop into the cake tin, level the top and bake for about 1 hour 15 minutes, placing the candied peel on top after 30 minutes. Check that the cake is cooked by inserting a thin metal skewer in the centre, which should come out clean.

4   Cool in the tin for 15 minutes, then turn out onto a wire rack to cool completely.

### VARIATION

#### Marmalade cake
Omit the lemon zest and candied peel and stir in 4 tbsp marmalade to the beaten eggs, chopping the peel if chunky.

## 294 Battenberg cake

**MAKES** 2 cakes  **PREPARATION TIME** 35 minutes  **COOKING TIME** 25 minutes

4 large eggs
350g (12oz) butter, softened, or soft
    margarine plus extra for greasing the tin
350g (12oz, 1¾ cups) caster sugar
350g (12oz, 2⅓ cups) self-raising flour
grated zest of 1 lemon and 2 tbsp juice

a few drops of edible red food colour or
    3 tbsp cocoa powder, sifted
500g (1lb 2oz) prepared marzipan, white
    or yellow
8 tbsp apricot jam, warmed and sieved
sifted icing sugar, to dust

1   Grease a shallow 17 x 24 cm (6½ x 9½in) cake tin. Fold a large sheet of baking
    paper in half and fold back on each side 5cm (2in) from the centre as a pleat. Place
    this into the tin, pressing against the base and sides, snipping the corners to fit, so
    that you have divided the tin in half. Preheat the oven to 180°C (350°F, Gas Mark 4).
2   Put the eggs, butter, sugar and flour into the bowl of an electric mixer and beat well
    for 3 minutes, scraping down the sides twice. Divide the mixture in two. Beat the zest
    and juice into one half and a few tiny drops of red food colour (or cocoa powder) into
    the other. Spoon the mixtures into each side of the paper-lined tin and level the top.
3   Bake for about 25 minutes, turning the tin for even cooking, until firm to touch.
    Cool for 10 minutes, then turn out onto wire racks and cool completely.
4   Trim the edges with a sharp knife to neaten. Cut each cake into 2 long halves and
    sandwich together with half the apricot jam glaze, alternating plain and coloured
    cakes so you have a simple chequer pattern.
5   Sprinkle icing sugar onto the worktop and roll out the marzipan to a rectangle large
    enough to enclose the whole cake. Brush the marzipan all over with the remaining
    jam and wrap over the cake, pressing well into the sides and top. Press the join
    together, and pinch the four edges to decorate. Wrap tightly in cling film until served.

# 295 Homemade Swiss roll

**MAKES** 1 x 23cm (9in) wide roll  **PREPARATION TIME** 25 minutes  **COOKING TIME** 10–12 minutes

3 large eggs
1 tsp vanilla extract
125g (4oz, ½ cup plus 2 tbsp) caster sugar
 plus 3 tbsp extra for rolling

85g (3oz, ⅔ cup) plain flour, sifted
3–4 tbsp jam (e.g. raspberry, apricot, plum
 or cherry)

1  Preheat the oven to 180°C (350°F, Gas Mark 4). Lightly oil a 30 x 23cm (12 x 9in) Swiss roll tin and line with baking paper, snipping at the corners to fit.
2  Put the eggs, extract and sugar into a large heatproof bowl and set over a pan of simmering water. Using a hand-held electric whisk, beat for about 7 minutes until you have a stiff pale golden foam that forms a firm trail.
3  Remove from the heat and beat for a further 3 minutes to cool. Sift over the flour and fold in with a large metal spoon. Scoop into the prepared tin, spread evenly and bake 10–12 minutes until risen and just firm when pressed on top.
4  Remove, cool for 5 minutes then turn out onto a wire rack. Peel off the paper and cool completely. Transfer to a large sheet of baking paper on a flat worktop sprinkled with the extra sugar.
5  Trim the edges and spread evenly with the jam. Roll up, using the paper, to a tight roll and leave for 30 minutes, then cut into 8 slices. Can also be used to make Old English strawberry trifle (see page 158).

# 296 Victoria sandwich

**MAKES** 1 x 20cm (8in) cake  **PREPARATION TIME** 20 minutes  **COOKING TIME** 20 minutes plus cooling

3 eggs, at room temperature
180g (6½oz, 1 cup) caster sugar
180g (6½oz) butter, softened,
 or soft margarine
180g (6½oz, 1¼ cups) self-raising flour
1 tsp baking powder
1 tsp vanilla extract

3–4 tbsp jam (raspberry, apricot, plum or
 strawberry) and/or buttercream made with
 50g (2oz) softened butter beaten with 40g
 (1½oz) sifted icing sugar
sifted icing sugar, to dust

1  Preheat the oven to 180°C (350°F, Gas Mark 4). Lightly oil and line 2 x 20cm (8in) sandwich tins with baking paper.
2  Put the eggs, sugar, butter, flour, baking powder and vanilla extract into a food processor or the bowl of an electric mixer. Beat well for a good 3 minutes, scraping down the sides twice.
3  Scoop into the tins, level the tops and bake for 20 minutes until the tops are golden and lightly springy. Cool in the tins for 10 minutes, then turn onto a wire rack and cool completely.
4  Spread jam on one cake and sandwich with the other, or spread jam on one and buttercream on the other and sandwich together.
5  Dust lightly with icing sugar tapped from a sieve and serve.

## 297 Date and walnut cake

**SERVES** 8   **PREPARATION TIME** 20 minutes plus soaking   **COOKING TIME** 40 minutes plus cooling

225g (8oz) stoned dates, chopped
1 tsp bicarbonate of soda
225g (8oz, 1²/₃ cups) soft brown sugar
85g (3oz) butter, softened
1 tsp vanilla extract
2 eggs, beaten
300g (10½oz, 2 cups) self-raising flour

125g (4oz, 1¼ cups) chopped walnuts plus
    extra for decorating

**ICING**
4 tbsp soft brown sugar
25g (1oz) butter, softened
2 tbsp double cream

1   Place the dates and bicarbonate in a bowl and pour over 200ml (7fl oz, ³/₄ cup) boiling water. Leave until cold, then mix well to a purée.
2   Meanwhile, preheat the oven to 180°C (350°F, Gas Mark 4). Lightly oil a 21 x 30cm (9 x 12in) rectangular non-stick cake tin and line with baking paper.
3   Cream the sugar, softened butter and vanilla then gradually mix in the eggs and flour alternately. Stir in the cooled date purée and chopped nuts. Spoon into the tin, level the top and bake for 35–40 minutes until the top is firm.
4   Cool for 10 minutes in the tin, then turn out onto a wire tray and cool completely.
5   For the topping, boil together the sugar, butter and cream for 2 minutes then cool for 2 minutes and spread over the top of the cake. Sprinkle with chopped nuts, cool until set then serve cut in slices.

## 298 Cherry cake

**MAKES** 1 x 20cm (8in) cake   **PREPARATION TIME** 20 minutes   **COOKING TIME** 1 hour 15 minutes plus cooling

175g (6oz) natural colour glacé cherries,
    quartered
180g (6oz, 1¼ cups) self-raising flour
125g (4oz) butter, softened

125g (4oz, ½ cup plus 2 tbsp) caster sugar
½ tsp vanilla extract or almond essence
3 eggs, beaten

1   Rinse the syrup from the cherries under warm running water. Pat dry on kitchen paper, then toss with 2 tbsp of the flour. Set aside.
2   Preheat the oven to 180°C (350°F, Gas Mark 4). Lightly oil a deep loose-bottomed 20cm (8in) cake tin and line with baking paper.
3   Cream together the butter and sugar with the extract, then gradually mix in the eggs and the remaining flour alternately. Fold in the cherries and spoon into the cake tin, levelling the top. Bake for 1 hour–1 hour 15 minutes or until a metal skewer inserted in the centre comes out clean. Cool for 30 minutes in the tin, then turn out and cool completely.

### VARIATION

#### Cherry and coconut cake
Fold in 25g (1oz, ⅓ cup) lightly toasted desiccated coconut with the flour.

# 299 Chocolate cake with fudge icing

**SERVES** 8 **PREPARATION TIME** 30 minutes **COOKING TIME** 35 minutes plus cooling

75g (3oz) dark chocolate, at least 60% cocoa
   solids, melted
5 tbsp double cream
175g (6oz) butter, softened
250g (9oz, 1¾ cups) muscovado sugar
3 eggs, beaten
250g (9oz, 1⅔ cups) plain flour
2½ tbsp milk

**ICING**
180g (6oz, 1¼ cups) icing sugar
50g (2oz, ⅔ cup) cocoa powder
85g (3oz) butter, softened
2 tbsp cold strong coffee
pistachio nuts, slivered, and Crystallized
   violets (see page 213), to decorate

1   Break up the chocolate into a bowl and melt with the cream in the microwave or
    over a pan of gently simmering water. Remove and cool.
2   Preheat the oven to 180°C (350°F, Gas Mark 4). Grease and line a deep 22cm
    (8½in) round cake tin. Cream the butter and sugar, then gradually mix in the eggs
    and flour alternately.
3   Stir in the melted chocolate and, finally, enough milk to make a smooth, soft dropping
    consistency. Spoon into the tin, level the top and bake for 30–35 minutes until the
    top is springy and just firm.
4   Cool in the tin for 10 minutes, then turn out and cool completely. Split in two.
5   For the icing, sift the icing sugar and cocoa powder into a large bowl, then beat in
    the softened butter and coffee until creamy. Cool until set.
6   Use half to sandwich the two cake halves together and spread the rest on the top,
    marking with a fork to decorate. Press on the nuts and violets.

## 300 Cornish saffron cake

**MAKES** 1 x 1kg (2lb) cake    **PREPARATION TIME** 30 minutes plus soaking and rising    **COOKING TIME** 50 minutes

2 good pinches of saffron strands  
500g (1lb 2oz) plain flour  
a little freshly grated nutmeg  
1/4 tsp ground cinnamon  
50g (2oz) lard  

100g (3 1/2 oz) butter  
1 sachet easy-blend yeast  
100g (3 1/2 oz, 1/2 cup) caster sugar  
200ml (7fl oz, 3/4 cup) warm milk  
150g (5oz, 1 cup) mixed dried fruit  

1 Crush the saffron strands into a cup with 2 tbsp boiling water, stir and stand for at least 1 hour.

2 Mix together the flour and spices, then rub in the lard and butter to fine crumbs. This can be done in a food processor. Stir in the yeast, then add the sugar. Tip into a large bowl.

3 Stir in the milk and saffron water. Draw together to a soft dough, kneading until smooth. Cover with cling film and leave at a warm spot until doubled in size, about 3–6 hours, depending on outside temperatures.

4 Preheat the oven to 200°C (400°F, Gas Mark 6). Lightly oil and line a 1kg (2lb) loaf tin. When the dough has risen, turn out onto a lightly floured board and punch it down to a flat oblong, then work in the fruit.

5 Shape into a fat roll that will fit inside the prepared loaf tin, cover again loosely with cling film and allow to rise by about half this time.

6 Bake for 30–35 minutes until golden on top and firm when pressed. Check it is cooked by tipping out the loaf and tapping on the base. It should sound hollow. Cool on a wire rack. When cold serve in slices, lightly buttered if liked.

## 301 Grace's Dundee cake

**MAKES** 1 x 20cm (8in) cake    **PREPARATION TIME** 30 minutes plus drying overnight    **COOKING TIME** 1 hour 45 minutes

175g (6oz) currants, preferably the small  
    Greek Vostizza variety  
175g (6oz, 1 cup plus 1 tbsp) sultanas  
12 natural colour red glacé cherries,  
    quartered  
about 12 whole blanched almonds  
a little milk  
white vegetable fat, for greasing  

175g (6oz) butter, softened  
125g (4oz, 3/4 cup) soft light brown sugar  
2–3 drops of almond extract  
200g (7oz, 1 1/3 cups) plain flour  
1/2 tsp baking powder  
25g (1oz, 1/4 cup) ground almonds  
3 large eggs, beaten  

1 Soak the currants and sultanas in enough boiling water to cover for 1 hour, then drain and squeeze dry. Rinse the syrup from the cherries under warm running water and pat dry on kitchen paper. Spread the fruits in a large roasting tin and leave in a warm place to dry out overnight. Soak the almonds in a little milk for 1 hour, then drain and split in half.

2 The next day, grease a deep, loose-bottomed 20cm (8in) cake tin and line with baking paper. Cream the butter and sugar with the almond extract in a large bowl until light and creamy.

3 Sift together the flour and baking powder over the fruits, add the ground almonds and stir to mix. Using a strong spatula, fold a third of this mixture into the butter and sugar then mix in about one-third of the beaten eggs. Repeat again with the floury fruits and egg, stirring to incorporate rather than beating.

4 Scoop the combined mixture into the prepared cake tin, level the top and bang it once or twice on the worktop. Set aside while you preheat the oven to 150°C (300°F, Gas Mark 2).

5 Dip the split almonds in a little milk and arrange, rounded side up, in 3 rings on top of the cake mixture. Bake for 45 minutes, then lower the temperature to 130–140°C (275°F, Gas Mark 1) for a further 50 minutes or until a clean thin metal skewer inserted in the centre comes out clean.

6 Cool in the tin for 30 minutes then turn the cake out on a wire rack to cool completely. Wrap well in foil for at least 2 days before cutting and eat within a week to 10 days.

## 302 Yorkshire ginger parkin

**MAKES** 12 **PREPARATION TIME** 15 minutes **COOKING TIME** 20 minutes

125g (4oz, ¾ cup plus 1 tbsp)
  self-raising flour
125g (4oz, 1⅓ cups) porridge oats
  or oatmeal
1 tsp ground ginger
50g (2oz) butter, softened

125g (4oz, ½ cup plus 2 tbsp) caster sugar
1 tbsp black treacle or molasses, spooned
  from a warmed tin
2 tbsp milk
1 egg, beaten
12 whole blanched almonds

1  Preheat the oven to 180°C (350°F, Gas Mark 4) and line a flat baking sheet with baking paper.

2  Mix the flour, oats and ginger in a large bowl. Rub in the butter and mix in the sugar.

3  Beat together the warm treacle and 1 tbsp milk, then beat in the egg and pour onto the dry ingredients. Mix well to a paste.

4  Divide into 12 soft balls and place on the baking sheet, spaced well apart. Dip the almonds into the remaining milk and press on top. Bake for about 20 minutes until flattened and firm on top. Cool and store in a tin for up to 1 week.

## 303 Christmas cake

**MAKES** 1 x 20cm (8in) round or 1 x 18cm (7in) square cake  **PREPARATION TIME** 30 minutes
**COOKING TIME** 2 hours 30 minutes

250g (9oz) butter, softened
250g (9oz, 1¾ cup) soft dark brown sugar
   or molasses sugar
4 eggs, beaten
1 tbsp warmed black treacle or
   molasses syrup
350g (12oz, 2⅓ cups) plain flour
1 tsp ground mixed spice

grated zest of 1 small lemon
1 kg (2lb 4oz) dried mixed fruit (including
   cherries, mixed peel and vine fruits)
75g (3¾oz) pack dried cranberries
50g (2oz) flaked almonds
2–3 tbsp milk (optional)
2–3 tbsp brandy or rum (optional)

1 Lightly grease a deep 20cm (8in) round or a 18cm (7in) square cake tin and line the base and sides with baking paper. Preheat the oven to 140°C (275°F, Gas Mark 1).

2 Cream the butter and sugar either by hand or with an electric mixer. Mix together the eggs and treacle. Sift together the flour, spice and mix in the lemon zest.

3 Add the egg and flour mixes alternately and, when smooth, stir in the fruits, cranberries and almonds. Mix in a little milk for a softer consistency if liked.

4 Scoop into the tin, level the top and bang the tin 2–3 times on the worktop to settle the mixture.

5 Bake for 1 hour 30 minutes, turning the tin once or twice for even browning, then reduce the temperature to 130°C (275°F, Gas Mark ½) for a further hour. Watch the top doesn't overcook – cover loosely with foil if necessary. When the cake is cooked a thin metal skewer inserted in the centre will come out clean.

6 Cool in the tin for 1 hour. While it cools, skewer the top several times and drizzle in the brandy if liked. Turn out and cool completely on a wire rack.


## 304 Simnel cake

**MAKES** 1 x 20cm (8in) round cake  **PREPARATION TIME** 30 minutes  **COOKING TIME** 2 hours 30 minutes

200g (7oz) butter, softened or soft margarine
200g (7oz, 1 cup) caster sugar
200g (7oz, 1⅓ cups) plain flour
½ tsp baking powder
2 tsp mixed spice
4 large eggs, beaten
250g (9oz, 1½ cups) sultanas

250g (9oz, 1½ cups) raisins
50g (2oz, ⅓ cup) chopped mixed peel
500g (1lb 2oz) prepared marzipan
a little sifted icing sugar, to dust
2 tbsp warmed Apricot glaze (see page 19)

1 Lightly grease a deep, loose-bottomed 20cm (8in) round cake tin and line with doubled baking paper. Preheat the oven to 150°C (300°F, Gas Mark 2).

2 Cream the butter and sugar either by hand or with an electric mixer. Sift together the flour, baking powder and spice. Mix in alternately the eggs and flour, then stir in the fruits and peel.

3 Cut off a quarter of the marzipan, roll into 11 balls (representing the apostles minus Judas) and set aside. Lightly dust the worktop with icing sugar, knead the remaining marzipan into 2 balls and roll into shapes the same size as the cake tin.

4 Scoop half the cake mixture into the tin, fit one marzipan piece on top and scoop in the remaining mixture. Level the top and bang the tin once or twice on the worktop.

5 Bake for approximately 2 hours or until a thin metal skewer inserted in the centre comes out clean. Cool in the tin for 30 minutes, then turn out onto a wire rack and allow to cool completely.

6 Brush the cooled cake top with apricot glaze and press on the remaining marzipan round. For an attractive finish, press the wire rack on top to mark a criss-cross pattern and pinch the edges to crimp. Press on the marzipan balls (moistening with a little extra egg white) and press lightly on top. The cake will keep for a good 2 weeks in an airtight tin.

## 305 Eggless vinegar fruit cake

**MAKES** 1 x 20cm (8in) cake  **PREPARATION TIME** 25 minutes  **COOKING TIME** 1 hour 15 minutes

125g (4oz) butter, softened
250g (9oz, 1²/₃ cups) plain flour
2 tsp ground mixed spice
125g (4oz, ³/₄ cup) soft dark brown sugar
grated zest of 1 lemon

250g (9oz, 1¹/₃ cups) dried mixed fruits
1 tsp bicarbonate of soda
150ml (5fl oz, ²/₃ cup) milk
2 tbsp malt vinegar

1  Preheat the oven to 170°C (325°F, Gas Mark 3). Grease a deep 20cm (8in) cake tin and line with baking paper.
2  Rub the butter into the flour and spice, either by hand or in a food processor, until it resembles fine crumbs. Mix in the sugar, zest and then the fruits.
3  Whisk the bicarbonate of soda into the milk, then mix in the vinegar. It will start to froth. Immediately beat into the dry ingredients, mixing well, then spoon into the prepared cake tin.
4  Level the top and bake for 1 hour–1 hour 15 minutes until the cake feels firm when pressed and a thin metal skewer inserted in the centre comes out clean.
5  Remove and cool in the tin for 30 minutes, then turn out on a wire rack to cool completely. Keeps for about 4 days in an airtight tin.

## 306 Pineapple and coconut upside-down cake

**MAKES** 1 x 18cm square (7in) or 20cm (8in) round cake  **PREPARATION TIME** 25 minutes  **COOKING TIME** 45 minutes

3 tbsp warmed golden syrup
1 x 225g (8oz) can pineapple rings in natural juice, drained
2 tbsp dried cranberries or 8 natural colour glacé cherries, halved
125g (4oz) butter, softened, or soft margarine

125g (4oz, ¹/₂ cup plus 2 tbsp) golden caster sugar
2 eggs, beaten
150g (5oz, 1 cup) self-raising flour
3 tbsp desiccated coconut

1  Lightly grease an 18cm (7in) square or 20cm (8in) round non-stick cake tin with a solid base. Preheat the oven to 180°C (350°F, Gas Mark 4). Spoon the syrup into the tin and warm it in the oven for 2–3 minutes until it is runny and coating the entire base.
2  Press the pineapple rings into the tin, cutting in half to fit, if necessary. Stick the cherry halves or cranberries in clusters into the ring centres.
3  Beat together the butter, sugar, eggs, flour and coconut in a large bowl and spread over the pineapple.
4  Bake for about 45 minutes until risen and firm. Stand for 15 minutes, then loosen the tin sides and invert the cake onto a plate.

**VARIATION**

### Rhubarb squashy cake
Follow the recipe above, but substitute 400g (14oz) Yorkshire pink rhubarb for the pineapple, use soft brown sugar instead of caster sugar and add 1 tsp ground ginger to the flour. Cut the rhubarb into small lengths and scatter over the syrup. Make up the cake mix, spread over the fruit and bake as above, standing the tin on a baking sheet to help cook the rhubarb. Good served with soured cream or crème fraîche.

## 307 Welsh bara brith

**MAKES** 1 large loaf  **PREPARATION TIME** 20 minutes plus soaking overnight  **COOKING TIME** 1 hour 30 minutes

400g (14oz, 2²/₃ cups) dried mixed fruit
75g (2¹/₂oz, ¹/₃ cup) caster sugar
250ml (9fl oz, 1 cup) hot black tea
500g (1lb 2oz, 3¹/₃ cups) self-raising flour
2 tsp mixed spice

2 tbsp orange marmalade, chopped if chunky
1 large egg, beaten
100g (3¹/₂oz) butter, softened
2 tbsp clear honey

1   Tip the dried mixed fruit and sugar into a large bowl and mix in the hot tea. Cover and soak overnight.

2   The next day, lightly grease a 1kg (2lb) loaf tin and line with baking paper. Preheat the oven to 170°C (325°F, Gas Mark 3). Mix the flour and spice together, then beat into the fruit mixture with the marmalade, egg and butter.

3   Scoop the mixture into the loaf tin, level the top and bake for 1 hour 15 minutes– 1 hour 30 minutes or until a thin metal skewer inserted in the centre comes out clean. Cool for 15 minutes in the tin, then turn out onto a wire rack. Glaze the top with the honey and cool completely. Store in an airtight tin and serve sliced, lightly buttered.

## 308 Lemon drizzle cake

**MAKES** 1 x 1kg (2lb) loaf tin  **PREPARATION TIME** 20 minutes plus cooling and soaking  **COOKING TIME** 45 minutes

150g (5oz) butter, softened, or soft margarine
150g (5oz, ¾ cup) caster sugar plus 2 tbsp
  for topping
2 eggs

grated zest and juice of 1 lemon
150g (5oz, 1 cup) self-raising flour
3 tbsp milk

1  Lightly grease and line the base of a 1kg (2lb) loaf tin. Preheat the oven to 180°C (350°F, Gas Mark 4).

2  Whiz together the butter, sugar, eggs, zest, flour and milk in a food processor or beat in a large bowl until smooth. Scoop into the prepared cake tin, level the top and bake for 40–45 minutes until risen and firm. Cool for 10 minutes.

3  Mix together the 2 tbsp sugar and the lemon juice and spoon over the loaf as it cools. Leave in the tin for a further 15 minutes, then turn out and cool completely.

## 309 Mrs Palmer's apple cake

**MAKES** 1 x 20cm (8in) round cake  **PREPARATION TIME** 25 minutes  **COOKING TIME** 45 minutes

75g (3oz) butter, softened, plus extra
  for greasing
125g (4oz, ½ cup plus 1 tbsp) caster sugar,
  plus extra to sprinkle
150g (5oz, 1 cup) self-raising flour
1 tsp ground mixed spice, plus extra
  to sprinkle

2 eggs, beaten
grated zest of 1 lemon or lime
500g (1lb 2oz) dessert apples, peeled and
  coarsely grated

1  Preheat the oven to 190°C (375°F, Gas Mark 5). Grease a 20cm (8in) cake tin and line the base with baking paper.

2  Beat the butter, sugar, flour, spice, eggs and zest together in a large bowl until creamy and smooth. Then mix in the apple and scoop into the tin, levelling the top.

3  Bake for 20 minutes, then mix together about 2 tbsp extra sugar and 2–3 pinches of spice. Sprinkle on top of the half-baked cake and return to the oven for a further 20–25 minutes until golden brown and firm. Cool for 10 minutes in the tin, then turn out onto a wire rack and cool completely.

## 310 Scotch pancakes

**MAKES** about 16 scones  **PREPARATION TIME** 5 minutes  **COOKING TIME** 10 minutes

125g (4oz, ¾ cup plus 1 tbsp)
  self-raising flour
1 egg
125ml (4fl oz, ½ cup) milk

1 tbsp caster sugar
few drops of vanilla extract (optional)
vegetable oil, for greasing

1  Put the flour, egg, milk, sugar and vanilla, if using, into a large bowl and use a whisk to beat to form a smooth batter. Alternatively, whiz everything in a food processor and pour into a jug or bowl.

2  Heat a large, heavy-based, non-stick frying pan until hot, brush quickly with a little oil using a folded piece of kitchen paper, then ladle in a generous tablespoonful of batter for 1 mini pancake. You can probably make 3–4 at a time. Cook until holes appear, then flip over for a few seconds to cook the other side.

3  Slide out the pancakes onto a clean tea towel and repeat with the remaining mixture. Serve immediately, allowing 4 pancakes per serving, spread with butter and jam or drizzled with honey or maple syrup and whipped cream.

# 311 The Connaught's carrot cake

**MAKES** 1kg (2lb) loaf  **SERVES** 8–10  **PREPARATION TIME** 25 minutes  **COOKING TIME** 1 hour 25 minutes

200g (7oz, 1½ cups) wholemeal plain flour
1 tbsp ground mixed spice
1 tsp bicarbonate of soda
250g (9oz, 1⅔ cups) soft dark brown sugar
150ml (5fl oz, ⅔ cup) sunflower oil
grated zest and juice of 1 large orange

2 eggs
225g (8oz) carrots, coarsely grated
110g (3½oz, ¾ cup) sultanas
50g (2oz, ⅔ cup) desiccated coconut
50g (2oz, ½ cup) chopped walnuts
1 tbsp fresh lemon juice

1  Grease a 1kg (2lb) loaf tin and line the base with baking paper. Preheat the oven to 150°C (300°F, Gas Mark 2).
2  Sift together the flour, spice and bicarbonate of soda. Beat two-thirds of the sugar with the oil and orange zest in a large electric mixer (not a food processor) or by hand until smooth.
3  Beat in the eggs one by one until light and creamy. Mix in the spicy flour until smooth, then fold in the carrots, sultanas, coconut and walnuts. Scoop into the prepared loaf tin, level the top and bake on a heavy metal baking sheet for 1 hour 20–25 minutes. Check the cake is cooked by inserting a metal skewer in the centre, which should come out clean. The top should also be quite firm when pressed.
4  While the cake is baking, heat the orange juice with the remaining sugar and lemon juice in a small pan. Do not let it boil, but heat it enough for the sugar to dissolve.
5  When the cake is cooked, remove from the oven and run a table knife around the edges to loosen. Skewer holes over the top, then slowly pour over the syrup into the holes and round the edges. It takes a little time for the cake to absorb this but eventually it all soaks in. Leave the cake in the tin until all the syrup is absorbed then turn out, remove the base paper and cool completely.

# 312 Passion cake

**MAKES** 1 x 20cm (8in) round cake  **PREPARATION TIME** 30 minutes  **COOKING TIME** 1 hour

200g (7oz, 1⅔ cups) plain flour
2 tsp baking powder
1 tsp ground cinnamon
¼ fresh nutmeg, grated
125g (4oz) butter, softened, or soft margarine
125g (4oz, ¾ cup) soft light brown sugar
grated zest of 1 lemon
2 large eggs, beaten
2 carrots, coarsely grated
1 large ripe banana, mashed
125g (4oz, ¾ cup) raisins

50g (2oz, ½ cup) roughly chopped walnuts
   or pecans
1½ tbsp milk

**TOPPING**
200g (7oz) cream cheese, softened
2 tbsp icing sugar
juice of 1 lemon
grated zest of 1 orange plus juice of ½
8 walnut halves, to decorate
coffee crystals, to sprinkle

1  Lightly grease the base of a deep 20cm (8in) round cake tin. Preheat the oven to 180°C (350°F, Gas Mark 4).
2  Sift together the flour, baking powder and spices. Cream the butter, sugar and lemon zest in a large bowl. Then mix in the eggs and spicy flour alternately, followed by the carrots, banana, raisins, nuts and milk.
3  Scoop into the prepared tin, level the top, bang the tin 2–3 times on the worktop and bake for about 1 hour or until firm and springy.
4  Cool upside down in the tin on a wire rack for 15 minutes, then turn out and cool completely.
5  To make the topping, beat together the cream cheese, icing sugar, lemon juice, orange zest and juice.
6  Split the cake in half. Sandwich together with half the topping and spread the remainder on the top of the cake, swirling the icing decoratively. Press on the walnuts and sprinkle with the coffee crystals.

# 313 Eccles cakes

**MAKES** about 16 cakes   **PREPARATION TIME** 25 minutes   **COOKING TIME** 12 minutes

500g (1lb 2oz) pack puff pastry,
  thawed if frozen
1 large egg white, lightly beaten
a little caster sugar, to sprinkle

**FILLING**
100g (3½oz) butter
100g (3½oz, ¾ cup) dark muscovado sugar
2 tsp ground mixed spice
100g (3½oz, ⅔ cup) currants
10 dried apricots, snipped into small bits
75g (3½oz, ½ cup) dried cranberries
grated zest of 1 small lemon

1   First make the filling. Cream together the butter, sugar and spice, then mix with the dried fruits and lemon zest.
2   Roll out the pastry on a lightly floured board to a thickness of 3mm (¼in). You may find this easier to do in two batches. Use a small coffee saucer or metal cook's ring to press out at least 16 x 10cm (4in) rounds – you might get up to 18 rounds. If you need to re-roll the pastry, simply stack the trimmings on top of each other; do not squash them into a ball (this helps keep the pastry light and crisp).
3   Spoon a good teaspoonful of the mixture into the centre of each pastry round. Brush lightly around the edges with egg white, then pull into the centre and press to seal, like a flattish pouch. Turn the little cakes over and place join side down on a non-stick baking sheet.
4   Flatten slightly using your fingertips. It looks nice if the filling pokes through a little. Then use the tip of a small sharp knife to make 3 slashes on top of each cake. Brush with more egg white and sprinkle with an even layer of caster sugar.
5   Let the cakes stand while you preheat the oven to 200°C (400°F, Gas Mark 6). Then bake for 10–12 minutes until golden brown, glistening and crisp. Slide onto a wire tray to cool.

### VARIATIONS

### Banbury cakes
Follow the recipe for Eccles cakes above but cut out 6–8 larger pastry rounds, about 18cm (7in) diameter. Spoon the filling down the centre, brush the edges with egg white and draw up the sides like an oval pasty. Turn over and press join side down to flatten, then slash 3 times, glaze with egg and sprinkle with sugar. Bake as above.

### Coventry godcakes
These are rounds of thinly rolled puff pastry with their centres filled with 1–2 tsp red berry or plum jam. The sides are drawn up into a three-cornered hat, pinched together and turned over join side down on a non-stick baking sheet to form triangles. Brush with egg white and sugar and bake as above.

# 314   The ultimate light scones

**MAKES** 18 medium scones   **PREPARATION TIME** 10 minutes   **COOKING TIME** 12 minutes

500g (1lb 2oz, 3⅓ cups) plain flour
2 tbsp baking powder
125g (4oz) butter, chopped

100g (3½oz, ½ cup) caster sugar
1 large egg
150ml (5fl oz, ⅔ cup) milk

1   Whiz together the flour, baking powder and butter in a food processor until fine
crumbs form. Add the sugar and pulse for a few seconds. Tip into a large bowl and
chill until ready to cook.

2   Beat together the egg and milk and reserve 2 tbsp for glazing. Preheat the oven to
200°C (400°F, Gas Mark 6). Lay a sheet of baking paper on a heavy baking sheet.

3   Mix the egg and milk into the crumb mixture using a table knife. Work quickly and
lightly and when forming soft clumps tip out onto the worktop and knead lightly to
a light dough. Do not overwork.

4   Lightly roll out to a thickness of about 1.5cm (⅝in). Using a scone cutter, cut out
12 x 5cm (2in) rounds. Lightly knead the remaining dough, roll out and cut out a
further 6 rounds.

5   Place on the prepared tray, brush the tops with the reserved egg and milk and bake
for 10–12 minutes, turning the tray once if necessary. The scones are cooked when
the centre springs back when pinched. Cool on a wire rack and serve split and
spread with butter or clotted cream and jam.

## 315 Fairy cakes or butterfly cakes

**MAKES** 18 individual cakes  **PREPARATION TIME** 20 minutes  **COOKING TIME** 15–20 minutes plus cooling

1 recipe quantity Victoria sandwich
  (see page 177)
150g (5oz, 1¼ cups) icing sugar, sifted
1 tbsp warm water
edible food colour
sugar flowers or edible flowers (e.g. violets,
  pansies) dipped in beaten egg white and
  caster sugar

or:
buttercream made with 50g (2oz) softened
  butter beaten with 40g (1½oz, ⅓ cup)
  sifted icing sugar

1 Preheat the oven to 190°C (375°F, Gas Mark 5). Prepare the cake mixture as in the recipe but spoon into 18 paper cake cases in 2 x 12-hole bun tins. Bake for 15–20 minutes until firm on top and golden. Cool in the cases.

2 For fairy cakes, mix the icing sugar with the water to make a thin glacé icing. Colour delicately pink, blue, yellow or green with food colouring, using a cocktail stick dipped into the colour. Spoon onto the cake tops, spreading with a small table knife. Decorate with edible sugar flowers or real flowers, such as small violas or pansies, dipped first in beaten egg white and then caster sugar and dried on a wire rack.

3 For butterfly cakes, slice off the top quarter of each cake. Spread buttercream on the cut cake, then cut each top in half. Fix back on the buttercream to resemble wings and dust the tops with icing sugar.

## 316 Coffee and walnut cake

**MAKES** 1kg (2lb) loaf  **SERVES** 8  **PREPARATION TIME** 15 minutes  **COOKING TIME** 40–45 minutes

175g (6 oz) butter, softened
175g (6 oz, 1¼ cups) soft brown sugar
1 tsp vanilla extract
3 large eggs
250g (9oz, 1⅔ cups) self-raising flour, sifted
  with ½ tsp sea salt

4 tsp instant coffee, dissolved in 5 tbsp
  hot water
75g (3oz, ¾ cup) chopped walnuts
100g (3½oz, ¾ cup) royal icing sugar
6–8 whole walnuts, to decorate

1 Preheat the oven to 170°C (325°F, Gas Mark 3). Grease a 1kg (2lb) loaf tin and line the base with baking paper.

2 Beat together the butter, sugar and vanilla until light and creamy, ideally using an electric mixer. Add the eggs, one at a time, alternating with the flour, then stir in 4 tbsp of the dissolved coffee.

3 Add the chopped walnuts and spoon the mixture into the tin. Level the top. Bake for 40–45 minutes until risen and firm. Insert a thin metal skewer into the centre; when cooked it should come out clean. Cool in the tin for 10 minutes then turn out onto a wire rack and allow to cool completely.

4 To make the icing, sift the icing sugar into a large bowl and gradually beat in the remaining coffee until you have a thick, just-runny mix. Add extra trickles of hot water if necessary. Use a teaspoon to drizzle the icing over the cake surface, allowing it to run down the sides. Press on the walnuts as the icing sets.

## 317 Cornish rock buns

MAKES about 18 buns   PREPARATION TIME 15 minutes   COOKING TIME 25 minutes

175g (6oz, 1½ cups) wholemeal flour
175g (6oz, 1½ cups) self-raising flour
1 tsp baking powder
1 tsp freshly grated nutmeg
175g (6oz) butter
175g (6oz, ⅞ cup) granulated sugar, ideally
  golden unrefined

100g (3½oz, ⅔ cup) currants
25g (1oz) chopped mixed peel
75g (3oz, 1 cup) desiccated coconut
50g (2oz, ⅓ cup) natural colour glacé
  cherries, quartered or chopped
1 large egg, beaten
4–6 tbsp milk

1   Preheat the oven to 190°C (375°F, Gas Mark 5). Line a heavy baking sheet with baking paper. Mix the flours, baking powder and nutmeg in a large bowl. Rub in the butter until fine crumbs form then stir in the sugar, currants, peel, coconut and cherries. Beat the egg with 3 tbsp milk and mix into the ingredients to form a soft dough, adding extra milk in trickles if necessary.
2   Spoon into rough mounds on the baking sheet, allowing room for expansion, and bake for 20–25 minutes until golden and firm. Transfer to a wire rack to cool.

## 318 Chocolate chip and nut cookies

MAKES about 20   PREPARATION TIME 15 minutes   COOKING TIME 15 minutes

100g (3½oz) butter, softened
100g (3½oz, ½ cup) caster sugar, ideally
  golden unrefined
100g (3½oz, ¾ cup) soft brown sugar
½ tsp vanilla extract
150g (5oz, 1 cup) self-raising flour
25g (1oz, ⅓ cup) cocoa powder

good pinch of fine sea salt
1 large egg, beaten
75g (3oz, ¾ cup) chopped roasted hazelnuts
  or walnuts
75g (3oz, ¾ cup) dark chocolate chips

1   Preheat the oven to 180°C (350°F, Gas Mark 4). Line 2 heavy baking sheets with baking paper.
2   Cream together the butter, two sugars and vanilla. Sift together the flour, cocoa powder and salt and beat into the butter-sugar mix alternately with the egg, then stir in the nuts and chocolate chips.
3   Drop spoonfuls onto the baking sheets allowing room for expansion. Bake for 12–15 minutes until firm. Cool for 1 minute on the trays then slide onto a wire rack using a palette knife to cool completely and crisp. Store in an airtight tin.

## 319 Melting moments

MAKES about 24   PREPARATION TIME 12 minutes   COOKING TIME 20 minutes

125g (4oz) butter, softened
75g (3oz, ½ cup) icing sugar
½ tsp vanilla extract
1 egg yolk

150g (5oz, 1 cup) self-raising flour
6 glacé cherries, quartered (optional)
small bowl cornflakes, crushed (optional)

1   Cream the butter, icing sugar and vanilla then mix in the egg yolk and flour to make a stiff, smooth dough. If liked, spoon into a piping bag fitted with a large star nozzle.
2   Preheat the oven to 190°C (375°F, Gas Mark 5). Line a heavy baking tray with baking paper. Either pipe 24 stars on the paper and press a quarter cherry on top, or roll into balls using floured hands and toss in the crushed cornflakes. Space out well on the baking sheet. Bake for 15–20 minutes, turning once until golden brown and firm. Remove to a wire rack to cool and firm until crisp.

## 320  Shortbread/petticoat tails

**MAKES** 1 x 20cm (8in) round/8 tails  **PREPARATION TIME** 15 minutes  **COOKING TIME** 20 minutes

125g (4½oz) unsalted butter, softened
50g (2oz, ¼ cup) caster sugar
150g (5oz, 1 cup) plain flour, plus extra
   for dusting

50g (2oz, ⅓ cup) ground rice
caster sugar, for dusting

1  Cream together the butter and sugar then gradually work in the flour and ground rice. Knead lightly until smooth.

2  Roll out to a 20cm (8in) round and lift onto a heavy baking sheet lined with baking paper. Pinch the edges to crimp and score almost through to the base to form 8 spokes of a wheel.

3  Prick evenly all over with a fork and chill while you preheat the oven to 170°C (325°F, Gas Mark 3). Bake for about 20 minutes, turning the baking sheet once or twice, until pale golden and just firm.

4  Remove and cool until crisp, dust with caster sugar, then slide onto a wire rack to cool completely. Break into triangles and serve or store up to 1 week in an airtight tin.

### VARIATIONS

#### Norfolk lavender shortbread
Grind 2 tsp dried lavender flowers with the sugar.

#### Hazelnut shortbread
Substitute ground toasted hazelnuts for the rice or semolina.

#### Chocolate chip shortbread
Add 50g (2oz, ⅓ cup) chocolate chips after working in the flour. Roll out and cut into rounds or triangles.

#### Millionaires' shortbread (illustrated)
Make up the shortbread as above but press into an 18cm (7in) square tin and bake for 25 minutes. Remove and cool and spread with a jar of Dulce de Leche, then top with 150g (5oz) melted milk or dark chocolate. Allow to set, then cut into squares.

## 321  Easter biscuits

MAKES about 24   PREPARATION TIME 20 minutes plus chilling   COOKING TIME 12 minutes

125g (4oz) butter, softened, or soft margarine
75g (3oz, 1/3 cup) caster sugar, preferably
  golden unrefined, plus extra for sprinkling
1 egg, separated
75g (3oz, 1/2 cup) plain flour, plus extra for
  dusting
2 1/2 tbsp cornflour, ground rice or fine
  semolina

1/2 tsp each ground cinnamon and ginger
75g (3oz, 1/2 cup) wholemeal flour
50g (2oz, 1/3 cup) currants
1 1/2 tbsp chopped mixed peel or grated rind of
  1 lemon
1 tbsp milk

1   Cream the butter and sugar, then stir in the egg yolk.
2   Mix together the plain flour, cornflour, spices, wholemeal flour, currants and peel.
    Stir into the butter and sugar, then mix in the milk. Knead lightly to a firm but not
    too dry dough ball. Cover with cling film and chill for 20 minutes. Preheat the
    oven to 200°C (400°F, Gas Mark 6).
3   Roll out the dough on a lightly floured surface to a thickness of 5mm (1/4in) and use
    a 6–7cm (2 1/2–3in) cutter to make several rounds. Re-roll the trimmings and cut out
    more rounds. Place on a non-stick baking sheets.
4   Lightly beat the egg white and brush over the biscuit tops then sprinkle with extra
    sugar. Bake for 10–12 minutes until the biscuits are lightly browned and feel slightly
    firm. Slide them onto a wire rack to cool and crisp.

## 322  Almond flapjacks

MAKES 12–16 slices   PREPARATION TIME 15 minutes   COOKING TIME 25 minutes

150g (5oz) butter or soft margarine
125g (4oz, 1/2 cup plus 2 tbsp) caster sugar,
  ideally golden unrefined
2 tbsp golden syrup

150g (5oz, 1 1/2 cups) porridge oats
50g (2oz, 1/2 cup) flaked almonds
50g (2oz, 1/3 cup) raisins (optional)

1   Preheat the oven to 170°C (325°F, Gas Mark 3). Line the base of an 18 x 25cm
    (7 x 10in) baking tin with baking paper. Melt the butter or margarine in a large pan
    then remove from the heat and stir in the remaining ingredients.
2   Tip into the tin and spread evenly. Bake for 20–25 minutes, then cut into 12–16
    portions and leave to cool in the tin for a further 20 minutes.
3   Tip out of the tin onto a wire rack, break into the cut portions and cool until firm.
    Store in an airtight tin for up to 1 week.

## 323  Coconut pyramids

MAKES 6–8   PREPARATION TIME 5 minutes   COOKING TIME 10–12 minutes

2 tbsp condensed milk
50g (2oz, 2/3 cup) desiccated coconut

1/2 tsp vanilla extract
3–4 cherries, halved

1   Preheat the oven to 170°C (325°F, Gas Mark 3). Line a flat baking sheet with
    baking paper.
2   Mix together the milk, coconut and vanilla essence. Spoon 6–8 mounds on the
    baking sheet, spaced well apart, and form into pyramids with your fingers.
3   Press a cherry half on top of each one. Bake for 10–12 minutes until golden and
    just firm. Let cool for 3 minutes before sliding onto a wire rack to cool completely.

## 324 Grasmere gingerbread biscuits

**MAKES** 16 squares    **PREPARATION TIME** 20 minutes    **COOKING TIME** 30–40 minutes

500g (1lb 2oz, 3⅓ cups) self-raising flour
½ tsp fine sea salt
2 tbsp ground ginger
180g (6oz, ¾ cup plus 1 tbsp) caster sugar,
   ideally golden unrefined
250g (9oz) butter, plus extra for brushing

2 tbsp warmed golden syrup
4 egg yolks plus 1 egg white
200g (9oz, 1¼ cups) chopped mixed peel
granulated sugar, ideally golden unrefined,
   to sprinkle

1    Preheat the oven to 170°C (325°F, Gas Mark 3). Sift the flour, salt and ginger into
   a large mixing bowl and mix in the sugar.
2    Melt the butter and syrup, then remove and cool until warm. Mix into the dry
   ingredients with the yolks to make a soft dough.
3    Brush the sides of a 20cm (8in) square gingerbread tin with softened butter and
   line the base with baking paper. Press half the dough into the base of the tin, using
   lightly floured hands, sprinkle the peel evenly then press the remaining dough on
   top. Brush with egg white and sprinkle an even layer of granulated sugar.
4    Bake for 30–40 minutes, turning the tin once or twice for even browning, until the
   top feels just firm. Remove, cool for 10 minutes, then cut into 16 squares. Cool for
   30 minutes then turn out on a wire rack and cool completely.

## 325 Brandy snaps

**MAKES** 10–12    **PREPARATION TIME** 10 minutes    **COOKING TIME** 25 minutes

50g (2oz, ⅓ cup) plain flour
½–1 tsp ground ginger
50g (2oz, ⅓ cup) soft light brown sugar
1½ tbsp golden syrup
50g (2oz) butter

squeeze of lemon juice
200ml (7fl oz, ⅔ cup) double cream
2 tsp caster sugar
½ tsp vanilla extract

1    Preheat the oven to 170°C (325°F, Gas Mark 3). Line 2 flat baking sheets with
   baking paper.
2    Sift together the flour and ginger. Melt the soft brown sugar, syrup, butter and lemon
   juice until just combined: do not boil. Beat into the flour as a thick batter. Cool for
   5 minutes. Have ready a wire rack and 1 thick long-handled wooden spoon.
3    Drop 3 dessertspoonfuls, well spaced apart, onto a prepared tin and bake for
   8 minutes to make thin lacy rounds. Cool on the tray 3 minutes until a round can
   be lifted up with a palette knife. Wrap it loosely around the handle of a wooden spoon
   to form a roll about 1.5cm (⅝in) in diameter. Push the round to the end of the spoon
   and wrap another lacy disc into a roll. Cool, join side down. Repeat in batches until
   all the mixture is used up. If any disc crisps before you can roll it, return it to the oven
   to soften for a few seconds.
4    When cool, store in an airtight tin until ready to serve. Whisk the cream to soft peaks
   with the caster sugar and vanilla and using a piping bag with a 1cm (½in) plain
   nozzle, pipe cream in at each end of a brandy snap roll. It doesn't have to reach the
   middle. Serve immediately.

### VARIATION

The baked discs can be pressed into small tartlet tins to cool as brandy snap baskets
and filled with whipped cream and soft red berries.

# SWEETS

Ideally, you will need a sugar thermometer for these recipes to test the temperature once the sugar solution has dissolved and boiled.

### To check for 'soft ball' stage
Have ready a large glass of cold water and drop a little of the hot sugary mixture into the water where it should form into a soft clump. Check the temperature on a sugar thermometer if you have one – it should read 115°C (240°F), or soft ball.

### To check for 'small crack' stage
Boil to 140°C (285°F) and drop a small trickle of syrup into cold water where it should form a hard brittle clump that cracks when snapped.


## 326   Vanilla fudge

**MAKES** 25 squares   **PREPARATION TIME** 15 minutes   **COOKING TIME** 15 minutes

500g (1lb 2oz, 2½ cups) caster sugar
200ml (7fl oz, ¾ cup) evaporated milk
50g (2oz) lightly salted butter

150ml (5fl oz, ⅔ cup) milk
1 tsp vanilla extract

1   Put all the ingredients except the vanilla extract into a large non-stick pan with 4 tbsp cold water. Heat gently, stirring until dissolved.
2   Lightly grease a 20cm (8in) square tin. When the mixture no longer feels gritty, increase the heat to medium and boil until the temperature reaches the soft ball stage (see above), 115°C (240°F) on a sugar thermometer – this takes about 10–12 minutes.
3   Remove from the heat and use a long-handled wooden spoon to mix in the vanilla. Beat well for about 7 minutes until the mixture thickens and starts to turn grainy. Immediately pour into the tin and set aside to cool and set.
4   Demould when cold and cut into squares.

### VARIATIONS

#### Nut and vanilla fudge
Add 100g (3½oz, 1 cup) chopped walnuts or macadamia nuts to the recipe above.

#### Rum 'n' raisin fudge
Add 125g (4oz, ¾ cup) raisins (which can be soaked in hot rum) to the recipe above.

#### Berry or cherry fudge
Add 125g (4oz, ¾ cup) cranberries or glacé cherries (or half and half) to the recipe above.

#### Chocolate fudge
Replace the evaporated milk in the recipe above with 100g (3½oz) dark chocolate and 3 tbsp clear honey.

# 327 Scottish tablet

**MAKES** about 16–20 bars   **PREPARATION TIME** 5 minutes   **COOKING TIME** 20 minutes

125g (4 oz) unsalted butter
1kg (2lb 4oz, 4¾ cups) granulated sugar
300ml (10fl oz, 1¼ cups) full-fat milk

pinch of fine sea salt
200ml (7fl oz, ¾ cup) condensed milk
1 tsp vanilla extract

1   Melt the butter in a large, non-stick, heavy-based pan, then stir in the sugar, milk and salt. Heat gently until the sugar has dissolved, stirring occasionally. Lightly grease a 23 x 33cm (9 x 13in) Swiss roll tin.

2   Bring to the boil and keep over a high heat, while you stir frequently with a long-handled wooden spoon for about 8 minutes.

3   Carefully mix in the condensed milk and simmer again, stirring most of the time for a further 8–10 minutes. Boil to soft ball stage (see left), 115°C (240°F) on a sugar thermometer.

4   Remove from the heat and mix in the vanilla. Change the wooden spoon for a hand-held electric mixer and beat on a medium speed for 4–5 minutes until the mixture begins to stiffen and become grainy.

5   Immediately pour into the tin and leave to cool, marking into squares when it is lukewarm. When quite cold, demould and break into squares. Wrap the squares in waxed paper if you have any.

# 328 Coconut ice

**MAKES** 16 squares   **PREPARATION TIME** 5 minutes   **COOKING TIME** 10 minutes

500g (1lb 2oz, 2½ cups) granulated sugar
150ml (5fl oz, ⅔ cups) milk

150g (5oz, 1⅞ cups) desiccated coconut
pink or yellow edible food colour

1   Lightly grease an 18cm (7in) square cake tin. Put the sugar and milk in a large non-stick pan and stir over a low heat until the sugar has dissolved.

2   Bring to the boil stirring once or twice then boil steadily, without stirring, for about 10 minutes or until the temperature reaches soft ball stage (see left), 115°C (240°F) on a sugar thermometer

3   Remove from the heat and stir in the coconut. Pour half the mixture into the tin and level the top. Dribble tiny drops of food colour into the remaining mixture in the pan and beat well until it is a pale pastel colour, then pour over the white coconut.

4   Leave until almost set then mark into 18 squares. When completely cold, turn out and cut into squares along the score lines.

# 329 Cinder toffee

**MAKES** about 18 squares   **PREPARATION TIME** 10 minutes   **COOKING TIME** 15 minutes

200ml (7fl oz, ¾ cup) warmed golden syrup
300g (10½oz, 1½ cups) caster sugar
50g (2oz) butter

1 tsp white vinegar
2 tsp bicarbonate of soda

1   Lightly grease an 18cm (7in) square cake tin. Put the syrup, sugar, butter, vinegar and 4 tbsp water into a large heavy-based pan. Heat slowly until the sugar has dissolved and is no longer gritty.

2   Increase the heat and boil to the small crack stage (see left), 140°C (285°F) on a sugar thermometer.

3   Remove from the heat and stir in the bicarbonate of soda using a long-handled wooden spoon. The mixture will rise up and froth. Pour immediately into the prepared tin and leave to cool.

4   Before the slab cools completely, mark into 18 squares. Break into squares along the score lines when cold.

# 330 Toffee apples

**PREPARATION TIME** 5 minutes  **COOKING TIME** 12–15 minutes

4 even-sized dessert apples, washed,
   stalks removed
5 tbsp warmed golden syrup
150g (5oz, 1 cup) soft brown sugar

good knob of butter
1 tsp white vinegar
4 thick wooden sticks or 8 wooden skewers

1  Push a thick wooden stick or 2 skewers into the centre of each apple. Lay a sheet of baking paper on a wooden board. Have ready a large bowl of very cold water.
2  Put the syrup, sugar, butter and 5 tbsp (or 4 tbsp) water into a heavy-based pan. Heat gently until the sugar dissolves, then raise the heat and boil to the small crack stage (see page 194), 140°C (285°F) on a sugar thermometer.
3  Working quickly, remove the pan from the heat and dip the apples one by one into the hot syrup, swirling to coat and tipping the pan slightly towards the end. Dip the apples immediately into the cold water, then place on the paper to cool. Overwrap in acetate film if not eating immediately so the toffee stays crisp.

## 331 Chocolate-dipped mint creams

**MAKES** about 20 sweets   **PREPARATION TIME** 20 minutes plus drying   **COOKING TIME** nil

250g (9oz, 2 cups) icing sugar, plus extra
   for rolling
1 tsp peppermint essence

1 egg white
green edible food colour
150g (5½oz) dark chocolate

1. Sift the icing sugar into a large bowl and, using an electric hand mixer on a slow speed, work in the peppermint essence and egg white until you have a firm but malleable paste.
2. Break off half and work in 1–2 drops of food colour to give a pale pastel shade. Shape both batches of mint paste to equal long rolls and press together to form a thick smooth roll about 4cm (1½in) thick. (Brush the edges lightly with water so they stick well.) Cut into 20 discs and place on a sheet of baking paper on a wire rack to dry out overnight.
3. Next day, melt the chocolate in a microwave on a low setting or in a heatproof bowl set over simmering water. Dip each mint cream half way up into the chocolate so that the undipped side shows half white, half green. Replace on the paper to set. Serve in small sweet cases.

## 332 Turkish delight

**MAKES** about 36 squaress   **PREPARATION TIME** 5 minutes plus overnight setting   **COOKING TIME** 30 minutes

4 tsp gelatine crystals
500g (1lb 2oz, 2½ cups) caster sugar
¼ tsp citric acid (available from Asian
   foodstores)
few drops of triple-strength rosewater or
   peppermint essence

pink or green edible food colour
4 tbsp icing sugar
4 tbsp cornflour

1. Lightly grease an 18cm (7in) square shallow tin. Put 300ml (10fl oz, 1¼ cups) water into a large pan and sprinkle over the gelatine. Wait a few moments until it begins to solidify, then stir in the sugar and citric acid.
2. Bring slowly to the boil, stirring with a long-handled wooden spoon until the sugar has dissolved, then boil for up to 20 minutes on a medium heat without stirring.
3. Add the rosewater or peppermint then add the appropriate food colouring using the point of a cocktail stick to match the flavour. Pour into the prepared tin and leave to set overnight.
4. Sift together the icing sugar and cornflour and sprinkle on a sheet of baking paper. Demould the Turkish delight onto the paper and cut into neat squares, tossing in the powdery sugar. Store in an airtight tin, dusted in between with more powdery sugar.

# CHAPTER 7

# PRESERVES, SAUCES & ACCOMPANIMENTS

Before the days of freezers, the autumn glut of orchard fruits, berries and garden produce could be made to last an entire year if cooked with sugar, vinegar, spices and honey. Jams, jellies, chutneys, pickles, sauces and relishes were used to liven up simple plain fare, spread on bread, baked in open tarts, or dolloped alongside chunks of cheese or cold meats. Neatly labelled jars packed with homemade goodies are such a source of pleasure. Nowadays, with globally sourced fresh produce we can make these preserves at any time of the year, a couple of jars at a time just enough to enhance a few meals. Refrigeration has meant the recipes require less of the preserving ingredients, so the amount of sugar and vinegar can be reduced to enhance the flavour.

Preserves are easy to make, store and transport, which has made them the focus of a growing band of small entrepreneurial food producers, including a number from India and the Middle East. The creative efforts of these groups have helped to contribute to a great British food tradition.

## 333 Summer fruits jam

**MAKES** about 4 pots   **PREPARATION TIME** 5 minutes   **COOKING TIME** 25 minutes plus cooling

1kg (2lb 4oz) mixed prepared summer
  berries, unblemished (choose 3 or 4 from
  strawberries, raspberries, cherries,
  redcurrants)

juice of 1 lemon
about 1kg (2lb 4oz, 5 cups) granulated
  or preserving sugar
small knob of butter

1  Place the fruits and lemon juice in a preserving pan or other large heavy-based pan. Add 1.5 litres (2½ pints, 6 cups) water and bring slowly to the boil, then lower the heat and simmer for about 15 minutes until the fruit is tender and the liquid has reduced by about half.

2  Remove from the heat and leave to cool, then measure the pulp and juice. Allow 800g (1lb 12oz, 4 cups) sugar per litre (1¾ pints, 4 cups) pulp. Sterilize 4–6 medium clean and washed jam jars (see page 15).

3  Heat the pulp and sugar slowly, stirring once or twice, to dissolve the sugar then increase the heat to boiling and cook for about 10 minutes and check for a set (see page 15).

4  When a set is reached, remove the pan from the heat, cool for 5 minutes, then stir in the butter to disperse the froth. Ladle into warm sterilized jars. Screw on the lids and cool.

## 334 Blackberry and apple jelly

**MAKES** 6 pots   **PREPARATION TIME** 30 minutes plus dripping   **COOKING TIME** 45 minutes

3 Bramley or other large cooking apples,
  about 750g (1lb 10oz)
1kg (2lb 4oz) blackberries/brambles,
  preferably wild

about 1.25kg (2lb 12oz, 5 cups) granulated
  or preserving sugar

1  Chop up the apple, including skins, cores and pips, and place in a preserving pan with the berries and 2 litres (3½ pints, 8 cups) water. Bring to the boil, stirring, then simmer gently for 25 minutes until the fruit is very soft and the liquid has reduced by half.

2  Suspend a jelly bag over a large bowl. Scoop in the hot pulp and leave to drip through the bag – this can take 2 hours or so.

3  Discard the pulp and measure the juice. Wash out the preserving pan. Sterilize 6 medium clean and washed jam jars (see page 15). Calculate the sugar, allowing 800g (1lb 12oz, 4 cups) sugar per litre (1¾ pints, 4 cups) juice. Bring slowly to the boil, stirring until the sugar dissolves, then cook on a medium boil for 15 minutes or longer until a set is reached (see page 15). Remove from the heat and ladle into warm sterilized jars. Screw on the lids and cool.

### VARIATION

#### Elderberry jelly
Replace the blackberries with wild elderberries stripped from their stalks.

## 335 Blackcurrant jam

**MAKES** about 5 pots    **PREPARATION TIME** 10 minutes    **COOKING TIME** 50 minutes plus standing

1kg (2lb 4oz) blackcurrants
about 1.25kg (2lb 12oz, 5 cups) granulated
    or preserving sugar

small knob of butter

1   Strip the currants from their stalks and place in a preserving pan with about 2 litres (3½ pints, 8 cups) water. Bring to the boil, then simmer for about 35 minutes until the fruit is soft and pulpy.
2   Measure the pulp and calculate the sugar, allowing about 700g (1lb 9oz, 3½ cups) sugar per litre (1¾ pints, 4 cups) pulp. Add the sugar, stirring until dissolved, then bring to the boil and cook for 10–15 minutes until a set is reached (see page 15). Sterilize 4–6 medium clean and washed jam jars (see page 15).
3   Remove the preserving pan from the heat, leave to stand for 10 minutes, then stir in the butter to disperse any froth. Ladle into warm sterilized jars. Screw on the lids and cool.

## 336 Freezer raspberry jam

**MAKES** about 6 small–medium pots/freezer tubs    **PREPARATION TIME** 15 minutes plus 7 hours standing and 24 hours setting    **COOKING TIME** nil

800g (1lb 12oz, 4 cups) caster sugar
500g (1lb 2oz) fresh raspberries
½ bottle liquid pectin (brandname Certo)
    or 1 sachet pectin crystals

juice of 1 lemon (about 3–4 tbsp)

1   Place the sugar in a shallow metal dish and warm for 10 minutes in the oven at 140°C (275°F, Gas Mark 1).
2   Crush the berries roughly in a large bowl, stir in the sugar and leave at room temperature for about 4 hours until the sugar has dissolved, stirring occasionally.
3   Add the pectin, stir well, then 3 tbsp of lemon juice.
4   Ladle the fruit crush into freezerproof containers. Cover loosely with cling film and leave at warm room temperature for about 3 hours, then check for a set. If it is still quite runny, tip the contents back into the bowl, mix in another 1 tbsp of lemon juice then re-pot.
5   Leave for at least 24 hours at room temperature by which time the mixture should have reached a soft set (see page 15. Cover tightly with cling film and freeze until required. Thaw a pot at a time as required. This will freeze for up to 6 months.

## 337 Damson and cinnamon jam

**MAKES** about 4 pots    **PREPARATION TIME** 20 minutes    **COOKING TIME** 50 minutes

2kg (4lb 8oz) ripe damsons
2 sticks cinnamon

about 1.5kg (3lb 5oz, 7¼ cups) granulated
    or preserving sugar

1   Wash the damsons and place in a preserving pan with the cinnamon and 3 litres (5¼ pints, 12 cups) water. Bring slowly to the boil, then simmer for about 40 minutes until the fruit is softened.
2   Cool until the fruit is comfortable enough to handle. Use your fingers (wear clean rubber gloves to avoid staining) to remove the stones from the soft fruit and discard. Return to the heat and stir in the sugar.
3   Bring to the boil then cook on a medium boil until a set is reached (see page 15), about 10 minutes. Discard the cinnamon and ladle into warm sterilized jars. Screw on the lids and cool.

## 338 Marrow and ginger jam

**MAKES** 2 pots    **PREPARATION TIME** 15 minutes plus overnight standing    **COOKING TIME** 50 minutes

1 large marrow, about 1.5kg (3lb 5oz)
750g (1lb 10oz, 3¾ cups) granulated sugar

3 lemons
75g (3oz) fresh root ginger, roughly chopped

1  Trim then halve the marrow, scoop out the seeds, peel off the thick skin and chop the flesh finely. Place in a large preserving pan with a third of the sugar, cover, and leave overnight.

2  Use a swivel peeler to remove strips of lemon zest and squeeze the juice. Tie the ginger and lemon zest in a small piece of muslin.

3  Stir the lemon juice into the steeped marrow and bring to the boil. Add the muslin bag and simmer for about 30 minutes until the marrow flesh is very soft. Stir in the remaining sugar, return to the boil, stirring until dissolved, then boil for a further 20 minutes or so until a set is reached. Sterilize 2 medium clean and washed jam jars (see page 15).

4  Remove the muslin bag and ladle into the warm, sterilized jars. Screw on the lids and allow to cool.


## 339 Redcurrant jelly

**MAKES** about 3 pots    **PREPARATION TIME** 10 minutes plus dripping time    **COOKING TIME** 30–40 minutes plus cooling

1kg (2lb 4oz) redcurrants
about 1kg (2lb 4oz, 5 cups) granulated
  or preserving sugar

1  Remove any leaves from the redcurrants, but leave the fruit on the stalks. Put the fruits into a large preserving pan with about 1.5 litres (2½ pints, 6 cups) water. Bring to the boil, then simmer gently for about 20 minutes until the fruits have burst and are pulpy.

2  Suspend a jelly bag over a large bowl. Scoop in the hot pulp and leave to drip through for at least 3 hours.

3  Discard the pulp and measure the juice. Wash out the preserving pan. Sterilize 3 medium clean and washed jam jars (see page 15). Calculate the sugar, allowing 800g (1lb 12oz, 4 cups) sugar per litre (1¾ pints, 4 cups) juice.

4  Return the juice and sugar to the pan, bring to the boil then cook at a medium boil for about 10 minutes or until a set is reached (see page 15). Remove from the heat, cool for 10 minutes then ladle into warmed sterilized jars. Screw on the lids and allow to cool.

### VARIATION

### Rowanberry or quince jelly
Make as above substituting an equal weight of rowanberries or peeled, cored and chopped quince for the redcurrants.

## 340 Seville orange marmalade

**MAKES** about 8 pots    **PREPARATION TIME** 30 minutes    **COOKING TIME** about 1 hour 30 minutes

1.25kg (2lb 12oz) Seville oranges, washed
3 lemons
10 whole cardamoms, pods crushed
2 tsp coriander seeds, roughly crushed

2.5kg (5lb, 12 cups) granulated or
preserving sugar
knob of butter

1   Halve the oranges and lemons then squeeze the juice and tip the pips into a piece of
muslin with the crushed spices. Using a sharp or serrated knife cut the fruit shells as
finely as possible into slices. (Alternatively, slice the fruit shells after simmering when
they will have softened.)

2   Put the juice, sliced peel and 6 litres (10½ pints, 24 cups) water into a large
preserving pan. Bring slowly to the boil. Tie the spices in the muslin with kitchen
string and add to the pan. Simmer very gently for about 1 hour or until the peel feels
very soft and the liquid is reduced by half. Sterilize 8–10 medium clean and washed
jam jars (see page 15).

3   Stir in the sugar until dissolved and raise the heat to a medium boil. Cook until setting
point is reached, about 15 minutes. Remove from the heat for 10 minutes, discard
the bag and stir in the butter to disperse any froth. Pot into warm sterilized jars and
screw on the lids.

## 341   Crab apple, mint and chilli jelly

**MAKES** about 3 pots   **PREPARATION TIME** 10 minutes plus dripping time   **COOKING TIME** 1 hour 10 minutes plus cooling time

1.5kg (3lb 4oz) crab apples or windfall apples
6–8 sprigs of mint
2 large fresh red chillies

about 1.25kg (2lb 12oz, 5 cups) granulated
or preserving sugar

1   Wash the apples and cut in half or quarters depending on size. Put into a large preserving pan with 2.5 litres (4½ pints, 10 cups) water. Bring to the boil. Add the stalks of the mint and 1 chilli, roughly chopped, then simmer for about 40 minutes until the liquid is reduced by half.

2   Meanwhile, slit the remaining chilli, shake out the seeds and finely shred the flesh. Boil for about 10 minutes in a little water until softened. Drain and reserve. Finely shred the mint leaves.

3   Suspend a jelly bag over a large bowl. Scoop in the cooked apple and allow to drip through for about 3 hours.

4   Discard the pulp and measure the juice. Wash out the pan. Sterilize 3–4 medium clean and washed jam jars (see page 15). Calculate the sugar, allowing 800g (1lb 12oz, 4 cups) sugar per litre (1¾ pints, 4 cups) juice.

5   Return the juice to the pan with the chillies. Add the sugar and bring to the boil, stirring. Boil for about 15 minutes until setting point is reached (see page 15). Stir in the shredded mint and ladle into warm sterilized jars. Screw on the lids and cool.

## 342   Grapefruit jelly marmalade

**MAKES** 8 pots   **PREPARATION TIME** 35 minutes plus dripping   **COOKING TIME** 2 hours 20 minutes

2kg (4lb 8oz) cooking or tart apples,
    roughly chopped
4 lemons, chopped
3 red or pink grapefruits, halved

1.5kg (3lb 5oz, 7¼ cups) granulated
or preserving sugar
knob of butter

1   Put the apples, lemons and grapefruit halves into a large preserving pan. Add 5 litres (8¾ pints, 20 cups) cold water and bring to the boil. Simmer, uncovered, for about 2 hours until the grapefruit skins are tender when pierced.

2   Remove from the heat and transfer the grapefruits to a plate and cool. Spoon the rest of the pulp into a jelly bag hung over a large bowl and allow to drip through for 2–3 hours. Wash out the pan.

3   When the grapefruits are cool, scrape out the flesh and tip into the jelly bag. Slice the grapefruit skin thinly, then chop into small pieces. Set aside. Sterilize 8–10 medium clean and washed jam jars (see page 15).

4   Measure the clear juice back into the preserving pan: you should have just over 2 litres (3½ pints, 8 cups). Stir in the sugar, heat until dissolved, then increase the heat and boil for about 15–20 minutes, stirring occasionally.

5   Test for setting point (see page 15) and, if ready, remove and mix in the chopped grapefruit skin. Stir in the butter to disperse any froth. Cool for 10 minutes then ladle into 8 warm sterilized jars. Screw on the lids and cool.

# 343 Lemon curd

**MAKES** about 5 pots    **PREPARATION TIME** 15 minutes    **COOKING TIME** 10 minutes

6 lemons
250g (9oz) unsalted butter

250g (9oz, 1¼ cups) granulated sugar
2 eggs plus 3 egg yolks

1   Grate the lemon zest and squeeze the juice. Place in a large heatproof bowl. Add
    the remaining ingredients and place over a pan of gently simmering water. Sterilize
    4–6 medium clean and washed jam jars (see page 15).
2   Stir the pan for 7–10 minutes until everything has dissolved and the mixture thickens.
    Remove from the heat and pour immediately into warm sterilized jars. Screw on the
    lids and cool. Keep in the fridge for 3–4 weeks and use as required. Once opened,
    use each jar within 1 week.

**VARIATION**
## Lemon and lime curd
Substitute 3 limes for 2 of the lemons.

## 344 Brandy or rum butter

**MAKES** 250g (9oz)　**PREPARATION TIME** 5 minutes　**COOKING TIME** nil

125g (4oz, 1 cup) icing sugar, ideally
  golden, sifted
125g (4oz) unsalted butter, softened

40g (1½oz, ½ cup) ground almonds
2 tbsp brandy or dark rum

1　Beat together the sugar, butter and almonds until creamy then mix in the spirit. Spoon into a small serving bowl or container. Cover or seal and store up to 2 weeks. Serve at cool room temperature.


## 345 Cranberry and port relish

**MAKES** 2 pots　**PREPARATION TIME** 5 minutes　**COOKING TIME** 20 minutes

250g (9oz) fresh cranberries
grated zest and juice of 1 orange
150g (5oz, ¾ cup) granulated sugar

small stick cinnamon
120ml (4fl oz, ½ cup) ruby port

1　Put the cranberries, orange zest, juice and sugar into a large pan and bring to the boil. Lower the heat, add the cinnamon stick, stir and simmer for about 15 minutes, stirring 2–3 times, until the berries have burst and the mixture is pulpy. Sterilize 2 medium clean and washed jam jars (see page 15).
2　Add the port, remove from the heat, cool for 5 minutes and pot in warm sterilized jars. Store in a cool dark cupboard.


## 346 Cumberland sauce

**MAKES** about 1 pot　**PREPARATION TIME** 10 minutes　**COOKING TIME** 7 minutes

zest of 1 orange, peeled in strips
zest of 1 lemon, peeled in strips
175ml (6fl oz, ¾ cup) red wine

½ x 340g (12oz) jar Redcurrant jelly
  (see page 202)
3 tbsp cranberry sauce (optional)

1　Slice the zest strips into thin julienne sticks. Boil in water for 2 minutes then drain and boil with the wine for 3 minutes. Sterilize 1 medium clean and washed jam jar (see page 15).
2　Stir in the jelly and sauce, if using. Reheat until bubbling, then remove and pot in the warm sterilized jar.


## 347 Pear, ginger and saffron chutney

**MAKES** 2 pots　**PREPARATION TIME** 15 minutes　**COOKING TIME** 20 minutes

4 large shallots, chopped
5cm (2in) fresh root ginger, peeled
  and chopped
3½ tbsp olive oil
4 large firm Conference pears, peeled, cored
  and chopped

½ tsp saffron strands
200g (7oz, 1 cup) caster sugar
150ml (5fl oz, ⅔ cup) cider vinegar

1　Sauté the shallots and ginger in the oil for 5 minutes, then add the pears and cook for 3 minutes. Crumble in the saffron then add the sugar. Sterilize 2 medium clean and washed jam jars (see page 15).
2　Stir and cook on a medium heat until the sugar begins to caramelize and the pears soften. Stir in the vinegar and cook for a further 2–3 minutes. Cool for 10 minutes and pot in warm sterilized jars.

## 348 Plum and chilli chutney

**MAKES** about 4 pots   **PREPARATION TIME** 20 minutes   **COOKING TIME** 30 minutes plus cooling

1.25kg (2lb 12oz) ripe but firm plums,
halved and stoned
500g (1lb 2oz) tart dessert or small cooking
apples, cored and chopped
500g (1lb 2oz) onions or shallots, chopped
2–3 large fresh red chillies, seeded
and chopped

175g (6oz, 1¼ cups) soft brown sugar
1 tsp ground ginger
1 tsp five-spice powder or ground allspice
¼ tsp ground cloves or 3 whole cloves,
crushed
¼ whole nutmeg, grated
¾ tbsp sea salt

1   Put everything into a large pan with 250ml (9fl oz, 1 cup) water. Heat until the
fruit begins to break down and soften and simmer gently for 30 minutes. Sterilize
4–5 medium clean and washed jam jars (see page 15).
2   Cool the chutney for 10 minutes then pot in warm sterilized jars.

## 349 Tomato and sweet pepper relish

**MAKES** 2 pots   **PREPARATION TIME** 20 minutes plus 15 minutes soaking   **COOKING TIME** 25–30 minutes

125g (4oz, ¾ cup) raisins
1 large onion, sliced
1 large red or yellow pepper or 2 small
peppers (1 of each colour)
3 large cloves garlic, chopped
1 large fresh red chilli, seeded and chopped
1 x 500ml (18fl oz) bottle or carton sugocasa
tomatoes (sieved tomatoes) or tomato juice

150ml (5fl oz, ⅔ cup) malt vinegar
1 tsp smoked paprika
2 tsp ground cumin
125g (4oz, ¾ cup) soft light brown sugar
1 tsp sea salt
3-4 tbsp chopped coriander

1   Cover the raisins with boiling water and leave to plump up for 15 minutes then drain.
2   Meanwhile, put everything except the fresh coriander into a medium pan. Bring to
the boil, and then simmer for 15 minutes, stirring occasionally, until softened and
reduced down. Sterilize 2–3 medium clean and washed jam jars (see page 15).
3   Stir in the raisins and cook for a further 10 minutes. Then add the coriander. Cool
and serve, or ladle immediately into warmed sterilized jars and seal.

## 350 Pickled grapes

**MAKES** 1 pot   **PREPARATION TIME** 5 minutes   **COOKING TIME** 10 minutes plus 1 week storing

400g (14oz) seedless grapes (ideally half
white and half red fruits)
125g (4oz, ½ cup plus 2 tbsp)
granulated sugar
150ml (5fl oz, ⅔ cup) white wine vinegar

150ml (5fl oz, ⅔ cup) dry white wine
1 tsp coriander seeds
1 large fresh green chilli
2 star anise or 1 stick cinnamon,
snapped in two

1   Pick the grapes from the stems and wash then pat dry. Tip into a large clean jam jar.
2   Put the sugar, vinegar and wine into a pan and heat until the sugar dissolves, then
add the coriander seeds and boil for 2 minutes.
3   Meanwhile, slit the chilli and remove the seeds then cut the flesh into thick strips.
Stick down the sides of the jar along with the star anise or cinnamon.
4   Pour the syrup over the grapes, pushing them down under the liquid. Seal and cool,
then store for about a week before serving.

## 351 Bread and butter pickle

**MAKES** 1 large pot   **PREPARATION TIME** 15 minutes plus draining   **COOKING TIME** 2 minutes

1 large cucumber
1 onion, sliced thinly
1 tbsp fine sea salt
150ml (5fl oz, ⅔ cup) malt vinegar
   or pickling vinegar

2½ tbsp granulated sugar
1 tsp fennel or celery seeds or crushed
   coriander seeds
1 tsp black mustard seeds or
   cumin seeds

1   Slice the cucumber about 3mm (¼in) thick, ideally using a mandolin or Japanese food slicer for neat even slices. Layer in a large colander with the onion slices, sprinkling salt in between the layers.

2   Leave to drain for at least 3 hours, stirring the slices occasionally in the colander. Then pat dry in a clean tea towel. Do not rinse.

3   Sterilize 1 large clean and washed jam jar or preserving jar (see page 15).Meanwhile, heat the vinegar (use pickling vinegar for a spicy flavour), sugar and spices in a pan until the sugar has dissolved, then bring to the boil and simmer for 2 minutes.

4   Pack the cucumber and onion into the sterilized jar and pour over the hot liquid. Press the slices well under the liquid. Seal, cool and store in a dark cupboard for at least a week before using.

## 352  Piccalilli

**MAKES** 2 large pots   **PREPARATION TIME** 20 minutes plus overnight draining   **COOKING TIME** about 25 minutes

1kg (2lb 4oz) mixed fresh vegetables
 (cauliflower florets, baby onions, red
 or green peppers, green beans,
 courgettes, etc), neatly chopped small
85g (3oz, ¼ cup) salt
500ml (18fl oz, 2 cups) white
 malt vinegar

125g (4oz, ½ cup plus 1 tbsp) sugar
¾ tbsp ground turmeric
1½ tsp dry mustard powder
2 whole cloves
1½ tbsp cornflour
1 large green chilli (optional)
1 tbsp chopped fresh root ginger (optional)

1   Layer the vegetables in a colander, sprinkling in between with salt. Leave to drain
    on a draining board or over a bowl overnight.
2   The next day, rinse off the salt under cold running water and pat the drained
    vegetables dry with a clean tea towel.
3   Put the vinegar in a large pan with the sugar, dried spices and cornflour. To spice up
    the mixture further, slit the chilli in half and tie in a piece of muslin with the ginger.
    Bring the mixture to the boil, stirring, and add the muslin bag.
4   Mix in the vegetables, return to the boil and simmer for about 20 minutes until the
    vegetables are just tender. Remove the bag and whole cloves and pot in warm jars.
    Cool and keep for 1 week before eating.

## 353  Red onion marmalade

**MAKES** 1 pot   **PREPARATION TIME** 15 minutes   **COOKING TIME** 20 minutes

4 tbsp olive oil
2 large red onions, halved, peeled and cut
 into thin wedges
1 small red pepper, cored, seeded and cut
 into small chunks
1 large red chilli, seeded and chopped
2 large cloves garlic, chopped

2 tbsp chopped fresh ginger
250ml (9fl oz, 1 cup) cider or malt vinegar
75g (3oz, ½ cup) soft light brown sugar
1 tsp five-spice powder or ground
 mixed spice
2 tsp fine sea salt

1   Heat the oil in a large pan and gently sauté the onion, pepper, chilli, garlic and
    ginger for about 5 minutes until just softened.
2   Pour in the vinegar and add the sugar, spice and salt. Bring to the boil, stirring, then
    lower the heat and simmer for 15 minutes until the vinegar has reduced down and
    the onions have softened.
3   Pour into a large, clean heatproof jar. Cover and seal while hot. Allow to steep
    for about 3 days before serving, if possible. Once opened, store in the fridge and
    eat within 2 weeks.

## 354  Pickled wild mushrooms

**SERVES** 8   **PREPARATION TIME** 10 minutes   **COOKING TIME** 10 minutes

about 500g (1lb 2oz) wild seasonal
 mushrooms and button mushrooms
1 recipe quantity Vinaigrette (see page 19)
2 fat cloves garlic, sliced

2 large sprigs of thyme
2 bay leaves
sea salt and freshly ground black pepper

1   Wash the mushrooms quickly and dry with kitchen paper. Trim the ends and slice
    any large ones.
2   Place in a large pan with the remaining ingredients. Bring to the boil, then cover and
    simmer gently for 5 minutes.
3   Tip into a large clean heatproof preserving jar and seal. Cool and store in the fridge
    for at least 1 week before using. Spoon out as required, topping up with more
    vinaigrette to cover.

## 355 Spiced pickled quail's eggs

**MAKES** 1 large jar **PREPARATION TIME** 15 minutes plus soaking overnight **COOKING TIME** 10 minutes

300ml (10fl oz, 1¼ cups) malt, cider or wine
vinegar, plus 2 tbsp for soaking
1 tbsp whole pickling spices
24 quail's eggs

2–3 mace blades
1 large fresh chilli, sliced in 3 lengthways
(optional)

1 Gently heat the vinegar until almost boiling then pour into a heatproof jug, add the pickling spices and cool overnight.
2 The next day, place the eggs in a pan of cold water with the 2 tbsp vinegar and soak for 20 minutes (this softens the shells for easy peeling). Drain and cover with fresh cold water. Bring to the boil and simmer for 3 minutes, then drain and plunge into a bowl of ice-cold water for 15 minutes to prevent a grey rim forming around the yolks.
3 Carefully peel the eggs and pop them into a large clean jam jar or a preserving jar large enough just to accommodate the eggs, along with the mace and chilli slices, if using. Pour over the vinegar, ensuring the eggs are well submerged, screw down the top or seal and store until required.

## 356 Old English salad dressing

**MAKES** about 150ml (5fl oz, ⅔ cup) **PREPARATION TIME** 10 minutes **COOKING TIME** nil

2 hard-boiled eggs, yolks only
2 tsp French mustard
1½ tbsp vegetable or light olive oil
pinch each of sea salt, caster sugar and
freshly ground white or black pepper

1 tbsp herb vinegar
4 tbsp single or double cream
1 tbsp chopped parsley, tarragon or dill

1 Cream together the yolks, mustard, oil, salt, sugar and pepper.
2 Beat in the vinegar then the cream and stir in the chopped herbs. Can be thinned down with a little tepid water to taste.

## 357 Mayonnaise

**MAKES** 300ml (10fl oz, 1¼ cups) **PREPARATION TIME** 15 minutes by hand or 5 minutes in food processor
**COOKING TIME** nil

2 egg yolks or 1 whole egg plus 1 yolk
¼ tsp fine sea salt
a little freshly ground white or black pepper
½ tsp mustard powder

250ml (9fl oz, 1 cup) vegetable oil and olive
oil mixed half and half
1 tbsp cider or white wine vinegar

1 To make by hand, place the 2 yolks in a medium bowl with the salt, pepper and mustard powder and 2 tsp of the oil. Beat until smooth with a whisk. Then gradually beat in the remaining oil, 1 tsp at a time at first, gradually adding more as the mixture gets thicker. Beat in the vinegar and continue with the oil until all is incorporated. Spoon into a jar and use as required. Will keep for up to 1 week in the fridge.
2 To make in a food processor or blender, use the whole egg and 1 yolk. Whiz with the seasonings and 1 tbsp oil until thick then, with the motor running, trickle in the oil until thick and add the vinegar.

## 358 Herb vinegars

**MAKE** as much as you require    **PREPARATION TIME** 5 minutes plus steeping    **COOKING TIME** nil

freshly picked herb sprigs, ideally gathered
  just before flowering (tarragon, rosemary,
  marjoram or thyme are ideal)

slivers of garlic and/or slices of fresh red
  chill can be added also
cider or white wine vinegar

1   Wash the sprigs quickly in cold water and pat dry. Place with the garlic or chilli,
    if using, in clean sterilized jars or glass bottles to come half way up and pour over
    cider or white wine vinegar. Screw on lids or stopper with corks and steep for at least
    2 weeks before using.

## 359 Berry fruit vinegars

**MAKES** 2–3 bottles   **PREPARATION TIME** 5 minutes plus steeping   **COOKING TIME** 5 minutes (for the cordials)

at least 600g (1lb 5oz) freshly picked
raspberries, loganberries, elderberries,
blackberries or gooseberries or a mixture

500ml (18fl oz, 2 cups) cider, or white
malt or white wine vinegar for every
600g (1lb 5oz) fruit

1   Tip the fruit into a large glass or china bowl, mix in the vinegar, stir and cover with a lid or large cloth.
2   Steep for about 3 days in a cool place (not the fridge). Sterilize 2–3 washed, clean bottles (see page 15). Strain off the vinegar, through a muslin-lined sieve, into the clean bottles, discarding the fruit. Seal with a screw top or cork and store.

### VARIATION

#### Fruit cordials

Measure the fruit vinegar and allow 400g (14oz, 2 cups) granulated sugar to each 500ml (18fl oz, 2 cups) vinegar. Bring to the boil and simmer for 5 minutes, then pour into clean bottles. Stopper and store in a cool dark cupboard. To serve, dilute to taste with water. These cordials make a refreshing summer drink and good old country cure for sore throats.

## 360 Sloe gin

**MAKES** about 750ml (1¼ pints, 3 cups)   **PREPARATION TIME** 30 minutes   **COOKING TIME** nil

350g (12oz) fresh sloes, washed
175g (6oz, ¾ cup) granulated sugar

1 tbsp blanched whole almonds
500ml (18fl oz, 2 cups) gin

1   Prick each sloe a couple of times with a large clean needle or skewer and tip into a large preserving jar, sprinkling with the sugar in between. Top with the almonds, then pour over the gin.
2   Seal tightly, store in a dark, cool cupboard and shake every month for 3 months, then leave alone for 9 months–1 year. Strain through a flannel jelly bag into a large old gin bottle, cork or seal and keep for a further 6 months before drinking.

### VARIATION

#### Damson gin

Replace the sloes with damsons. The alcoholic fruit, once you strain off the gin, can be used to make a most delicious pie or can be spooned over icecream.

## 361 Elderflower champagne

**MAKES** about 5 litres (8¾ pints, 20 cups)   **PREPARATION TIME** 25 minutes plus resting   **COOKING TIME** nil

4–5 large heads elderflowers
2 large unwaxed lemons

500g (1lb 2oz, 2½ cups) granulated sugar
60ml (2fl oz, ¼ cup) cider vinegar

1   Shake the elderflower heads to remove any stray insects. Snip off the stems. Place in a clean bucket.
2   Peel the zest from the lemons with a swivel peeler and squeeze the juice. Place both in the bucket along with the sugar and vinegar.  Pour over 5 litres (8¾ pints, 20 cups) cold water.
3   Cover and leave in a cool spot for 24 hours, stirring every 6 hours or so. Meanwhile, sterilize 5 x 1 litre (1¾ pints, 4 cups) glass bottles with boiling water or baby bottle sterilizing solution (rinsing after).
4   Remove the elderflower heads and lemon zest strips with a skimming spoon then decant the liquid through a sieve and funnel into the bottles. Seal with screw tops or corks and store in a cool shaded room, or shed or garage for at least 2 weeks, or up to 6–12 months for a more mature flavour.

## 362 Rosehip syrup

**MAKES** about 700ml (1 pint 4fl oz, 2¾ cups)   **PREPARATION TIME** 10 minutes plus standing and dripping
**COOKING TIME** 25 minutes

500g (1lb 2oz) fresh rosehips, rinsed              250g (9oz, 1¼ cups) granulated sugar

1   Bring 1 litre (1¾ pints, 4 cups) water to the boil in a large pan and reduce to a
    simmer. Blitz the rosehips quickly in a food processor to a chunky pulp and tip into
    the water. Return to the boil, remove from the heat, and let stand for 15 minutes.
    Suspend a jelly bag over a large bowl and allow the juice to drip through. This can
    take about 2 hours.
2   Wash the pan and pour the juice back into it and boil until reduced by half. Sterilize
    1 medium clean and washed glass bottle (see page 15).
3   Stir the sugar into the pan and boil for a further 5 minutes. Pour into the warmed,
    sterilized bottle and seal with a screw top or cork. Store in a cool, dark cupboard.
    Dilute with cold water to drink.

## 363 Christmas punch

**MAKES** about 3 litres (5¼ pints, 12 cups)   **PREPARATION TIME** 20 minutes   **COOKING TIME** 20 minutes

2 small oranges, sliced thinly                     small knob of fresh root ginger, halved
2 litres (3½ pints, 8 cups) red wine               1 wine glass (175ml, 6fl oz, ¾ cup) brandy
200g (7oz, 1 cup) golden granulated or                or rum
   caster sugar                                    1 wine glass (175ml, 6fl oz, ¾ cup) Cointreau
8 whole cloves                                     2 small Cox's apples, quartered, cored and
8 allspice or juniper berries                         thinly sliced
1 stick cinnamon

1   Place the oranges, wine, sugar, spices and root ginger into a large pan or preserving
    pan with 2 litres (3½ pints, 8 cups) water. Bring to the boil then lower the heat and
    simmer gently for 15 minutes.
2   Remove from the heat, stir in the spirits and apple slices and cool for 10 minutes.
    Place a silver spoon into the glass before ladling in the punch (to prevent it cracking).

## 364 Irish coffee

**SERVES** 1   **PREPARATION TIME** 3 minutes   **COOKING TIME** 1 minute

1 measure (75ml, 3fl oz, ⅓ cup) Irish whiskey      a little sugar, to taste
1 small coffee cup of espresso-strength            1 tbsp double or whipping cream,
   hot coffee                                         lightly whipped

1   Heat a tall heatproof Irish coffee glass with hot water and tip out. Fill with the whiskey
    and hot coffee and add sugar to taste.
2   Hold the back of a spoon just above the coffee and slowly pour in the cream so it
    floats on the coffee. Serve immediately.

## 365 Crystallized violets and other flowers

**MAKE** a batch in season   **PREPARATION TIME** 20 minutes plus drying   **COOKING TIME** nil

small edible flowers (e.g. violets, primroses,     1 egg white, lightly beaten with
   primulas, rose petals, freesias), a mixture        1 tsp water
   looks pretty                                     caster sugar

1   Pick off the stalks from the flowers. Tip the egg white into a saucer. Sprinkle sugar
    into another saucer to a depth of 5mm (¼in).
2   Dip the flowers face down first in the egg white, then dip quickly in the sugar to
    coat well. Shake off the excess and lay out to dry on tray lined with baking paper. If
    wished, the next day dip the stalks in egg white and sugar and dry for a further day.
    Store in an airtight tin until ready for use.

# Index

## Author's acknowledgements

I would like to acknowledge the many cooks, friends and family past and present whose inspiration for many of the recipes in this book I have absorbed over the years. In particular, the following friends allowed me to use their actual recipes – Sue Lawrence (in Edinburgh), Grace Mulligan from Yorkshire, Sallie Morris, Wendy Godfrey, Jane Avery and Angela Hartnett in London. I owe much to the team behind this book – Grace Cheetham for her enthusiasm, Stephanie Evans for editing, Bridget Sargeson for the beautiful food styling and William Lingwood for the photographs. Lastly, my daughter Clemmie Jacques and her friend Bex Ferguson, two young cooks who tested many of the recipes and had a lot of fun discovering their Great British culinary heritage.